TABLE OF CONTENTS

CHEAPIES, FREE GOODIES AND GIVEAWAYS

Introduction

3. Clothing Cheapies

4. Money Matters: Banking, Credit Cards, Investing, Taxes And Insurance

5. Car Buying

6. Health Care Cost Cutters

7. Travel On The Cheap

8. College Cheapies

9. Government Goodies

10. Miscellaneous Cheapies & Free Stuff

I N T R O D U C T I O N

CHEAPIES, FREE GOODIES AND GIVEAWAYS

Do you find it difficult to get out of the supermarket without spending more money than you intended? Is your bank taking money out of your pocket with excessive fees and charges? Are you paying more taxes than you should? Are you struggling to find money to send your kids to college? Have you put off a vacation because you don't think you can afford it? Are your insurance premiums too high? Can you afford to visit a doctor's office? If you answered yes to some or all of those questions, this book is for you!

In this edition of "Cheapies and Free Stuff" you'll find information and tips designed to help you get the best deals on food, clothing, banking services, credit cards, a new car, insurance, and travel. You'll also learn how to cut your taxes, utility bills, medical bills, college costs, and more. In addition, there are over 100 sources of wholesale bargains, almost 200 things you can get absolutely free, and scores of addresses and phone numbers for free and low-cost goods and services.

Used wisely, the information, tips and suggestions provided in this book can help you find bargains on virtually all of your personal needs and cut your bills by 30 to 40 percent a year. Of course, the key to successful bargain hunting and savings is smart shopping. And as a consumer, you can apply the shopping techniques described on the following pages to get the cheapies that are out there waiting for you.

C H A P T E R   1

Cul 1-10-97

CHEAPIES, FREE GOODIES
AND GIVEAWAYS

Consumer Savvy

As a consumer, you're faced with countless decisions. Whether or not you get the most for your money depends on how you make those decisions.

An appealing product and a "too-good-to-be-true" sales pitch are not reasons enough for you to spend your hard-earned money. In order to get the best bargains, you'll need to make all your buying decisions based on accurate consumer knowledge and facts. Ask the right questions before you buy and shop around. It's the best way to avoid impulse buying. Which seldom comes cheap it's also your best defense against consumer fraud and rip-offs which can turn a bargain into a consumer's nightmare.

Before You Hand Over Your Money

Whether you're buying from a retail outlet or shopping by mail, you should practice the following "smart shopping" techniques from the U.S. Office of Consumer Affairs:

1) Take advantage of sales, but compare prices. Don't assume an item is a bargain just because it's advertised as one.

2) Don't rush into a large purchase because the "price is good only for today ."

3) Check to see if the company is licensed or registered at the local or state level.

4) Contact your consumer protection office or Better Business Bureau (BBB) for complaints recorded against any company. Request any consumer information they might have on the type of purchase.

5) Be aware of extra charges, such as delivery fees, installation charges, service costs, and postage and handling fees. Be sure to add them into the total cost.

6) Ask about the seller's refund or exchange policy.

7) Read the warranty. Be aware of what is covered and what is

not. Find out what you must do and what the manufacturer or seller must do if there is a problem.

8) Don't sign a contract without reading it. Don't sign a contract if there are any blank spaces in it or if you don't understand it. In some states, it is possible to sign away your home to someone else.

9) Before buying any product or service, contact your consumer protection office to see if there are automatic cancellation periods for the purchase you are making. In some states, there are cancellation periods for dating clubs, health clubs, and time-share and campground memberships. Federal law also gives you cancellation rights for certain door-to-door sales.

10) Walk out or hang up on high-pressure sales tactics. Don't be pressured into buying something you really don't need or want.

11) Do business over the telephone only with companies you know.

12) Be suspicious of P.O. Box addresses. They might be mail drops. If you have a complaint, you might have trouble locating the company.

13) Don't respond to any prize or gift that requires you to pay even a small amount of money.

14) Use unit pricing to compare what items cost. Unit pricing allows you to compare the price ounce-for-ounce, pound-for-pound, etc. For example, bigger packages are not always cheaper than smaller ones.

15) Don't rely on a salesperson's promises. Get everything in writing.

After You Buy

Consumer savvy also means protecting yourself after you've parted with your money. Even the best bargains sometimes require service after the sale. Here are several things you can do to protect your purchase and make sure it remains a bargain:

1) Read and follow all product and service instructions carefully.

2) Be aware that how you use and take care of a purchase might affect your warranty rights.

3) Keep all transaction documents— sales receipts, warranties, service contracts, and instructions.

4) If you have a problem contact the company as soon as possible. Don't try to fix the product yourself; you might cancel your right to service under the warranty.

5) Keep a written record of each contact you have with the company.

6) If you have a problem, contact your consumer

protection office to find out about the warranty rights in your state (See the Appendix for state-by-state listing of consumer protection agencies).

7) Check your contract for any statement about your cancellation rights. Contact your consumer protection agency to find out whether or not a cancellation period applies.

8) If you take a product in for repair, be sure the technician understands and writes down the problem you have described.

Fraud Alert

Unfortunately, as a consumer, you also must be on guard against the sellers of bogus bargains. A savvy consumer always looks at the total price before deciding and checks out the company and product before buying. Remember, if a deal sounds too good to be true, it probably is.

Consumer protection offices advise consumers to be aware of the following signs of potential fraud:

— Pressure from a salesperson that "if you don't buy right now, the price will increase". The indication is that it's a once-in-a-lifetime bargain and you'll be making a major blunder if you don't hand over your money right away. Maybe so, but then it's more likely that the salesperson is a crook.

— Any offer that starts out, "You have been specially selected..."

In most cases you have been "specially selected" because some-how your name wound up on a mailing list of potential suckers. Be sure to look at such offers with a very critical eye.

— Telemarketers who want to: send a representative or courier service to pick up your money, have you send money by wire , automatically withdraw money from your checking account, give you a "free prize", but charge handling and shipping fees, get your credit card number, checking account or savings account number, social security number or other personal information ,have you send payment in advance, especially for employment referrals, providing a loan or credit card, or credit repair ,involve you in pyramid schemes and multi-level sales schemes.

Keep in mind that the savvy consumer always looks at the total price before deciding. And if there is any doubt at all, he/she checks out the company and product before buying. You also should keep any purchase-related paperwork in a file. Your records should include copies of sales receipts, repair orders, warranties, canceled checks, contracts, and any letters to or from the company. If you do have a problem, you should take the following action:

— Contact the company that sold you the item or performed the service. In a calm manner, accurately describe the problem and what action you wish taken.

— Maintain a record of all your efforts to resolve the problem. Write to the company and describe the problem, your efforts so far to try to resolve it and what solution you want. For example, do you want the product repaired or exchanged? Or do you want your money back?

— Give the company time to resolve the problem. Keep notes of the name of the person you spoke with, the date of your conversation and what action was taken.

— Contact the company headquarters if you are unable to resolve your problem at the local level. Many companies have toll-free 800 numbers which often appear on their package labeling. You also can find 800 number directories in the reference section of your local library, or you can call 1 (800) 555-1212 to see if the company has a toll-free number. When writing a company's headquarters, address your letter to the consumer office or the company's president.

More Smart Shopping Techniques

Some of the factors involved in being a savvy consumer and getting the best bargains possible include practice, ingenuity, patience, and sometimes a little luck. By combining the smart shopping techniques described at the beginning of this chapter with those factors, you can realistically expect to save $2000 or more each year. The following suggestions can help you save even more:

— Devise a budget and stick to it. Whenever you're planning a purchase consider whether or not the cost falls within the limits of your budget. If it doesn't, don't buy it. Regardless of the temptation, don't stray from your budget.

— Be ever alert for bargains and sales (see the "Smart Shopping

Calendar" at the end of this chapter). If you're paying attention, all sorts of cheapies will come your way. In fact, you seldom should have to pay full price for anything.

— Shop for major purchases near the end of the month. Since many retailers have monthly sales quotas they want to meet, you're likely to get a better deal just before the month ends. This is especially true for major purchases such as appliances and furniture.

— Prepare a shopping list before you hit the stores. Whether you're going grocery shopping, shopping for clothes at an outlet center, or heading to your nearest computer store, shopping from a list can save you a bundle of money. If you stick to the list and avoid temptation, you'll get only those things you need and resist costly impulse purchases.

— Give yourself enough time to find the best buys. One of the biggest mistakes many shoppers make is being in a hurry. Under the pressure and constraints of time, these shoppers are likely to make split second decisions and spend a lot more money than they have to. Whenever possible, allow yourself several hours to find the bargains and cheapies that are out there.

— Avoid appliance service contracts. Such contracts are generally a waste of your hard-earned money.

— Use low-rate bank credit cards rather than store cards if you don't pay your bill in full each month. Most store cards charge interest of more than 18 percent a year. A low-rate bank card, on the other hand, can charge as little as 8 percent.

— Avoid accepting store credit on returned merchandise. If the store gives you a choice, ask for your money back. Accepting a store credit simply means you're allowing the store to keep your money until you make another purchase there.

— Keep all tags and receipts. You'll need them in case you want to return an item. This is especially important if you buy an item at one store and then find the same thing in another store at a lower price. You can return the first item and buy the second at a lower price.

Savvy Shopper's Calendar

January: This is a great month for sales and getting various items cheaply. Most stores offer discounts on items not sold during the holiday season. Watch for bargains on holiday supplies, bicycles and toys (left over from December), clothing, footwear, jewelry, coats, china and glassware, cosmetics, and books.

February: Since most stores are getting ready to begin displaying spring and summer fashions, February is a good month to find bargains on winter clothing. You also can find bargain prices on air conditioners, fans, luggage, and certain home furnishings.

March: Winter clothing values are still available in March. You'll also find good prices on some of the latest spring and summer fashions. Ski equipment, ice skates, small appliances, and children's shoes also can be good values in March.

April: April showers bring May flowers and sale prices on

rain coats and umbrellas. Also look for discounts on jewelry, outdoor furniture, and sleepwear.

May: Generally, many stores offer sale prices on housewares (china, pots and pans, various kitchen utensils, etc.) during the month of May. Other possible May bargains include blankets, sleepwear, carpeting, and luggage.

June: Look for sales prices on gardening equipment, lingerie, carpeting, rugs, and radios and stereos.

July: This is a good month to get that bathing suit you've been wanting at a sale price. Also shop for savings on major appliances, such as refrigerators, freezers, dishwashers, and washers and dryers. You also may find some super values on men's and women's undergarments during the month of July.

August: Another great month for sales, August is a good time to find values on summer clothing, outdoor furniture, bathing suits, air conditioners, sporting goods, and camping equipment.

September: It's back to school in September with sales on children's clothing at many stores. Also look for savings on fall and winter clothing, lawn mowers, paint, and china.

October: Children's shoes, clothing and school supplies are likely bargains in October. Any remaining summer clothing will be available at discounted prices this month. Winter coats, fishing equipment, and some power tools also can be found at sales prices in October.

November: If you don't mind the crowds and standing in long lines, the last week in November is a great time to shop for bargains. Stores are competing for the holiday trade and offer sale prices on a number of items. Look for special bargains on clothing, bedding, bicycles, and home furnishings.

December: Shopping for Christmas is on everyone's mind now. Savvy shoppers will be able to find bargains on men's, women's and children's footwear; quilts and bedding, cosmetics, coats, party favors, used cars, and furniture. Shop early to find the best bargains.

NOTES

_____

_____

_____

_____

_____

_____

_____

C H A P T E R   2

CHEAPIES FREE GOODIES & GIVEAWAYS

Food Savings

How many times have you been to the supermarket within the past week? How much money did you spend? If your answers are "several" and "more than I planned," you're doing something wrong. While it may seem impossible, especially if you have a teenager or two constantly raiding the cupboards and refrigerator, there are many easy ways to cut your food costs and actually spend "less than you planned." In fact, with careful planning and smart shopping you should be able to cut your food bills by 30 percent or more and not give up any of your favorite foods.

The following tips and suggestions can help you cut down

on the number of trips you make to the supermarket each week, as well as how much you spend each trip.

Supermarket Set-Up

The next time you go to the supermarket to pick up staples such as bread and milk, check out the store's layout. Most likely, you'll have to walk from the front of the store to the back just to get the few things you need. Along the way, you'll have to walk down at least one aisle of products and be enticed by eye-catching packaging and professional marketing techniques. Such store design and product placement is not mere chance. It's part of a shrewdly planned technique designed to slow you down and get you to spend more of your money on impulse purchases.

Such a technique may seem underhanded, but it's commonplace in most supermarkets. After all, supermarkets, like other stores, are businesses trying to make as much profit as possible. However, as a consumer with cost-cutting in mind, you should be aware of a store's techniques to get your money.

The overall layout of a typical supermarket follows a general design. The first things you'll encounter upon entering are non-staples such as seasonal products (cookout and picnic supplies in summer, etc.) and soft drinks. You'll usually also find fresh produce close to a store's entrance. These are all often impulse purchases and by placing them "in your face" as soon as you walk in, supermarkets are taking advantage of consumer impulsiveness.

Also near the entrance in many supermarkets are bakeries. As soon as you enter the store, you're tempted by the aroma of freshly-baked bread, rolls, pies and other pastries. You normally don't "need" these items, but the mouth-watering smell can often tempt you into making an impulse purchase. And that's exactly what near-the-entrance supermarket bakeries are designed to do.

Here are several other features of a typical supermarket set-up:

— End-of-aisle displays. Most shoppers expect to find sale items in these displays, and sometimes they do. More often, however, these displays are stocked with high-profit, non-sale items to take advantage of consumer perception that such attractive displays are for weekly bargains.

— Side by side display of related products. This is another technique designed to encourage impulse buying. The idea is that you are more likely to purchase salad dressing if it's located next to salad makings such as lettuce, radishes, tomatoes and so on. Likewise, you're likely to find ice cream toppings alongside the ice cream freezer. Admittedly, such product placement offers convenience, but it also stimulates more purchases.

— Front-of-the-store floral displays. You'll find these in most supermarkets— another tactic designed to attract consumer attention and encourage impulse buying. After all, how often do you really need a floral display?

— Eye-level displays. High-profit items such as convenience

foods are typically placed at eye level, while staples such as flour, sugar and canned fruit are usually placed on harder-to-see-and- reach bottom shelves.

— Check-out counter displays. Before you can check out, supermarkets "offer" you the opportunity to purchase high profit items such as magazines, candy bars, gum, film, cigarette lighters and other items not on most grocery shoppers' lists. Again, these items are generally impulse purchases and can be found cheaper elsewhere.

The typical supermarket is set up to get you to spend more of your money on products you don't need. In effect, as a shopper, you are "set up" to make impulse purchases as soon as you walk in. Being aware of the tactics supermarkets use to manipulate you into spending your money can help make you a smarter shopper. If you know what a store is up to you're less likely to succumb to its tricks. And you'll end up saving money and having a much lower grocery bill.

10 Smart Strategies For Lower Grocery Bills

1) Comparison Shop: The first step to cutting your grocery bill is to shop where you get the best values. Compare the prices of items you buy frequently at your regular supermarket with the prices for the same items at other area supermarkets.

Be sure to compare the prices and quality of food items in a variety of forms— fresh, frozen, canned, etc. You may find that you can shop for less by switching supermarkets. Or you may discover that you can get the best value for your money by shopping at two or three stores.

2) Always Shop from a List: The best way to avoid distractions and costly impulse purchases is to shop from a list of items you need. Shopping from a list also helps prevent the necessity of making extra shopping trips to "pick up" something you forgot. If you can do all your shopping in one trip, and get only the items you need, you can save yourself a bundle on your monthly grocery bill.

3) Avoid Impulse Purchases: Impulse buying can play havoc with your grocery budget. As noted earlier, the entire layout of most supermarkets is designed to get you to spend money, on anything. So shop from your list and, if necessary, keep repeating to yourself, "I will not buy anything I don't need and can't use."

4) Choose Store Brands: Most store brands, while cheaper, are just as good as their pricey name-brand counterparts. Store brands are generally cheaper because they come in less expensive packaging and are not heavily advertised. You pay for the product itself, not for the product, packaging and advertising. What's more, most store brands are produced by the same manufacturers who market the name brands. They're virtually the same products with the same ingredients- but minus the frills.

Store brand canned vegetables, cold cuts, bread, snacks, soft drinks, and many other items are available at most supermarkets. Admittedly, some are inferior to brand-name products, but you'll never know until you make a comparison. And you could end up saving as much as 20% to 40% on your grocery bill buying by price whenever you have no definite preference for a brand name product.

When looking for cheaper less-known brand products, keep this in mind: the more expensive, nationally advertised brands are usually shelved at an adult's eye level, the cheaper store brands above and below them.

5) Compare Unit Prices: Unit pricing is an excellent way to compare the cost of items that are priced differently and packaged in differently sized containers. Many stores provide unit pricing, making it relatively easy for you to find the cheapest items. However, some don't.

If your supermarket doesn't offer unit pricing, take along a pocket calculator when you go shopping. Divide the cost of the product by the number of ounces in the container to get the price per ounce. For example, a 16 ounce can of peaches priced at 89 cents would cost $.056 per ounce. A 12 ounce can priced at 75 cents would cost $.063 per ounce. Your unit pricing comparison shows that the 16 ounce can is the better bargain.

Unless you don't like a particular brand, the best food buys are generally those that sell for the least amount per unit.

6) Take Advantage of Sale Prices: By taking advantage, we mean stocking up on high-priced items, especially staples and dry goods such as cereal, coffee, sugar, flour, and aluminum foil when they're offered at sale prices. Canned goods also are often discounted by the case and are good values, if you like canned corn, or whatever is being offered. While buying large quantities of sale-priced items may be more expensive at the outset, it could save you a lot of money in the long run.

Of course, you'll need to be certain you can use these items before you buy them in large quantities. You'll also need to have adequate storage space in the pantry, freezer or elsewhere to keep your bargains until you can use them. The key to saving with this strategy is in stocking up on only those sale items you're certain you'll use.

7) Get A Supermarket "Frequent Shopper Card": Some grocery stores offer frequent or preferred shopper programs to their regular customers. Generally, you fill out an application and then get a membership card which entitles you to bonus discounts on selected items and automatic coupon discounts. Membership in such a program can mean considerable savings.

Check with the management at the store where you shop most frequently about the availability of a frequent or preferred shopper program. If such a program is offered, you can save even more money on your grocery bill by becoming a member.

8) Check Out Warehouse Membership Clubs And Co-ops: For an annual fee of $25 to $40, you may be able to get big savings on many food items through a membership club or a food co-op.

Warehouse membership clubs offer an assortment of items (including non-food items) you can buy in bulk— some for a savings of 50% or more. If you don't mind shopping in a no frills setting, you'll likely be able to save on everything from ketchup to paper towels. You'll also need adequate storage space for bulk purchases of dry goods and plenty of refrigerator and freezer space to store fresh foods. Again, this strategy is economical only if you buy foods you will really use.

Food co-ops also can provide savings of 50% or more on some items. Such savings are possible because the co-op gets food products at discount prices by purchasing in large quantities. The discount purchases are then divided up among co-op members. As a member of a co-op, you'll likely be involved in some of the labor— ordering, picking up and delivering, etc.— but it can be a great way to save on an assortment of food items.

You can find out whether or not there's a food co-op in your area, by calling the Co-op News Network at (207) 948-6161. To get information on starting a food co-op in your area, write to the National Co-operative Bureau Association, 1401 New York Avenue NW, Suite 1100, Washington, DC; or call (800) 636- 6222.

9) Clip And Redeem Coupons: "Couponing" can be an effective money-saving technique, especially if you have a lot of time to look for and clip numerous coupon offers. The average shopper, with limited time to spend on coupon hunting and clipping, can find valuable coupons in newspapers, store circulars, Sunday paper inserts, and magazines.

To make it worth your while, clip and redeem coupons for only those food items you and your family like and will use. Otherwise, the money you save will be wasted. The best rule to follow is to clip coupons only for products you normally buy.

10) Pay Attention To the Check-out Scanner: Yes, even computerized scanners make mistakes. Sometimes these scanners are programmed with incorrect prices. Sometimes they scan the bar code wrong. Sometimes they "forget" about sale prices, ringing

up regular prices instead. Sometimes cashiers make mistakes. And unfortunately, when such mistakes are made, they are much more likely to be in the store's favor.

To protect yourself from an unreliable scanner, make a note of all prices as you fill your shopping cart. Unless the items are marked individually, write the prices on your shopping list. Then, keep your eyes on the register as the scanner rings up the prices.

The best defense against being overcharged by a mistake-prone scanner is to go over your receipt when you get home. Double-check the prices you were charged for every item you buy. If you find any mistakes, take the receipt back to the store and have the charges corrected. Some stores may even give you the item free, in apology for overcharging you.

More Cheap Grocery Shopping Tips

Leave The Kids At Home

Sure you love your children. You want to spend as much time with them as you can. But whenever possible, spend time with them some place other than the supermarket.

Think of grocery shopping as a mission to get the things you need at the lowest possible prices. It's hard to accomplish such a mission with the distraction of keeping an eye on your children. They wander up and down the aisles, beg for candy or some new cereal they've seen advertised on TV, and in general distract you from the business at hand. As result, you'll probably spend more than you planned on items you don't really need.

The Best Time To Find Coupons

You'll find more coupons good for bigger savings between June and October. That's when magazines and newspapers feature the most coupons and biggest discounts on a number of products. According to manufacturers who issue coupons for money-off on their products, May is the next best month for coupon clipping, followed by September and November. You're less likely to find great coupon values in July and December.

When looking for coupons, check the following sources:

— Free-standing inserts (FSI'S): You'll find FSI's in Sunday newspapers. In fact, over one-third of all manufacturer's coupons are distributed in such a manner. Clip them from your own paper and from any papers you can collect from friends, neighbors, co-workers, etc. You also may check with your local library and find out what happens to the inserts from the Sunday papers it receives. If the inserts are routinely thrown away, ask if you can have them instead.

— Daily newspapers and magazines: Look for these coupons in local newspapers. They will often be available about mid-week when many stores distribute their advertising circulars. These coupons often appear one-per-page. You'll also find "in-ad" coupons, which typically offer money off when used in a particular store.

You also can leaf through certain magazines for coupons. Some of the best sources include "women's magazines," such as "Ladies Home Journal," "McCalls," "Family Circle," and "Woman's Day." Money-saving coupons also appear in a few general interest magazines, such as "Reader's Digest."

— In-store coupons: You usually can find in-store coupons on product packages or inserted inside packages. These coupons are to be used when making another purchase of the same product.

— Home mailers: Large marketing firms, manufacturers and their representatives send out packets of coupons as a means of promoting their products. The packets may be addressed to "occupant" or to specific individuals. In either case, they may contain coupons which could help you save on some items you buy regularly.

— Immediate Use Coupons: Also known as manufacturer's "hang-tags," these coupons often are found hanging from the necks of bottled products or attached with removable adhesive to the sides of product packages. They are to be redeemed immediately at the check out counter. Pay close attention as these items are being scanned at the check out counter. The coupons will often go unnoticed by the person working the scanner, unless you call his/her attention to them.

— Instant coupon machines: A fairly recent innovation, instant coupon machines now can be found in thousands of stores throughout the United States. The machines are typically located at the end of aisle displays. Customers press a button on one of these machines and receive a coupon for money off on a particular product being promoted.

— Direct from the manufacturer: You won't always be able to get coupons this way, but it's worth a try. Contact the manufacturers of some of the products you use most frequently and ask them for coupons. Some manufacturers will be agreeable to such a request, others will not. You can contact product manufacturers by calling or writing the numbers and/or addresses listed on product packages.

Double Or Triple Your Coupon Savings

Take advantage of "double coupon" days whenever offered by your supermarket. Some stores even offer triple coupon days, making it possible for you to redeem your coupons for three times their face value. For example, at a store offering double coupon days, a 30-cents-off coupon is actually worth 60 cents off; on triple coupon days, that same coupon is good for 90 cents off. This is a great way to use coupons to get the best possible bargains.

Try Refunding For Extra Savings

The first thing you should know about refunding is that it takes time and effort. In order to be effective, refunding requires daily clipping, saving UPCs (Universal Product Codes), product labels, and cash register tapes (CRTs). You'll also have to use national brand products almost exclusively, and sometimes you'll have to buy in bulk. In addition to all the clipping, saving and buying, you'll need to locate required forms (FRs), fill them out properly and send them in before the expiration dates. If you have the time and you're willing to do all that, you can make an extra $150 to $200 a month by taking advantage of refund offers.

In order to get a refund, you'll usually have to send a product label, UPC or other "proof of purchase" (POP) to a product clearinghouse. In some cases, refund offers require recipients to fill out and send in forms, which are usually found in the supermarket near the product which is subject to the refund offer. About two months later, you'll receive a refund check or "money-off" coupons. Refund checks typically range from $1.00 to $5.00.

Here are six examples of refund offers for everything from cash to coupons. Most are "form required" (FR) offers. Note the expiration date at the end of each offer. Some of the offers may have expired by the time you read this information.

— Capri Sun $1 Refund, P.O. Box 490436, El Paso, TX 88549-0436. Send Universal Product Codes (UPCs) from two purchases of Capri Sun Drink 10-pack (any flavor), a cash register tape, and a properly completed form required (FR) to receive a $1.00 refund check. Offer expires 6/01/96.

— Chef Boyardee $1.50 Refund Offer, P.O. Box 7830, Young America, MN 55573-7830. Send UPC symbols from any 5 packages of Chef Boyardee 7 1/2 ounce Microwave Meals or 10 1/2 ounce Main Meals to get a $1.50 refund check. Be sure to include the completed FR which should be available at the supermarket near the Chef Boyardee Products. Offer expires 3/31/96.

— Cracker Jack Refund Offer, P.O. Box 7767, Clinton, IA 52736-7767. Send the 20-count UPC from Cracker Jack Pack and the Cash Register Tape (CRT) for a $1.50 refund check. Include the properly-completed FR. Offer expires 3/31/96.

— Crosse And Blackwell Sauce/Glaze, P.O. Box 14182, Baltimore, MD 21265. Send a UPC symbol from any Crosse And Blackwell sauce or glaze product, a cash register tape and the required store form for a refund of $2 for the purchase of seafood or ham. Offer has no expiration date.

— Maxwell House Cappuccino $1 Refund Offer, P.O. Box 490512, El Paso, TX 88549-0512. Send the Proof of Purchase (POP) from the plastic outerwrap of a 3-pack of Maxwell House Cappuccino Mocha, a CRT and a completed FR for a $1.00 refund check. Offer expires 12/31/95.

— Shake 'N Bake Coating Mix Offer, P.O. Box 490413, El Paso, TX 88549-0413. Send UPC symbols and completed FR for coupons from Shake 'N Bake. Send three UPC symbols for a $1 coupon; 5 UPC symbols for two $1 coupons; 8 UPC symbols for four $1 coupons. Offer expires 12/31/95.

Don't Buy Nonfood Items At A Supermarket

A good way to run up your grocery bill is to buy nonfood items— toothpaste, shampoo, bath soap, shaving cream, after shave, aspirin, etc.— at a grocery store. Grocery stores typically put high markups on these and other non-food items. Generally, you can get those items much cheaper at a discount store or a drugstore. Shop at each store and compare prices. Buy your nonfood items wherever you get the best value for your money. More often than not, won't be a supermarket.

Cheaper Meat, Fruit And Vegetables

One way to save on meat, fish and poultry is to buy on the last day of their "to-be-sold-by" date. They may not be the best selections, but they are usually marked down by as much as 50 percent. These items are still perfectly safe and tasty. Of course, you should eat whatever you buy within a day or two. But it's still a good way to get the cheapest meat for an evening meal.

The same is true for fruit and vegetables. Just because they've been on display under fluorescent lights for a few days doesn't mean that fruits and vegetables have lost their flavor if used right away. You can often get these items at greatly reduced prices if you know where to look. Ask someone in the produce department to show you where these dated items are kept.

Buy Potatoes A Lot Cheaper By The Bag

Although they may look more appealing, loose potatoes are generally overpriced. In fact, a 10-pound bag of potatoes is typically priced about the same as two pounds or so of loose potatoes. And, there's little, if any, difference in quality between loose and bagged potatoes.

If you use a lot of potatoes, they're definitely cheaper by the bag (10 pounds or more).

Look Closely For The Lowest Prices

When food items are newly marked with higher prices they are placed at the front of shelves for easy access. Look behind those items and you may find a few were missed in the markup and still are marked with the old price.

Salad Savers

Eliminate high-priced lettuce from your salads by replacing it with spinach, cabbage, cucumbers and other vegetables. You also may visit your market's salad bar (if available) and buy only the small quantity of individual vegetables you need. Overall, you'll be saving money and avoiding waste.

Another way to eat a cheaper salad is to make your own salad dressing. It doesn't take much time and you can save $2.00 a bottle or more making your own. Here are a couple of easy recipes:

— Homemade Italian Dressing

Mix the following ingredients: 2 cups of vegetable oil; 1 cup of wine vinegar; 1 teaspoon each of oregano, basil and celery seed; 1/3 cup of grated onion. Add sugar to taste.

— Homemade Blue Cheese Dressing

Mix the following ingredients: 2 ounces of crumbled blue

cheese; 1/2 teaspoon salt; 1/4 teaspoon pepper; 1 1/2 cups mayonnaise. Stir well and keep refrigerated.

You also can save by eating regular white bread with your salad, rather than French, Italian or other specialty breads. These specialty breads may go well with salads, but they are typically much more expensive than white bread.

Avoid Convenience Foods

Convenience foods may indeed be convenient, but they're also costly. You'll have to determine for yourself whether or not the convenience is worth the added expense. If not, buy the ingredients and make your own. For example, instead of buying vegetables with butter or sauce added, try buying vegetables plain and making your own sauces. Once you get the hang of it, you'll find that making your own sauce doesn't take much time and it's a definite money-saver.

When To Get The Best Buys On Fresh Fruits And Vegetables

Generally, you'll pay less for fresh fruit and vegetables during the peak harvest season. Check the following seasonal buying guide for the best times to buy these fruits and vegetables at the lowest prices.

Seasonal Buying Guide for Fresh Fruits and Vegetables

Fruits	Peak Harvest Season
Apples	September - March

Apricots	June - July
Cantaloupes	June - August
Cherries	June, July
Cranberries	September - December
Grapefruit	October - May
Nectarines	July, August
Peaches	July, August
Pears, Anjou	October - April
Pears, Bartlett	July - October
Plums	May - September
Rhubarb	May
Strawberries	April - June
Watermelons	June - August

Vegetables

Asparagus	April, May
Beans	May - September
Beets	June - October
Broccoli	October - April
Brussels sprouts	September - February
Cauliflower	October
Corn	May - September
Okra	June - August
Peas	May - September
Sweet Potatoes	September - December
Tomatoes	May - August

Pick Your Own Fruits And Vegetables And Save

Admittedly, some people consider picking fruits and vegetables back-breaking work. But, with a minimum of labor, you
can save a bundle on these items. In season, many vegetable
and fruit farmers allow you to pick your own beans, peas,
apples, strawberries, blueberries, oranges, and other fruits and
vegetables. For your labor, you get garden fresh foods for much
less than you'd pay in a supermarket. And, you can buy by the
pound, bushel, quart, bagful, or whatever amount you can pick.
You'll not only save on fresh foods, you'll get some exercise as
well.

Many farms which offer "pick-your-own" vegetables and
fruits advertise in the classified sections of local newspapers.
Check these ads whenever your favorite foods are in season.

Think Twice Before Buying Bottled Water

Americans drink over $2.5 billion worth of bottled water
every year. That's a lot of money to spend on water that may
actually come from common water supplies. According to the
Food and Drug Administration, as much as 25 percent of the
bottled water on the market is drawn from municipal supplies.
The water is then filtered, bottled in expensive-looking containers and sold by bottlers for $1 to $4 a gallon. Since it costs bottlers an average of 50 cents per gallon to bottle, market and distribute their product, bottlers can make a nifty profit for their
high-priced drink.

On the other hand, household tap water, which comes from

the same municipal supplies, is a lot cheaper. Consumers typically get several hundred gallons of tap water for $1. So, the next time you're tempted to buy some high-priced bottled water, open the tap instead and get a much cheaper thirst quencher.

Start A Food Co-op In Your Area

As noted earlier in this chapter, being a member of a food co-op can mean a considerable savings on your grocery bills. If there are no food co-ops convenient to where you live, you may want to consider starting your own.

The first thing you'll need to do is locate a good and cheap, source of food and dry goods. Local distributors and manufacturers (if any) are good places to start. Once you're certain of your source, the next step is to solicit members. Of course friends, relatives, neighbors and co-workers are likely candidates to join your co-op, but you also can post notices on community bulletin boards as a way to attract members.

You can get free information on how to set up a food co-op by writing to National Cooperative Business Association, 1401 New York Avenue, NW, Suite 1100, Washington, DC 20005; or calling (800) 636- NCBA (6222).

Free Food For Women, Infants And Children

There's a little-known government-sponsored program that provides free food for women, infants and children. The program, called WIC, is a nationwide nutrition education program which provides supplemental foods which provide good health for pregnant women, breastfeeding women, and their infants and children to age five.

To qualify for WIC assistance, family incomes must fall below a level established in USDA regulations and recipients must be residents in the state in which they receive benefits. However, the income guidelines for this program are generally quite liberal.

Qualified families receive coupons for such food items as eggs, cereal, milk, peanut butter, and juice. In addition to these supplemental foods, WIC also provides nutrition education and referrals for health care. In some states, the free food may even be delivered to the recipient's home by human services agencies. And with the money saved by not having to purchase the food provided by WIC, qualified families can purchase more fresh fruits, vegetables, meats, baby foods and other foods that the program does not provide.

To find out whether or not you qualify for the WIC program, contact a local human service agency. You also may check your telephone directory for a listing of a WIC clinic in your area.

For more information about government-sponsored food programs such as WIC and the Commodity Supplemental Food Program, see chapter 10, "Government Goodies."

CHAPTER 3   **3**

CHEAPIES, FREE GOODIES & GIVEAWAYS

Clothing Cheapies

There doesn't seem to be much middle ground when it comes to shopping for clothing. For some people it's a pleasurable adventure, for others an uncomfortable necessity. But while one person's pleasure is another person's pain, everyone feels the same when it comes time to pay the bill.

Regardless of whether you're a slave to fashion or you just buy what you need, there are many ways to cut your clothing costs and still look your best. The following tips and suggestions can help even the most reluctant shoppers put together a stylish wardrobe at bargain prices.

Smart Shopping Tips

1) Plan your wardrobe. Before you go on a shopping spree look in your closet and check out what's there. Instead of buying a whole new outfit, buy separate items and accessories that coordinate with the items you already have. As a result, you'll look and feel like you're wearing a new outfit, but you won't be dreading the bill.

2) Look for the best quality at the lowest prices. The key to getting the best clothing for your dollar is quality. Poor quality merchandise, regardless of the cost, is never a bargain. When shopping for clothing, here are some signs of quality you should look for:

— Clean, odor-free fabric that doesn't stay wrinkled after being crushed by hand.

— Smooth linings that are invisible from the right side.

— Evenly matched plaids, stripes, and cross seams.

— Flat, smooth seams with finished edges.

— Unbroken stitches that are straight and smooth.

— Hems and seams that are even in width and suitable for alterations.

— Zippers that work smoothly and lie flat.

— Securely held pockets, buttons, fasteners, and trims.

3) Try it on. Many clothing manufacturers use different cuts on their clothing. That could result in size variations you won't notice unless you're wearing the item. Unless you're buying through the mail, try on each article of clothing and make sure you get a proper and flattering fit. Otherwise you'll be wasting your money on clothes you may wear only one time before sending them to a "bottom drawer" or "back-of-the-closet" exile.

When planning a shopping trip, be sure to wear garments that are easy to remove, and the same type of undergarments and shoes you intend to wear with your new clothing.

4) Take a friend along. You may enjoy shopping alone, but an honest friend can help you avoid impulse purchases that may not fit properly, are unflattering or flawed. It's also nice to have help finding the size and color you need. And, with a friend at your side, you can take advantage of occasional "2 for 1 sale.".

5) Don't buy something you can't use. Brand-name clothing bargains are great as long as you'll wear them. However, if you pay $10 for a designer shirt you'll never wear, you're not getting a bargain. Make sure you need and can use whatever you buy, regardless of the price.

6) Consider the care involved before you buy. Read a garment's label to determine how much time and money will be required to keep it clean. If it has to be dry-cleaned, you'll need to figure that into the overall cost. It may not be such a great buy after all. Clothing that is machine-washable may be the best buy. It also may be a good idea to avoid whites and pleats as much as possible.

7) Buy in bulk. When you find items you like and will wear, such as socks, shirts and undergarments on sale, buy several. You'll save money in the long run. Some stores even offer discounts if you buy in quantity.

8) Buy shoes early in the day. You're not likely to get as good a fit later in the day when your feet have swollen slightly as you will in the morning hours. If you do try on shoes late in the day, make sure you allow for the swelling of your feet.

9) Shop for girl's clothing in the boy's department. Boy's clothes are often cheaper than similar clothing for girls. Women also can save on cotton shirts and T-shirts by shopping in the men's department.

10) Ask for a refund. Instead of bemoaning your bad luck the next time you buy an item at the regular price only to have it go on sale the next day, ask the store for a refund. Many stores, especially larger ones, will refund the difference. At any rate, you have nothing to lose by asking. And while you're at it, try to find out when the store's next sale is scheduled and what items will be marked down. If you can get the information, you can hold off on making your purchases until you can buy at lower prices.

11) Know a store's return policy. Most stores allow full exchanges or refunds if you return the clothes with receipts and tags. Don't cut off the tags until you try on the clothing at home and are completely satisfied with your purchase.

12) Check out private-label clothing. Many discount stores offer

their own labels for considerably less than similar brand-name items. Be sure to check out the quality before you buy.

13) Don't buy expensive items at full price. If you're patient, you can find items such as winter coats marked down well below their regular prices. Check the shopping calendar in chapter 1 for the best times to find specific items on sale.

Make Your Own Clothing And Sew Up The Savings

If you sew you can save hundreds of dollars by making your own clothing. Or if you know someone who sews you can invest in patterns, fabrics and the like and have your clothes made to order cheaper than buying them already made. And you can get discounts of 20% to 50% on patterns, fabrics and other necessities by joining a fabric club, such as those listed below:

— Barbeau Fine Fabrics, 1308-N Birch St., Fort Collins, CO 80521; Phone: (800) 766-5588. Membership in this swatch service is $12. Members receive four swatch mailings and a binder to keep them in. That way you can look and feel before you buy at discount prices. Call or write for information.

— Famous Labels Fabric Outlet, 2155 E. Burnside, Gresham, OR 97030; Phone: (503) 666-3187. Formerly known as the Activewear Fabric Club, Famous Labels Fabric Outlet now offers designer fabrics, including rayons, cottons, wools, lycra, knits and wovens, at outlet prices. Members receive monthly mailers of Designer Sportswear and Famous Activewear fabric swatches. Call or write the company for information.

— Fashion Fabrics Club, 10490 Baur Boulevard, St. Louis, MO 63132; Phone: (800) 468-0602. Offers discounts on hundreds of designer fabrics, including worsted wool, cotton prints, ultra suede, microfibers, silk prints, silk tweed, and more. Members receive free monthly swatch kits, free frequent buyer's plan, 24-hour telephone service. Contact the company for more information.

— G Street Fabrics, 12240 Wilkins Avenue, Rockville, MD 20852; PHONE: (301) 231-8960. This club offers fabrics by mail to all its members. Membership entitles you to 60 swatches every month, monthly mailings, and free custom samples. Call or write for more information.

— Nantucket Sewing Centre, P.O. Box 99, Nantucket, MA 02554; Phone: (508) 228-3846. Members pay an annual fee of $10.00 and receive access to "sensational fabrics" and "natural fibers." Call or write the company for information.

— Stretch and Sew Fabrics, 19725 40th Avenue W., Lynnwood, Wa 98303; (206) 774-9678. Subscription to this national mail order fabric service is $24 a year. Members receive a bi-monthly newsletter which features patterns, new ideas, fabric specials, garment ideas and more. Call or write for information.

— Thai Silks, 252 State Street, Los Altos, CA 94022; Phone: (800) 722-Silk. Annual membership in this silk fabric club is $20. Members receive access to a large selection of velvets, chiffons, prints, satins, suitings, scarves and more. Call or write to request a free brochure.

Discount Sewing Supplies

Many companies also offer fabrics, patterns, sewing supplies and notions at discount prices. Most, including the following, have product catalogs available upon request.

— Apparel Component Supply (A.C.S.), 447 West 36th Street, New York, NY 10018. A.C.S. offers notions, thread, lining, pattern making supplies, fasteners, cutting tools and other sewing supplies at wholesale prices. Write the company to order a product catalog for $3.00 (refundable with first order).

— Button Factory, 8205 Santa Monica Blvd., Unit #1-212, West Hollywood, CA 90046-5912; Phone: (310) 659-7307. Offers a huge selection of buttons— wood, metal, plastic, cotton, rubber and aluminum—at wholesale prices. No catalog is available, but the company will send samples upon request. No minimum orders required. Contact the company for more information.

— Fabric Depot Inc, 700 SE 122nd Ave, Portland, OR 97233; Phone: (800) 392-3376. Offers discounts of 40% to 50% on fabrics, notions, thread, zippers and other sewing supplies. Call or write for information.

— Feminine Touch Fabrics, 8453, Seneca Turnpike, New Hartford, NY 13413; Phone: (315) 793-0623. Offers designer fabrics at discount prices. Send $2.00 and a large SASE for brochure.

— National Thread & Supply Corp., 695 Red Oak Road, Stockbridge, GA 30281. Phone: (800) 331-7600 Ext. A-225.

Offers direct savings on notions, thread and other sewing supplies. Call or write to request a free catalog.

— Sewin' In Vermont, 84 Concord Avenue, St. Johnsbury, VT 05819; Phone: (800) 451-5124. Offers sewing and serger equipment, presses, vacuums, dress forms, and other sewing equipment at discount prices. Call or write for information.

— Solo Sewing Supplies, P.O. box 378A, Foxboro, MA 02035. Offers a large inventory of zippers, thread and notions at wholesale prices. A 60-page catalog is available for $1.00 (refundable with first order).

Where To Buy Clothes For Less

When it comes to buying clothing, it really pays to shop around. You may find bargains in your own backyard, or you might be able to attire yourself in splendor for less by driving to the nearest outlet shopping center. One thing's for certain, there's no shortage of stores in competition for your money.

Outlet Shopping Centers

The popularity of outlet shopping can be seen in the increasing number of outlet centers in the United States. According to industry insiders, there were 275 outlet shopping centers nationwide at the end of 1993. Today, there are over 300 outlets, offering savings on a wide assortment of merchandise, including brand-name clothing and footwear for men, women and children.

Savings at outlets typically range from 25 to 70 percent on merchandise that sometimes includes seconds, but generally consists of manufacturers' overruns and closeouts. Such discounts are possible because manufacturer-owned outlets sell their merchandise directly to customers, eliminating the middlemen and 50 to 100 percent markups at many clothing and department stores. Most outlet centers also are located "off the beaten path" away from downtown shopping areas where it doesn't cost as much to operate. Depending on where you live, you should be prepared to travel 30 to 50 miles or more to reach an outlet shopping center.

While you can get some remarkable bargains at outlets, you'll need to exercise caution and use smart shopping techniques. Be especially careful when buying seconds. These are items that fail to meet the maker's quality control standards and are generally sold "as is" with "no returns" accepted. You should inspect for size, flaws in the fabric, tears, broken zippers and so on. Some outlets will mark such items as "flawed," others however, do not.

To locate a specific outlet store in your area, call (800) 555-1212. If the outlet store you're trying to locate doesn't have an 800 number, try calling directory assistance in the largest city near where you live. You also can find listings of outlet centers nationwide in the following publications: "The Joy of Outlet Shopping" (1-800-344-6397; $6.95); and "Outletbound, Guide to the Nation's Best Outlets" (1-800-336-8853; $7.95).

Here's a sample list of factory outlet stores located across the country:

— Children's Clothing: Baby Bliss Outlet Store; Boston Traders Kids; Brooks Brothers Factory Store; The Eagle's Eye Kids; Hang Ten; Kids Xpress; LaPetite Factorie; Today's Child.

— Women's Clothing: Ann Taylor Clearance Centers; Anne Klein Factory Stores; Carroll Reed Catalog Outlet; Euro Collections; First Choice; French Connection Outlet; J. Crew Factory Store; J & F Factory Outlet; Large Sizes for Less; Laura Ashley; Liz Claiborne Outlet Stores; Maternities Factory Outlet.

— Men's Clothing: Arrow Factory Stores; Banana Republic Outlet; Bugle Boy Outlet; Calvin Klein Outlet; Country Road Australia Outlet; Dickies Factory Outlet; Eddie Bauer Outlet Store; European Designer Outlet; Geoffrey Beane Company; John Henry & Friends for Men.

— Family Apparel (Men's, Women's, Children's Clothing): B.U.M. Equipment; Fruit of the Loom; The Gap Outlet; Gitano Factory Outlet; Guess? Factory Outlet; Jordache; L.L. Bean Factory Outlet Store; Levi's Outlet; London Fog Factory Stores; OshKosh B'Gosh Factory Stores.

— Underwear/Lingerie/ Hosiery: Appel-Jones New York Intimates; Barbizon Lingerie Co., Inc.; Formfit; Jockey; LaLingerie; The Robe Outlet; The Sox Market.

— Footwear: Bostonian Factory Outlet; Converse Factory Outlet Stores; Nike Factory Store; Buster Brown; Endicott Johnson; Florsheim Factory; Naturalizer Outlet; Perry Ellis Shoes.

— Jewelry And Accessories: Charles Jourdan Factory Outlet; Coro Fashion Jewelry; L'ccessory; London Fog Factory Stores; Tower Jewelry Outlet.

Designer Outlet Locations

You can avoid paying full price for designer clothing by shopping at a designer outlet. There are scores of designer outlets across the country. Check the following list of four of the most popular designer labels for an outlet location near you:

— Anne Klein

AL: Boaz; AZ: Casa Grande, Sedona; CA: Barstow, Cabazon, Gilroy; CO: Silverthorne; FL: Naples, Orlando; GA: Calhoun; IN: Michigan City; ME: Freeport, Kittery; MD: Perryville, Queenstown; MI: Birch Run; MO: Osage Beach; NH: North Conway; NJ: Flemington, Secaucus, Shrewsburry; NY: Central Valley, Lake George; NC: Blowing Rock; OK: Stroud; PA: Lancaster, Tannersville; SC: Hilton Head, Myrtle Beach; TN: Pigeon Forge; TX: San Marcos; VT: Williamsburg, Woodbridge; WI: Kenosha.

— Calvin Klein

AL: Foley; FL: Orlando; ME: Freeport, Kittery; MA: New Bedford; MI: West Branch; NH: North Conway; NJ: Flemington, Secaucus; NY: Central Valley, Niagara Falls; PA: Reading; VT: Manchester Center; VA: Williamsburg, Woodbridge; WI:

Kenosha.

— Liz Claiborne

AL: Boaz, Foley; AZ: Casa Grande; CA: Gilroy, Lake Elsinore; CO: Silverthorne; GA: Calhoun, Commerce; IA: Williamsburg; LA: Gonzalez; ME: Kittery; MD: Perryville, Queenstown; MA: Buzzards Bay, Medford; MI: Birch Run; MN: North Branch: NH: North Conway; NJ: Secaucus; NY: Central Valley; NC: Burlington; OK: Stroud; PA: Mt. Pocono, Reading; TN: Pigeon Forge; TX: Conroe, Hillsboro; VT: Manchester; VA: Waynesboro, Williamsburg; WA: Burlington; WV: Martinsburg; WI: Kenosha.

— Ralph Lauren

AL: Boaz, Foley; AZ: Page; CA: Anderson, Barstow, Eureka; Mammoth Lakes, Redding; CO: Durango; GA: Valdosta; IN: Michigan City; IA: Williamsburg; KN: Colby; KY: Eddyville; ME: Freeport, Kittery; MA: Lawrence; MI: West Branch; MO: Osage Beach; MT: Billings; NH: North Conway; NY: Cohoes, Lake George, Niagara Falls, Plattsburgh, Watertown; NC: Blowing Rock; PA: Reading, Somerset; SD: Rapid City; TN: Chattanooga, Pigeon Forge; UT: St. George; VT: Manchester; VA: Williamsburg; WV: Martinsburg; WI: Appleton; WY: Jackson.

Off-Price Chain-Store Bargains

Off-price chains, such as Filene's Basement, T.J. Maxx, Syms, Burlington Coat Factory, Ross Dress For Less, and

Marshall's, offer prices up to 60 percent below typical retail on clothing for men, women and children. These are "no-frills" stores which feature factory overruns and closeouts from leading designers. While some off-price clothing may be end-of-the-season goods, you'll also find current, in-season styles from designers such as Calvin Klein, Perry Ellis, Armani, Anne Klein, and many others.

While you can find some genuine bargains at off-price apparel stores, you'll need to shop around and try items on before you buy. Otherwise you could end up with poor quality merchandise. Also be sure to find out about a store's return policy before you buy. Some off-price stores don't accept returns, while others may have very limited return policies. If you're persistent and careful, you can find some exceptional values at off-price stores, such as those listed below:

— Filene's Basement; (800) 666-4054. Offers discounts on men's and women's clothing in more than 30 stores throughout the Northeastern and Midwestern United States.

— Loehmann's; (212) 902-0800. There are Loehmann's off-price stores located throughout the U.S. offering clothing for women only.

— Marshall's; (800) 627-7425. This leading off-price chain has stores throughout the U.S. which offer men's, women's and children's clothing at discount prices.

— T.J. Maxx; (800) 926-6299. Offers men's and women's clothing at stores located nationwide.

Thrift Shops

These stores offer used clothing obtained through donations. They're sponsored by agencies such as Goodwill and the Salvation Army, and can provide some decent bargains on children's clothing. Since most children outgrow their clothing before they wear them out, the selection at thrift stores can be especially good. You also may be able to find other once-worn or infrequently worn clothing that still looks like new. And thrift shop prices are hard to beat.

Consignment Shops

Consignment shops offer some very good bargains on barely worn clothing, generally for women and children. While some consignment offerings are dated and no longer stylish, much of what you'll find in these stores is not only fashionable but of good quality as well. Nothing showing signs of excessive wear or of poor quality is accepted for resale. That means the overall selection at consignment shops is from good to excellent. Of course the prices are well below retail, as well.

The clothing is sold on a consignment arrangement between the original owner and the consignment shop owner. The original owner generally gets 40 to 50 percent of any of his/her items that are sold. The following shopping tips can help you get the best bargains at your favorite consignment shops:

— Shop as often as you can to know what consignment bargains are being offered. Consignment offerings change frequently, and if you shop only once in a while, you're bound to miss out on some good bargains.

— Don't wait too long to buy an item you want. Since most consignment offerings are "one-of-a-kind" items, you'll have to be first in line to cash in on many of the items you want. In other words, "first come, first served." If you wait too long, someone else is likely to get your bargain.

— Get to know the owners and managers of the consignment shops in your area. Ask them to put you on a list of customers to notify whenever they receive new consignments of the kind of clothing you're likely to buy.

— Compare all the consignment stores in your shopping area to find out which store(s) generally has the clothing and accessories that suits your needs.

Warehouse Clubs

Major warehouse buying clubs, such as BJ's Wholesale Club, Price-Costco (Price Clubs and Costco Wholesale Clubs), and Sam's Club are warehouse-sized stores which offer wholesale bargains to club members. These huge stores offer deep discounts of 30 to 50 percent off retail on all sorts of merchandise, including clothing. But don't expect department store ambiance— warehouse clubs are generally "no frills" stores with racks and racks of merchandise.

Most of the merchandise offered at warehouse clubs is first-quality, but the selection of clothing is generally limited. You'll usually be able to find casual wear clothing, undergarments, and sportswear. Little if any dress clothing is available. However, if you're persistent, and don't mind the lack of fitting rooms and salespeople, you could discover a real bargain or two.

In order to "get in" on the wholesale savings at a warehouse club, you'll have to become a dues-paying member. Membership fees generally range from $25 to $35 a year, with membership usually limited to businesses and certain groups and organizations, such as senior citizens or members of a credit union. However, anyone who is willing to pay the membership fee is likely to be accepted.

Check the Yellow Pages to find a warehouse club operating in your area. If you can find one within a couple of hours driving distance find out whether or not you can "look it over" before becoming a member. Some clubs will allow you to visit and shop on a trial basis before charging a membership fee. That's a good way to find out whether or not the club has the kind of clothing and other items you want. You also may visit a warehouse club in your area with a friend or a relative who is a member.

While you're making your trial visit, be sure to compare prices, products and quality with those at area retail stores. Remember, comparison shopping is a key to getting the best values on everything you need regardless of where you shop. You also should find out whether or not the club accepts credit cards, and if so, which cards. Some warehouse clubs will not accept credit cards. Other clubs will accept only one credit card. If the club doesn't accept a card you use, you'll need to take along a pocketful of cash in order to make any purchases.

Discount Department Stores

Discount department stores, such as Wal-Mart, Kmart, Ames, and Target offer a wide variety of merchandise at prices that are generally lower than they are for the same merchandise in "old-fashioned" department stores. Discount stores are able to offer these lower prices because they provide fewer customer services and take smaller markups.

Generally, these stores buy in quantity from manufacturers and offer their merchandise in a basic self-service setting. Salespeople usually are available in only a few departments, such as jewelry and electronics. By buying and selling in volume, and saving on overhead, discounters are able to operate on smaller profit margins than regular department stores and as a result can offer most of their merchandise at lower prices.

Most discount stores offer some name brands along with their own store brands, but generally, discount store quality is a cut below that offered in department stores. The best clothing values at such stores include casual clothes (jeans, sweatshirts, pajamas, work clothes), undergarments, and sportswear. Be sure to compare quality and prices with other retail outlets before making your purchase from a discounter.

Mail-Order Clothing Discounts

Shopping by mail can save you time as well as money. Regardless of your clothing needs, there's a mail-order company that has what you want, and in many cases at prices far below retail. You can browse through several product catalogs until you find the item you want at the price you want to pay, and then place your order either by phone or by mail. The merchandise you order will be shipped right to your door. You don't have to face gridlock or the thundering herd of fellow bargain hunters. You can order virtually anything you need without ever leaving your easy chair.

Of course, you should take precautions before ordering anything from a mail-order catalog. Just because a catalog listing appears to be the greatest bargain of all time doesn't mean that it is. Remember, you'll be paying good money to buy merchandise you've only seen on paper. With that in mind, here are some extra precautions you can take to protect yourself and your mail-order purchases:

— Calculate the final purchase price before you buy. Include shipping fees and state sales tax (if applicable). Then decide whether or not you're getting a bargain.

— Pay by credit card whenever possible. Avoid paying with check or money order if you can, and NEVER send cash through the mail. Using a charge card also can help minimize any problems that may arise if the merchandise is defective or otherwise unsatisfactory.

— Find out about the company's return policy. Most companies publish their policies on returning merchandise in their product catalogs. Make sure you understand and agree with the company's policy, including who pays the shipping charges for returned items, before you place an order.

— Open all your packages immediately. You should make sure you receive exactly what you paid for and that it is in perfect condition. If there is a problem with the merchandise, contact the company as soon as possible.

— Keep copies of all paperwork involved in the transaction in case there is a problem with the merchandise you receive. You should keep a record of the name, address and phone number of the company, name of the salesperson if you ordered by phone, goods you ordered, the date of your order, the amount you paid and the method of payment.

The following mail-order sources offer clothing and accessories for men, women and children. Most of the companies provide product catalogs free of charge. Some companies may require a nominal charge of $1 to $5 for their catalogs, but those charges are usually refunded with your first order (for an additional listing of mail-order sources, see chapter 10, "Miscellaneous Cheapies And Free Stuff").

Men's, Women's And Children's Apparel

— Baby Clothes Wholesale, 60 Ethel Road, West Piscataway, NJ O8854; Phone: (800) 568-1930; (800) 568-1940. This company offers wholesale savings by mail on clothing for girls and boys from newborn to size seven. Send $3.00 for the Baby Clothes Wholesale Catalog.

— Basic Brilliance, P.O. Box 1719, Port Townsend, WA 98368; (360) 385-3835. Offers a selection of children's clothing for both girls and boys sizes infant through 10. Many items including quality dresses are priced at around $20 or less. Call or write the company to request a free catalog.

— Chadwick's of Boston, One Chadwick Place, Box 1600, Brockton, MA 02403; Phone: (508) 583-6600. Offers savings of up to 50 % on brand name women's apparel. Brand names include Ellen Ashley, Ease Sport, Oleg Cassini, Bill Blass, Abernathy, Erika and Co. and many others. Call or write the company and request a free product catalog.

— D & A Merchandise Company, 22 Orchard Street, New York, NY 10002; Phone: (212) 925-4766. Offers most brand name lingerie for women and men's and women's underwear at savings of up to 35% off regular retail prices. Call or write the company to order a product catalog ($2.00).

— J.M. Originals, 70 Berme Road, Ellenville, NY 12428; (914) 647-1111. Offers fashionable clothing for children at 50 to 75 % off typical retail prices. Sizes range from infant to 14. Call or write the company and provide specific brand names and sizes for price quotes.

— Land's End, Inc., Land's End Lane, Dodgeville, WI 53595-0001; Phone: (800) 332-4444. Land's End offers mail-order savings of up to 40% on men's, women's and children's clothing. Several catalogs are available free upon request.

— Old Pueblo Traders, Palo Verde at 34th, P.O. Box 27800, Tucson, AZ 85726-7800; Phone: (520) 748-8600 . Old Pueblo Traders offers women's clothing—casual and dress— as well as women's footwear at savings of up to 30 % off typical retail prices. Call or write the company to request a product catalog.

— Olsen Mills Direct; (800) 829-4979. Offers children's clothing by Osh-Kosh at discount prices. Call the toll-free number to order a catalog ($2.00 refundable).

— Paul Frederick Shirt Company, 140 West Main Street, Fleetwood, PA 19522-9989; Phone: (800) 247-1417. This company manufactures its own quality dress shirts and offers them factory direct at savings of up to 50% off typical retail prices.

— Quinn's Shirt Shop, Rt. 12, Box 131, North Grosvenordale, CT 06255; (508) 943-7183. Offers irregular shirts by Arrow at prices up to 60% lower than typical retail. Send $2 (credited to your first order) and a SASE for a current price list.

— Rubens & Marble, Inc., P.O. Box 14900, Chicago, IL 60614-0900; (312) 348-6200. Offers discounts on clothing for infants. as well as on crib and bassinet items. Send a SASE and request a free product brochure.

Men's, Women's And Children's Footwear

— Gene's Shoes Discount Catalog, 126 N. Main Street, St. Charles, MO 63301; (314) 946-0804. Offers discounts of up to 30 % on dress and casual shoes for men and women. Brand names include Hush Puppies, Selby, Soft Spots, Easy Spirit, Devon Park and many others. Send $1 to order a discount catalog.

— Justin Discount Boots and Cowboy Outfitters, P.O. Box 67, Justin, TX 76247; Phone: (800) 677-2008. This company offers savings of up to 30% on men's and women's western style boots and clothing.

— Lee's Comfort Shoes, P.O. Box 126, S. Sandusky Avenue, Bucyrus, OH 44820; (800) 753-4736. Offers discounts on women's shoes in hard-to-find sizes. In stock are a selection of walking shoes, sandals, casuals, dress shoes, oxfords and other styles by Easy Spirit, Selby, Clinic, Soft Spots, Cobbie and other famous makers. Call or write the company and request a free catalog.

Hosiery And Ladies Intimate Apparel

Many women can order panty hose and other undergarments from mail order companies, such as those listed below. Some mail-order companies specialize in irregulars or imperfects, selling them at deep discounts. If you don't mind a few minor flaws in these garments, you can save up to 50% off regular retail prices on brand name merchandise. You may find it's cheaper to buy such brands as L'eggs, No Nonsense, Hanes and Bali through the mail. Contact any of the following companies to request their mail-order catalogs.

— Kayser-Roth Corporation, P.O. Box NN-1, Burlington, NC 27220; Phone: (919) 229-2246. Offers discounts on No Nonsense panty hose.

— Lady Grace Intimate Apparel, 61 Exchange Street, P.O. Box 128, Malden, MA 02148; (800) 922-0504. Offers a full line of women's intimate apparel with savings of up to 35% on some items. Brand names include Bali, Maidenform, Warners, Olga, Carnival, Hanes, Roxanne, Playtex, Vanity Fair and others. Write or call to request a catalog.

— L'eggs Hanes Bali Playtex Outlet Catalog, L'eggs, Brands, Inc., P.O. Box 843, Rural Hall, NC 27098-0843; (910) 744-1170. Offers a large selection of first-quality women's hosiery and intimate apparel at discounts of up to 60 %.   Brand names include Bali, Hanes, Isotoner, L'eggs, Playtex, Underalls and others. Some "slightly imperfect" hosiery and underwear also are available. Call or write the company and request a free product catalog.

— National Wholesale Company, 400 National Boulevard, Lexington, NC 27294; Phone: (704) 249-0211. Offers savings of up to 50% on some items.

— No Nonsense Direct, Box 26095, Greensboro, NC 27420-6095. This company offers No Nonsense panty hose, as well as imperfects at savings of up to 60% off typical store prices.

— Roby's Intimates, 121 S. 18th Street, Philadelphia, PA 19103; Phone: (800) 878-8272; (215) 751-1730 (in PA). Offers a selection of ladies intimate apparel by manufacturers such as Bali, Chantelle, Christian Dior, Lady Marlene, Maidenform, Playtex and others at savings of up to 25%.

— Showcase of Savings, P.O. Box 748, Rural Hall, NC 27098; Phone: (919) 744-1170. Offers imperfects of famous brands such as Hanes, L'eggs, Underalls and Bali.

— Smart Saver, P.O. Box 209, Waso, IL 60183. The Smart Saver offers intimate apparel by Playtex, Exquisite Form, Vanity Fair and other famous makers at savings of up to 30% off typical retail prices.

CHAPTER 4

CHEAPIES, FREE GOODIES
AND GIVEAWAYS

Money Matters: Banking, Credit Cards, Investing, Taxes And Insurance

Before you pat yourself on the back for saving money on your grocery bill, consider your overall personal finances. How much of your money is your bank getting through high fees and interest charges? How much do your credit cards cost each month? What financial investments have you made? Are you paying more taxes than you should? Are you paying too much for inadequate insurance coverage? The point is, the money you may be squandering through poor management of your personal finances may add up to much more than you save at the grocery store or elsewhere.

How you save money is important, but your overall financial security depends more on how you manage your money. You can save hundreds, even thousands of dollars every year by choosing the right bank, credit card(s), insurance polices, and by taking advantage of available tax breaks. You can plan for your future financial security by choosing the right investments. This chapter describes these and other money-management choices available, and how, by taking control of your own personal finances, you can save (and make) hundreds or thousands of dollars every year.

Banking Bargains: How To Choose The Right Bank

"Here's the deal: high fees, low returns, and poor service." Does that sound like a "true" advertisement for your bank? If so, you're doing business with the wrong institution. Here are several suggestions for finding the best deal on the banking services you need:

1) Comparison shop. As all savvy consumers know, comparison shopping is the key to finding the best deals. When shopping for a bank to handle your money, be sure to shop around and compare the terms and prices of all the services you need. Compare them on the basis of how you spend your money. Don't choose the first bank that appears eager to have your business. Consider carefully the services and fees offered by several banks in your area. Find out how much each bank charges for such services as check printing and processing, deposits, monthly

maintenance, ATM use, processing bounced checks, stopping payments, and any other services you might need.

2) Look for a bank that is federally insured. Check the front door to see if the bank displays a government logo of the Federal Deposit Insurance Corporation (FDIC). If the institution is insured by the federal government, an individual is covered for up to $100,000 in deposits if the institution fails.

3) Choose a bank that offers "free" checking. The Truth in Savings Act prohibits institutions from advertising free checking if there are hidden charges or requirements. For example, you aren't getting free checking if you're required to maintain a minimum balance to qualify. Likewise there should be no monthly service charges or per-check fees. A genuine free checking account comes with no strings attached.

4) Ask about charges for ATM withdrawal. These days it may be difficult to find a bank that doesn't charge for ATM withdrawals. Some banks may not charge for withdrawals from their own ATMs, but do charge for withdrawals from ATMs that are not their own. If you can't find a bank that offers free ATM withdrawals, look for one that charges $1.00 or less.

5) Banking-by-phone service. Full service banking by phone may include allowing you to pay your bills, transfer money from checking to savings, and phoning the bank to check on your balance. While these services are convenient, they aren't free. If you prefer to do a lot of your banking by phone, choose a bank that offers the services you want and will use, and at reasonable fees. Banking-by-phone services will vary from bank to bank so shop around for the best deal.

6) Extras. Look for a bank that provides free checks, free money orders, free or discounted traveler's checks, and other extras at no or low fees. Such perks can make other banking fees a little more palatable.

Bank Account Charges You Can Avoid

Take a careful look at your bank statement. You may be surprised at the number and dollar amount of bank fees being charged to your account. You could be paying more for printed checks, more for your checking account balance, higher ATM fees, more for bouncing a check, or even paying a fee for each deposit you make.

A recent government study confirms that bank fees on checking and savings accounts jumped by an unprecedented 50% between 1989 and 1993. A portion of that increase comes from new fees added to accounts, while the rest comes from raising existing fees. And if that isn't bad enough, you may have been paying these fees without being aware you're doing so. That's because most banks don't send customers separate notices whenever new fees are added or old fees are increased. In most cases, a notice of a change in fees can be found written in legal language and with small print, on a card that arrives with your monthly statement. You probably don't pay much attention to such a card, and as a result may not realize for months that you're paying for a service that used to be free or that you're paying one or more new fees.

Some banks have made the news lately by levying fees on customers who choose to use human tellers rather than ATMs.

Even "checking free" accounts, with no minimum balance or monthly fees, may be misleading. You may be paying more for other services such as replacement checks or using an ATM.

The best way to avoid such fees and save money is to find out as much about your account as possible. You can start by getting a list of all your bank's fees (see below). Then study your most recent bank statement carefully. Circle every fee you find and add them up. Be prepared. You may be in for a shock.

Once you have this information, contact a bank employee and ask about getting the fees reduced or the availability of "no frills" accounts which cost less.

Here are some other ways to cut your banking costs:

— Ask questions first. Before you open a checking account, find out what the fees will be for writing checks, for bounced checks, for the checks themselves and for other services. The Truth In Savings Act requires that financial institutions have available a list of their fees for bounced checks, stop payment orders, certified checks, wire transfers, and similar items. Ask for the list.

— Make a written summary of how you will use the account. The summary should include the following:

* how many checks you write each month
* how often you use a teller or an ATM
* how low your monthly balance goes
* the other incidental services you use

* the amount of your savings deposit
* how often you make deposits
* whether or not the amount of interest you've earned
  on your interest- paying checking account exceeds
  the fees you're being charged.

— Avoid interest-payment checking. In order to earn interest, your balance can't fall below a set amount— usually $500 to $1000. If it does, you can be charged a fee of $6 or more each month. Unless the interest you earn exceeds the fees you're being charged, look for an account with no minimum balance required.

— Consolidate all your accounts. You'll stand a better chance of getting a reduction in fees if you maintain all your accounts— checking, savings, certificate of deposit, etc.— in one bank. In appreciation for your business, the bank is more likely to give you a break on fees.

— Go easy on your debit card. Debit cards act like checks, and you'll usually pay a fee for using them. In many cases, you may find it cheaper to use your credit card for purchases, then pay off the card balance monthly.

— Use ATMs less. One way to avoid numerous ATM fees is to withdraw your weekly cash all at once. Don't make several trips to the ATM. You also can look for a bank that offers free, or at least some free use of the leading ATM network where you live. If you do a lot of traveling, find a bank that will give you at least a few free transactions on one of the leading national ATM networks.

— Try direct deposit. This is one of the best banking deals available. You can have your paycheck deposited directly into your account. There's no charge for direct deposit, and your funds will be available for use the morning of your payment date. Ask a bank officer about setting up a no fee, no-minimum account in exchange for direct deposit of your paycheck or government check.

In addition to making payments into your account through direct deposit, you also can withdraw money electronically from your account to pay your bills. All you need do is authorize a withdrawal for a specific amount at a predetermined date each month. Your bills will be paid and you won't have to write and mail checks. This automated method of paying bills saves time and money spent on postage. It also guarantees that your bills will be paid promptly.

If all else fails, try finding a new bank. Compare the terms and prices of all services you need. In many cases, smaller banks and credit unions offer the best deals.

Credit Unions Offer A Cheaper Banking Alternative

If you qualify, a credit union account may be a cheaper alternative than most banks or savings and loans. They offer share draft (checking), share (savings), share certificate (certificate of deposit) accounts, as well as personal loans and mortgages, usually at lower fees than banks. Credit unions can offer better deals because they're non-profit financial institutions which operate for the benefit of their members.

You may qualify for membership in a credit union if you work for a particular company or government agency; or belong to a sponsoring labor union, trade association, church or synagogue. In fact, there's such a proliferation of credit unions that your chances of qualifying for membership are better than you might expect. Some credit unions even accept relatives of current members.

Currently, more than 35 million Americans are members of federally chartered credit unions, including those from the sample list below. The Credit Union National Association (CUNA), P.O. Box 431, Madison, WI 53701; (800) 358-5701, can provide you with more information about institutions in your area. CUNA is the national trade association for credit unions and can provide you with appropriate referrals.

— Navy Federal Credit Union, Vienna, VA; (800) 656-7676. This is the world's largest credit union, with more than 1.5 million members. It accepts Navy and Marine personnel, as well as family members who have lived in the same household.

— American Baptist Credit Union, Covina, CA; (800) 347-2228. This credit union accepts members of American Baptist churches in every state except Massachusetts and Rhode Island.

— Pentagon Federal Credit Union, Alexandria, VA; (800) 247-5626. Welcomes anyone who has ever served in the Army, Air force, National Guard or who has worked at the Pentagon. Relatives of Pentagon Federal members also are generally accepted.

— Artists Federal Credit Union, New York, NY; (212) 366-

5669. Open to all artists— writers, painters, sculptors, musicians, etc. who reside in the U.S.

Pay Less For Bouncing A Check

It's probably happened to everyone who's ever had a checking account— the dreaded bounced check. And when it happens, the bank is right there to claim its "bounced check" fee. The only way to avoid that fee is to make sure you never bounce a check, or consider overdraft protection.

Most banks charge a high interest rate for overdraft protection, (some banks charge as much as 15% to 20%) but you won't have to pay it if you don't use it. And even if your account is overdrawn for just a few days, an overdraft loan will likely be much cheaper than the bank's fee for bouncing a check. It's worth checking into.

Get Checks At Least 50% Cheaper By Mail

Forget about your bank when it comes time to order replacement checks. Instead, buy your checks from a mail order vendor and save at least 50%. That's because most banks, who buy from these same low-cost vendors, mark up their checks by 50% to 100% and more. You, the bank's "loyal" customer, are in turn charged an exorbitant price for replacement checks. When you buy direct from the printers, you avoid your bank's high markup.

For example, many mail order vendors offer 200 checks

for as low as $4.95. That's a typical introductory offer, with regular replacement orders of 200 checks priced at around $7.00. You can usually get 400 replacement checks for under $15. Compare those prices with your bank's charges for replacement checks.

There are many such vendors who guarantee that your mail-order checks will work wherever you bank and wherever you shop. You can order personal checks, home desk checks, business checks, continuous computer checks, laser checks for use with a laser printer— whatever type checks you need. If you write a lot of checks, buying direct from a vendor is a cheapie you will truly appreciate.

Here are several reputable vendors who offer checks by mail (You can contact these companies and request free brochures and price lists. Compare the products and prices with those offered by your bank.):

— Artistic Checks, A Division of Artistic Greetings, Inc., Department #09-5189, One Artistic Plaza, P.O. Box 1501, Elmira, NY 14902-1501.

— Checks In The Mail, 5314 N. Irwindale Ave, Irwindale, CA 91706; Phone: (800) 733-4443.

— The Check Store, 790 Quail Street, P.O. Box 5145, Denver, CO 80217-5154; Phone (800) 424-3257.

— Current, Check Products Division, P.O. Box 19000, Colorado Springs, CO 80935-9000; Phone:

(800) 533-3937.

— Safeguard Business Systems, P.O. Box 2045, Tustin, CA 92681-2045; Phone: (800) 523-9108.

— American Check Printers (computer checks), 2197 East Bayshore Road, Palo Alto, CA 94303-0818; Phone: (800) 262-4325.

— Intuit (computer checks), Supplies Department, P.O. Box 50930, Palo Alto, CA 94303; Phone: (800) 433-8810; Fax: (415) 852-9146.

— NEBS Computer Forms & Software, (computer checks), 500 Main Street, Groton, MA 01471; Phone: (800) 225-9550.

Credit Card Cheapies

How To Choose And Use The Cheapest Credit Card

How you plan to use a credit card should determine what card you choose. For example, if you're a "convenience user," that is, you always pay your bill in full every month, the cheapest card to use is one that has no annual fee and offers a grace period for paying your bill without paying a finance charge. Since you pay your monthly bill(s) in full (within the grace period allowed), the card's interest rate isn't an important consideration.

However, if you can't pay off your credit card balance each month, the cheapest card to use is one that offers the lowest interest rate. If you hardly ever pay off your monthly balance, choose a card with no grace period— such cards typically offer the lowest interest rates.

For a small fee you can purchase a list of the cheapest credit cards in the country and find out how to qualify for the lowest rate possible. To get the latest list of low rate/no fee credit cards, send $4 to Bankcard Holders of America, 560 Herndon Parkway, Suite 120, Herndon, VA 22070; Phone: (800) 553-8025. RAM Research Corporation, (800) 344-7714 also will send you a list of low-rate cards for a modest fee.

Here are several other money-saving tips for choosing and using a credit card:

— Make sure you understand the terms of a credit card offer before you accept the card. Study the disclosure information regarding terms and fees that must appear on credit-card offers you get in the mail. Those diclosures are usually found in small print on the back of the credit-card application. Review several credit card plans and choose the one that offers terms that are best for you.

— Once you begin using a card, pay monthly balances in full or pay as much as you can promptly to keep finance charges as low as possible.

— Keep copies of all sales slips and compare charges as soon as your bills arrive.

— Go easy on credit-card cash advances. Most credit card issuers charge a fee for cash advances, as well as interest from the time you receive the money. It's usually cheaper to withdraw any cash you need from your checking or savings account.

— Use only one or two cards. You can save more than $100 a year in credit card fees by getting rid of all but one or two cards, and by avoiding over-the-credit-limit fees.

— Take care to prevent your credit card(s) and account numbers from being used without your consent. Draw a blank line through spaces above the total when you sign receipts. Destroy or keep in a safe place all carbons.

— Keep a record of your credit card numbers and the telephone numbers of each credit card issuer in a safe but convenient place in case your cards are lost or stolen.

— Report a lost or stolen card as soon as possible by calling the issuers 24 hour telephone number. You're responsible for the first $50 of any charges made on your card before you report it missing.

Free Benefits For Credit Card Users

No doubt about it, used wisely, credit cards are a great benefit when it comes to buying the things we need. But they also offer other benefits which we sometimes overlook. For example, most credit cards feature enhancements such as insurance and purchase protection. These enhancements are automatic when you accept and use the cards. In other words, they're free, if you take advantage of them.

So when you're considering the credit line, interest rate, and annual fee offered by a particular credit card, also consider the free benefits it offers. The automatic enhancements will vary, depending on the card you use, but here are some of the most common free benefits to look for:

— Buyer protection. Many buyer protection plans protect most purchases (made with the credit card) against damage and theft for up to 90 days and up to $1,000.

— Extended Warranty: In most cases, this doubles the manufacturer's warranty for up to one additional year on most purchases made with the credit card.

— Automatic Travel Accident Insurance: This automatic insurance can provide up to $100,000 if you charge your common carrier tickets (airline, rail, bus, or boat) to your credit card.

— Collision/ Loss Damage Insurance. This is an automatic service that protects you and saves you money when you rent a car with your credit card.

Be sure to read your brochures or contact your card's customer representatives to find out what automatic enhancements your card provides. And take advantage of them whenever the need arises.

Investment Tricks

The prospect of a quick profit can be tempting to many first-time investors. If you're a beginner, you should keep in mind that there's no such thing as "a sure thing." Every investment comes with some degree of risk. The key to successful investing is information. The more you know about investing, the better your chances of making informed decisions about how and where to spend your investment dollars.

Five Rules For Successful Investing

Here are five basic rules for investing that can help you cut your investment expenses and increase your returns:

1) Build a cash reserve before you begin investing. Most experts recommend putting aside at least six months living expenses. Of course, this suggestion depends on the size of your investment. If you're planning on a small investment ($1,000 or less), a smaller cash reserve may be adequate. However, if you plan to invest a large sum of money, your cash reserve should be large enough to cover any potential losses.

2) Set your investment goals. Determine what you want out of your investment. For example, do you want an investment that will give you a steady income after you retire? Are you saving for a vacation next year? Do you want an investment to help pay for a college education in several years? Your goals should tell you whether or not you should plan to invest for a short term or over the long haul.

3) Be sure you understand what you're getting into. Remember, it's your money at risk. Ask questions about anything you don't understand. Make sure you get a clear explanation of what the investment product offers, what it will cost, and what risks are involved. In the case of investments, what you don't know can hurt you, financially.

4) Diversify your investments. The best way to reduce the risk of loss is to spread your investment money among several stocks, bonds, cash, real-estate, and mutual funds. While the minimum investment at many mutual funds is $1,000, there are funds that let you begin with less than $50 if you agree to invest on a regular basis.

5) Begin with low-risk investments. Keep in mind the following rule: the higher the potential return, the riskier the investment. It takes experience to choose such investments wisely. If you aren't ready to take on a lot of risk with your money, consider low-risk investments, such as U.S. Treasury Bonds and Notes, money-market mutual funds, and individual common stocks.

Use Discount Brokers And Save 50%

One way to invest for less is to use discount brokerage firms. Brokers at such firms can save you 50% or more on typical commissions charged by full-service brokers. However, most discount brokers don't provide investment advice as part of their services. You'll make your own decisions on what and/or when to buy and sell.

Generally, full service brokerage firms provide execution

services, recommendations, investment advice, and research support. Discount brokers typically provide execution services but do not make recommendations regarding which stocks and bonds you should buy or sell. If you feel you are capable of making these decisions yourself, using a discount broker can be the cheapest way to invest.

You can find discount brokerage firms through advertisements in financial sections of most major newspapers. Listed below are several of the leading discounters and their toll-free numbers:

— Brown & Company, (800) 776-6063.

— Charles Schwab & Company, (800) 435-4000.

— Fidelity Brokerage Services, (800) 544-7272.

— Jack White & Company, (800) 233-3411.

— K. Aufhauser, (800) 368-3668.

— National Discount Brokers, (800) 888-3999.

— Pacific Brokerage Service, (800) 421-8395.

— Wall Street Equities, (800) 447-8625.

— Waterhouse Securities, (800) 930-4410.

Buy No-Load Mutual Funds And Avoid Paying Commission

If you've bought mutual funds through stockbrokers or salespeople, you're likely paying a commission of 3% to 8%. You can avoid those charges altogether by purchasing "no-load" funds directly from fund companies. By purchasing mutual funds directly, you eliminate salespeople and their commissions.

Many investment experts agree that no-load funds generally perform as well as "load" funds with a flat up-front sales commission. And if you do your homework, you may be able to find a no-load fund that performs better than a fund recommended by a commissioned salesperson.

Here are some companies which offer no-load mutual funds:

— Dreyfus, (800) 645-6561.

— Invesco, (800) 525-8085.

— Janus, (800) 525-8983.

— Neuberger & Berman, (800) 877-9700.

— T. Rowe Price, (800) 638-5660.

— Scudder, (800) 225-2470.

— Strong, (800) 368-1030.

— SteinRoe, (800) 338-2550.

— Twentieth Century, (800) 345-2021.

— USAA, (800) 531-2021.

— Vanguard, (800) 523-2566.

How To Buy Treasury Notes And Bonds At No Charge

One of the smartest investments you can make is buying U.S. Treasury notes and/or bonds. Both are guaranteed by the government and yield 6% to 7%. They also can be purchased in denominations as small as $1,000. You can purchase these Treasury securities through commercial banks, brokers, securities dealers or directly from the Federal Reserve. Banks and brokers will charge you anywhere from $25 to $50 for the transaction. You can avoid those costs by purchasing notes and bonds free of charge directly from Federal Reserve Banks and Branches, or the Bureau of the Public Debt.

In order to purchase notes and/or bonds directly through the Federal Reserve or the Bureau of Public Debt, you'll need to complete a "Treasury Direct" tender form. These forms are available at any Federal Reserve or Branch, or from the Bureau of Public Debt. The government agencies must receive tenders by the deadlines established in public announcments through press releases and major newspapers.

The schedule for the sale of Treasury notes and bonds is generally as follows:

1) Two-year notes and five-year notes are usually issued on the final business day of each month;

2) Three-year notes and ten-year notes are typically issued every three months on the 15th of February, May, August and November;

3) Thirty-year bonds are usually issued on the 15th of February and August.

If you wish to purchase Treasury securities direct, contact your bank for the address or phone number of the Federal Reserve Bank nearest you (A listing of Treasury Direct Servicing Offices, including Federal Reserve Banks and Branches and the Bureau of Public Debt is provided at the end of this chapter). You then can contact the Federal Reserve and request the necessary tender forms and additional information on how to purchase notes and bonds direct without being required to pay a fee.

For additional information, contact the Federal Reserve Bank of Richmond, VA, which offers a booklet titled, "Buying Treasury Securities at Federal Reserve Banks". The booklet explains how to buy Treasury notes and bonds directly from the government. To get the booklet, send $4.50, payable to the Federal Reserve Bank of Richmond, P.O. Box 27471, Richmond, VA 23261.

How To Replace Lost Savings Bonds At No Cost

You can get lost, stolen or otherwise destroyed Savings Bonds replaced free of charge simply by filing an application establishing the loss. The completed application, which details the loss, along with partially destroyed Bonds if mutilated or burned, should be sent to the Bureau of the Public Debt, Savings Bond Operations Office (SBOO), Parkersburg, WV 26106-1328. You then will be reissued new Bonds. The reissued Bonds are given the original issue date of the Bonds they replace.

You can help speed the free replacement of lost or stolen Bonds by filling out and submitting form PD-F1048. In the case of partially destroyed Bonds, completion of form PD-1934 will help speed the replacement process. These forms are generally available from local banks and Federal Reserve Banks and Branches.

Tax Savings

Reducing your tax burden will require aggressive planning and strategy. You'll need to keep abreast of the latest tax laws and be able to recognize IRS-approved tax breaks. There's a big payoff in the form of lower tax bills for taxpayers who are willing to invest the time and effort to find out what legal deductions are available.

For many people, accelerating deductions and deferring income is the most effective tax-saving tactic. For example, you can accelerate deductions by paying your state tax in December rather than in January. By drawing tax-deductible expenses into the current tax year and postponing income to the following year, you can lower your current tax bill and gain the use of your money for an additional 12 months. On the other hand, if you expect to be in a higher tax bracket next year, you may want to reverse this tactic and accelerate income and defer deductions. The income you accelerate into the current year will be taxed at your current lower rate. And any deductions you can defer will be more valuable to you next year.

Whichever strategy you choose, begin your tax-planning well before the end of the year and be ready to take advantage of any tax breaks you discover. There are scores of IRS-approved deductions available that could save you several thousand dollars on your tax bill. The fifteen tax-cutting tips that follow are all based on IRS-approved deductions. You won't qualify for all of these deductions, but you should be eligible for two or more that could help you reduce your tax bill significantly.

Fifteen Tips For Lower Taxes

1) Contribute to a tax-deferred retirement plan. You can't go wrong putting money into a retirement account. Besides building a nest egg for your future, all contributions to such an account are tax-deferred, meaning lower taxes now.

You may be eligible to participate in one or more of the following retirement plans:

— 401K and other employer retirement plans: Employer retirement plans enable you to make contributions which are deducted from your pay before taxes. Your taxable income is reduced by whatever amount you contribute. This could drop you into a lower tax bracket. What's more, many companies match a portion or all of your contribution increasing the value of your account, which continues to grow tax-deferred until you retire.

— Individual Retirement Accounts (IRAs): Contributions to an IRA also are tax-deferred for some taxpayers. You may be able to contribute up to $2,000 of earned income into a deductible IRA every year.

— Keogh Account: Keoghs are available to individuals who have any amount income from self-employment. Generally, if you qualify, you can contribute and deduct up to 25 percent of your net self-employment income, or $30,000, whichever is less.

2) Shift Income. One way to reduce your overall tax bill is to transfer assets to your child. The income generated from the transferred assets will be taxed at the child's lower rate. However, if a child under age 14 has more than $1,200 in unearned income a year, the excess will be taxed as if it were an addition to your income. Children 14 and over are taxed at their own rate, which is well below their parents' rate.

3) Hire Your Child. If you own a business, consider hiring your child as an employee. Your child will earn an income and you can take a deduction for the salary.

4) Donate to charity. Donations to charity are fully deductible, up to 50 percent of your income, as long as you itemize your deductions. Keep in mind that the IRS requires written documentation for any donation of $250 or more. A cancelled check is no longer enough proof for tax purposes.

5) Donate appreciated property. You may be eligible for a double tax break if you donate appreciated property to charity. If you've held the property for more than one year, you can take a deduction for its fair market value and you don't have to pay tax on its appreciation.

6) Take advantage of home-business deductions. If you operate a home business you can deduct your cost for maintaining part of your home as an office, as well as your costs for supplies, telephone, business cards, and mileage when you drive your car on business.

7) Use your home for a tax break. You can deduct your mortgage interest, points paid to secure a mortgage and property taxes. Remember, however, that points paid on refinanced mortgages are usually not deductible immediately. Generally, you must deduct the amount equally each year over the term of the loan.

8) Consider a home-equity loan. You can trade high-interest, non-deductible credit-card debt for a home equity loan and reduce your taxes. That's because the interest rates on home equity loans are generally much lower and the interest payments are tax-deductible.

9) Use Series EE Bonds as a tax break. Income from series EE bonds may be fully tax free if they are used to pay for your child's college education. Be aware that income limits apply to this tax break in order to qualify.

10) Write off moving expenses. For a work-related move, you can deduct the cost of transporting you, your family and your belongings from your former residence to your new home.

11) Deduct educational expenses. These expenses are deductible if they are incurred while you are employed or self-employed. Certain educational fees and costs also may be deductible if you're taking courses as a requirement of your pre-

sent job or to improve your skills.

12) Keep track of your medical expenses. Be aware that only medical expenses that exceed 7.5 percent of your adjusted gross income (AGI) are deductible. You should total these expenses in November or early December to see if you are near the limit. If you are, pay as many medical expenses as you can before the end of the year to increase your deduction. You may even consider accelerating elective medical procedures into the current year to maximize your deduction.

When calculating your medical expenses be sure to include doctors' bills, prescriptions, insurance premiums, and transportation costs to and from medical facilities. Other, often overlooked medical expense deductions include:

— Childbirth preparation classes
— Contact lenses
— Acupuncture treatments
— Psychotherapy
— Contraceptives (if purchased with a prescription)
— Braces
— Orthopedic shoes
— Prescribed and special diet foods
— Alcoholism and drug abuse treatment

13) Deduct child and dependent care expenses. You may qualify for this credit if you pay someone to care for your dependent who is under age 13, your disabled dependent, or your disabled spouse.

14) Claim credit for the elderly or the disabled. Generally, you

can qualify for this credit if you're 65 or older, or if you are retired on permanent and total disability.

15) Write off miscellaneous expenses. You may be able to deduct any miscellaneous expenses you incur in excess of 2 percent of your adjusted gross income. Expenses that qualify as miscellaneous generally fall into one of three categories: employment or business, investment, or tax.

For more information on these and other tax breaks available to individual taxpayers, contact the IRS at (800) 829-3676 to order any of its informational publications. The publications are all available free of charge.

Get Up To $105 A Month Added To Your Take Home Pay

It's true. If you qualify, you could receive extra money in your paycheck every month. The extra money is possible because of a special tax break called Earned Income Tax Credit (EITC). This special tax credit is available to certain lower-income people who are employed. The credit is deducted from the amount of tax you owe, so you end up paying less tax or you may get a refund.

Depending on whether or not you qualify, there are two ways you can claim EITC. You can get it all at once in the form of a refund when you file your tax return next year, or you can get up to $105 a month added to your take home pay by having EITC paid to you "in advance." To qualify for the advance payment, you must expect to earn less than $24,396 in 1995 and have at least one child living with you in the U.S.

To receive the advance EITC payment (if you qualify), you'll need to complete IRS Form W-5 ("Earned Income Credit Advance Payment Certificate") and give it to your employer. Then, based on what you earn, your employer adds a portion of the EITC to each paycheck you receive. However, if your only 1995 income is derived from self-employment, you cannot receive the advance EITC payment.

If you don't qualify to get the advance EITC payment, you still might be eligible to claim EITC on your 1995 tax return and get a refund if in 1995:

1) Your earnings are less than $26,673 and you have two or more children.

2) Your earnings are less than $9,230, you have no qualifying children, are between the ages of 25 to 64, and you are not claimed as a dependent by another person.

3) You are eligible for EITC, but you are self employed.

The IRS can give you detailed information about the EITC and whether or not you qualify. Call (800) 829-1040.

Save $50 to $100 By Preparing
Your Own Tax Return

Professional tax preparers charge from $50 to $100 to prepare tax returns, even the one-page 1040EZ. If your finances are not particularly complicated, with no itemizing, you can avoid such an expense by doing your own return. The IRS provides many free instructional and informational pamphlets (see chapter 10,("Government Goodies") that can help you prepare your return. For example, IRS Publication 17, "Your Federal Income Tax" is a good source of information for preparing your own tax return. You also can find many books at your local library which offer step-by-step instructions for filling out returns.

If you've been paying a preparer to do your returns, study his/her work line by line. Chances are, you'll discover you could have filled out the return accurately on your own.

How To Get Cheaper Insurance Coverage

Insurance. The mere mention of the word sends many people running for cover. And it's no wonder. Not only are there hundreds of confusing plans to choose from, the costs are often beyond imagination. What coverage do you need? How much should you pay for adequate coverage? The following tips and suggestions can help you answer these and other questions about homeowners, life and health insurance coverage (for information on automobile insurance, see chapter 5 "Car Buying"), as well as reduce the cost of your current policies.

Homeowners Insurance

If you're a homeowner you need adequate insurance to protect your property and possessions against unexpected loss. If you're not careful, you could end up overpaying an insurer for such protection. Fortunately, homeowners have many choices when it comes to insurance, and many easy ways to keep costs low. Here are some cost-cutting tips:

— Have your home and personal property appraised. You can hire your own appraiser or have the insurance company conduct the appraisal free of charge. Your appraisal should include an inventory of all your household possessions— furniture, clothing, appliances, TV, jewelry, silverware, etc.— as well as the structure itself.

It's also a good idea to take photographs and/or make a videotape of your home and your possessions. Combined with your written inventory record, a visual record can serve as positive evidence should you ever need to prove that a loss occured. You should keep these records in a safe place other than your house.

— Insure your home for its true replacement value, not its market value. You should know how much it would cost you to completely replace your home (the structure and possessions) if for some reason you have to rebuild, and insure it for the full amount.

— Raise your deductible. Increasing your deductible even a modest amount can yield substantial savings. For example, increasing a typical $250 deductible (which most homeowners can pay "out-of-pocket") to $500 or $1,000 would reduce your premium by 10% to $25%.

— Buy your policy direct from an insurance company. If you don't buy through an agent, you don't have to foot the bill for an agent's commission. When you buy a policy direct from the company, you eliminate the "middleman" and lower your own costs significantly.

— Buy from a reputable company which offers the best rates. Once again, you're reminded to shop around for the best deal. Look for a company which is rated "A" or "A+" by two or more of the leading insurance ratings services (see "Insurance Rating Agencies Listed Below).

— Take advantage of homeowner discounts. Insurers offer a variety of discounts for qualified homeowners. You may qualify for a discount of 2 to 5 percent if your home is equipped with working smoke detectors and/or an approved burglar alarm system. An in-house sprinkler system may also qualify you for a discount with some companies.Some insurers also offer "non-smoker" discounts to homeowners who don't smoke, as well as discounts for homes made of fire-resistant materials. A few companies offer discounts of up to 10 percent to retired homeowners who are age 50 or older. These are some of the discounts that may be available, but don't wait for an agent to bring up the subject. Ask what discounts are offered and find out whether or not you qualify for reduced rates.

— Earn a discount by having more than one policy with the same company. Many insurers offer reduced rates to loyal customers who purchase homeowner's, automobile and other policies from their company.

— Update your policy annually. Delete any items you no longer have and reappraise the values you've given to other possessions. Make sure the replacement values on your written record remain accurate.

Life Insurance

Most experts agree that much of the nearly $7 billion Americans spend each year on life insurance premiums is not necessary. While most policyholders know that the main purpose of life insurance is to provide financial security for their dependents, many don't fully understand what they buy. As a result, they end up being "overinsured" and paying high premiums. You can avoid those high premiums by shopping around for the coverage that fits your needs and your budget. Here are several proven life insurance cost cutters:

— Don't buy more life insurance than you really need. After all, the purpose of life insurance is to protect those people who are financially dependent on you in the event of your death. So, how much life insurance do you really need? If you're single and have no dependents, the answer is simple— you don't need life insurance. If you do have dependents, consider what financial resources they would require if your income is suddenly lost. Keep in mind, your life insurance policy should be just enough to provide for the financial well-being of your beneficiaries, not put them in a higher tax bracket. Buy only the amount of life insurance you need and can afford.

— Shop around and get an analysis and comparison of several life insurance policies. Insurance comparison services such as TermQuote (800) 444-8376; SelectQuote (800) 343-1985; and InsuranceQuote (800) 972-1104, will provide you with a list of competitively priced life insurance policies free of charge. The information can help you locate the policy that covers your needs at the lowest cost.

— Consider buying your policy direct from an insurance company. There are several large insurance companies which offer "low-load" policies for both term and cash-value life insurance direct, meaning no agents and no agents' commissions. Insurers such as USAA Life (800) 531-8000; Ameritas (800) 552-3553; Geico (800) 824-1247; and Amica Mutual (800) 242-6422, sell such policies. Such policies purchased direct are generally a lot cheaper than policies purchased through an agent.

— Don't Buy Life Insurance For Your Children. Remember, the purpose of life insurance is to protect one's dependents against a sudden loss of income— in your dependents' case, your income. It'll cost you $200 or more per year to get life insurance for a child who doesn't need the coverage anyway. Let your children buy their own life insurance when they have dependents.

— Don't Buy Credit Life Insurance. This type of insurance, which you buy from a lender to pay off a loan or a mortgage should you die, is generally overpriced. You can get the same type of protection at a lower price by increasing your basic life and disability coverage.

— Ask about discounts. You may qualify for lower rates if you're a nonsmoker or if you participate regularly in organized physical fitness programs.

— Contact the National Insurance Consumer Organization (NICO) for more information about life insurance. Write to NICO, 121 North Payne Street, Alexandria, VA 22314. You also can call the National Insurance Consumer Helpline at (800) 942-4242 for more information. The Helpline is available from

8 a.m. to 8 p.m., Eastern Time, Monday through Friday.

The American Council of Life Insurance, 1001 Pennsylvania Avenue, N.W., Washington, DC 20004-2599 also can answer general questions about life insurance, as well as provide referrals to other agencies. You also can get a free copy of the booklet, "A Consumer's Guide To Life Insurance" by writing to the American Council of Life Insurance at the above address.

Health Insurance

Obviously, the cheapest way to get health insurance coverage is to let someone else pay for it— like your employer. However, if you're not covered by a group policy where you work or through a trade association, paying for adequate coverage can be a major financial burden. The biggest headache is finding adequate coverage at rates you can afford. Here are some insurance industry insider suggestions that can help you do just that:

— Consider raising your deductibles. Higher deductibles can lower your premiums substantially. Consider how much you can afford and are willing to pay out-of-pocket to take care of medical expenses. Whether or not you can "self-insure" the first $500 or the first $1,000, you should raise your deductible as high as possible. The result will be significantly lower premium costs.

— Don't buy special "disease" policies. Special policies for cancer and other diseases generally are not cost effective. Instead, consider a health care plan that provides comprehensive cover-

age. You'll save money and have complete co'
of cancer or other specific illnesses.

— Ask about health club rebates. Some insur
members of approved health clubs. Regular
a club is generally a requirement to quality for this type of
rebate.

— Pay your premium annually in one lump sum. Depending on
your policy, you may be able to save $50 to $100 a year by
avoiding the service charges for premium payments made in
installments either monthly or quarterly.

— Contact the Health Insurance Association of America, 1025
Connecticut Avenue, NW, Suite 1200, Washington, DC 20036
for more information about health insurance.

— Contact your state insurance department (see appendix) and
find out whether or not an insurance company you are considering is licensed in your state. You could lose a lot of money buying insurance from a "fly-by-night" company that is exempt from
your state's control.

You can get more information about health and disability
insurance by contacting the Health Insurance Association of
America, the trade association of insurers. The Association provides a toll-free hotline with answers to questions about health
and other insurance topics. Call the hotline number at (800)
942-4242 or write to: Health Insurance Association of America,
1025 Connecticut Avenue NW, Washington, DC 20036-3998.

Insurance Rating Agencies

— A.M. Best Company, (900) 420-0400: Publishes annual reports rating life insurance companies and property liability companies. "Best's Insurance Reports" are available at many local libraries. You also can get a verbal report from Best for $2.50 per minute by calling the above 900 number.

— Duff & Phelps, (312) 368-3157: Offers a free rat ing report.

— Moody's, (212) 553-0377: Publishes ratings reference volumes available at many local libraries. Also offers a free rating report.

— Standard and Poor's, (212) 208-1527: Offers a free verbal report on up to five insurers.

— Weiss Research, (800) 289-9222: Charges $15 for a rating over the phone.

Free Credit Counseling

The key to successful money management is budgeting. If you can establish a monthly budget that allows you to pay all of your bills in a timely manner, you're not likely to have too many financial headaches. However, if you have trouble paying your bills, even with the help of a monthly budget, credit counseling may be the answer.

Credit counseling services may be able to help you fix bad credit, or set up a budget that will enable you to pay off your creditors and get your finances in order. And you should be able to get such assistance at little or no cost.

Free or low-cost credit counseling is available through a number of sources. The non-profit Consumer Credit Counseling Service (CCCS) offers budget counseling and financial guidance in most states. For more information and/or to locate the CCCS office nearest you, write to the National Foundation for Consumer Credit, Inc., 8611 Second Avenue, Suite 100, Silver Spring, Maryland 20910; or call (800) 388- CCCS [2227].

You also may be able to take advantage of non-profit credit counseling programs operated by the Legal Aid Society, local colleges and universities, credit unions, military bases, and county agencies, such as the Cooperative Extension Service. Check your phone directory for listings or contact your local credit bureau for possible referrals.

Free Credit Rating Review

If you haven't seen a copy of your credit rating report, you might want to consider contacting TRW, one of the country's three main credit reporting bureaus (along with Equifax and Trans Union). Upon your written request, TRW will send you a copy of your credit rating report at no cost (Equifax and Trans Union both charge a small fee for credit reports).

You can request the free report by writing to TRW,

Consumer Assistance, Box 2350, Chatsworth, CA 91313. Include your full name, addresses for the past five years (with zip codes), year of birth, Social Security number, and a copy of a document that provides proof of your identification. TRW will send you this report free once a year provided you furnish the required information.

You also can write to Equifax (P.O. Box 740241, Atlanta, GA 30374-0241) and/or Trans Union (P.O. Box 390, Springfield, PA 19064) and request a copy of your credit report. Both charge $8, the maximum allowed by federal law.

Treasury Direct Servicing Offices

If you're interested in purchasing Treasury securities direct from the government, you can contact the office nearest you from the list below.

Federal Reserve Banks and Branches

— ATLANTA: 104 Marietta Street, NW, Atlanta, GA; Phone: (404) 521-8657 (recording) or 8653. Or write to: Federal Reserve Bank, Securities Department, 104 Marietta Street, NW, Atlanta, GA 30303.

— BALTIMORE: 502 South Sharp Street, Baltimore, MD; Phone: (410) 576-3500 (recording) or 3300. Or write: P.O. Box 1378, Baltimore, MD 21203.

— BIRMINGHAM: 1801 Fifth Avenue, North, Birmingham, AL; Phone: (205) 731-8702 (recording) or 8708. Or write: P.O. Box

830447, Birmingham, AL 35283-0447.

— BOSTON: 600 Atlantic Avenue, Boston, MA; Phone; (617) 973-3800 (recording) or 3810. Or write to: P.O. Box 2076, Boston, MA 02106.

— BUFFALO: 160 Delaware Avenue, Buffalo, NY; Phone: (716) 849-5158 (recording) or 5000. Or write to: P.O. Box 961, Buffalo, NY 2214240-0961.

— CHARLOTTE: 530 East Trade Street, Charlotte, NC; Phone: (704) 358-2424 (recording) or 2100. Or write to: P.O. Box 30248, Charlotte, NC 28230.

— CHICAGO: 230 South LaSalle Street, Chicago, IL; Phone: (312) 786-1110 (recording) or (312) 322-5369. Or write to: P.O. Box 834, Chicago, IL 60690.

— CINCINNATI: 150 East 4th Street, Cincinnati, OH; Phone: (513) 721-4787 Ext. 334.

— CLEVELAND: 1455 East 6th Street, Cleveland, OH; Phone: (216) 579-2490 (recording) or 2000. Or write to: P.O. Box 6387, Cleveland, OH 44101.

— DALLAS: 2200 North Pearl Street, Dallas, TX; Phone: (214) 922-6100 (recording) or 6770. Or write to: P.O. Box 655906, Dallas, TX 75265-5906.

— DENVER: 1020 16th Street, Denver, CO; Phone: (303) 572-2475 (recording) or 2470. Or write to: P.O. Box 5228, Denver, CO 80217-5228.

— DETROIT: 160 West Fort Street, Detroit, MI; Phone: (313) 963-4936 (recording) or (313) 964-6157. Or write to: P.O. Box 1059, Detroit, MI 48231.

— EL PASO: 301 East Main, El Paso, TX; (915) 521-8295 (recording) or 8272. Or write to: P.O. Box 100, El Paso, TX 79999.

— HOUSTON: 1701 San Jacinto Street, Houston, TX; Phone:(713) 659-4433.

— JACKSONVILLE: 800 West Water Street, Jacksonville, FL; Phone: (904) 632-1178 (recording) or 1179. Or write to: P.O. Box 2499, Jacksonville, FL 32231-2499.

— KANSAS CITY: 925 Grand Avenue, Kansas City, MO; Phone: (816) 881-2767 (recording) or 2883. Or write to: P.O. Box 440, Kansas City, MO 64198.

— LITTLE ROCK: 325 West Capitol Avenue, Little Rock, AR; Phone: (501) 324-8274 (recording) or 8272. Or write to: P.O. Box 1261, Little Rock, AR 72203.

— LOS ANGELES: 950 South Grand Avenue, Los Angeles, CA; Phone: (213) 624-7398. Or write to: P.O. Box 2077, Terminal Annex, Los Angeles, CA 90051.

— LOUISVILLE: 410 South 5th Street, Louisville, KY; Phone: (502) 568-9240 (recording) or 9236. Or write to: P.O. Box 32710, Louisville, KY 40232.

— MEMPHIS: 200 North Main Street, Memphis, TN; Phone:

(901) 523-
9380 (recording) or 7171 Ext. 423. Or write to: P.O. Box 407,
Memphis, TN 38101.

— MIAMI: 9100 NW Thirty-Sixth Street, Miami, FL; Phone:
(305) 471-6257 (recording) or 6497. Or write to: P.O. Box
520847, Miami, FL 33152.

— MINNEAPOLIS: 250 Marquette Avenue, Minneapolis, MN;
Phone: (612) 340-2051 (recording) or 2075. Or write to: 250
Marquette Avenue, Minneapolis, MN 55480.

— NASHVILLE: 301 Eighth Avenue, North, Nashville, TN;
Phone: (615) 251-7236 (recording) or 7100. Or write to: 301
Eighth Avenue, N., Nashville, TN 37203-4407.

— NEW ORLEANS: 525 St. Charles Avenue, New Orleans, LA;
Phone: (504) 593-5839 (recording) or 3200. Or write to: P.O.
Box 61630, New Orleans, LA 70161.

— NEW YORK: 33 Liberty Street, New York, NY; Phone: (212)
720-5823 (recording) or 6619. Or write to: Federal Reserve,
P.O. Station, New York, NY 10045.

— OKLAHOMA CITY: 226 Dean A McGee Avenue, Oklahoma
City, OK; Phone: (405) 270-8660 (recording) or 8652. Or write
to: P.O. Box 25129, Oklahoma City, OK 73125.

— OMAHA: 2201 Farnam Street, Omaha, NE; Phone: (402)
221-5638 (recording) or 5636. Or write to: 2202 Farnam
Street, Omaha, NE 68102.

— PHILADELPHIA: Ten Independence Mall, Philadelphia, PA; Phone: (215) 574-6580 (recording) or 6680. Or write to: P.O. Box 90, Philadelphia, PA 19105.

— PITTSBURGH: 717 Grant Street, Pittsburgh, PA; Phone: (412) 261-7988 (recording) or 7802. Or write to: P.O. Box 867, Pittsburgh, PA 15230-0867.
— PORTLAND: 915 S.W. Stark Street, Portland, OR; (503) 221-5931 (recording) or 5932. Or write to P.O. Box 3436, Portland, OR 97208-3426.

— RICHMOND: 701 East Byrd Street, Richmond, VA; Phone: (804) 697-8355 (recording) or 8372. Or write to: P.O. Box 27622, Richmond, VA 23261.

— SALT LAKE CITY: 120 South State Street, Salt Lake City, UT; Phone: (801) 322-7844 (recording) or 7882. Or write to: P.O. Box 30780, Salt Lake City, UT 84130-0780.

— SAN ANTONIO: 126 East Nueva Street, San Antonio, TX; Phone: (512) 978-1330 (recording) or 1303. Or write to: P.O. Box 1471, San Antonio, TX 78295.

— SAN FRANCISCO: 101 Market Street, San Francisco, CA; Phone: (415) 974-3491 (recording) or 2330. Or write to: P.O. Box 7702, San Francisco, CA 94120.

— SEATTLE: 1015 Second Avenue, Seattle, WA; Phone: (206) 343-3615 (recording) or 3605. Or write to: P.O. Box 3567, Seattle, WA 98124.

— ST. LOUIS: 411 Locust Street, St. Louis, MO; Phone: (314)

444-8703. Or write to: P.O. Box 14915, St. Louis, MO 63178.

Bureau of Public Debt

Bureau of the Public Debt, Division of Customer Services, Washington, DC 20239-0001.

NOTES

C H A P T E R   5   5

CHEAPIES, FREE GOODIES
AND GIVEAWAYS

Car Buying

Down payments, financing, monthly payments, insurance, cost of operation, maintenance and repair— these all are important considerations when you're shopping for a new or used car. Indeed, the financial aspects of car-ownership can be intimidating. But, they don't have to be. There are ways to get the car you want, without spending your life savings. This chapter offers some suggestions and tips for getting the car you want, cheap.

Buy A New Car Cheap

For most people, buying a new car is a major financial decision. Besides the purchase price, there's financing, insurance, and the cost of operation and maintenance to consider. Without careful planning and smart shopping, those considerations could end up costing you hundreds, even thousands of dollars a year more than you should have to pay.

The biggest savings on a new car come with the selection of a model that combines a low purchase price with low financing, insurance, gasoline and maintenance and repair costs. With a little preparation, you can find a new car that meets those qualifications and then negotiate a good deal that could save you thousands of dollars over the lifetime of the car.

The following tips offered by industry insiders can help you locate and buy the new car you've been wanting at the lowest possible price:

— Find out the dealer's invoice price for the car and options. The invoice price represents the manufacturer's initial charge to the dealer, including freight. To get the best deal, you should pay as little over invoice price as possible. You may be able to find dealer costs in various new car guides available at your local library. For a fee, you also can get valuable "inside" information on actual dealer costs for a new car from a car pricing service. Armed with such information, you'll be better prepared to negotiate with new car dealers.

Here are some car pricing services you might try:

AAA Auto Pricing Services, (800) 933-7700. Offers AAA members price and other comparison information.

Car Price Network, (800) 227-3295. Charges $7 each for individual new car reports.

Consumer Reports New Price Service, (800) 395-4400. Charges $12 for the first pricing report and $10 for each additional report.

Fighting Chance, (800) 288-1134. Charges $19.95 for the first new car pricing report and $7 for each additional report. There's also a $3 handling fee for each order.

IntelliChoice, (800) 227-2665. Charges from $14.95 to $19.95 per pricing report.

— Find out whether or not the manufacturer of the car you're considering is offering any rebates or incentives that will lower the cost of the car.

— Comparison shop for the best deal. Once you've selected the model you want, get price quotes from at least five dealers. Be sure to let each dealer know you're shopping around for the best deal. Also find out if the amounts quoted by each dealer are the prices before or after any applicable rebates are deducted.

— Inspect and test drive the car you're interested in buying. Don't buy on impulse. Make sure it's a car you'll be comfortable driving and that it has all the options you want. Also inspect the car again before you drive it off the lot after the deal has been made.

— Keep your trade-in negotiations separate from the main deal. Negotiate and agree on the price of the car you plan to buy before you get a price for your trade in. Otherwise, the salesperson may simply quote you a trade-in price and then add that amount onto the price of the new car. To get the best deal, agree on the price of the new car first, then get a price for your trade-in. That way, the dollar amount of your trade-in will be deducted from the already agreed upon price of the new car.

— Forego some of the expensive extras. Consider whether or not you really need extras such as credit insurance, service contracts, rustproofing and so on. In most cases, such extras probably aren't needed and serve only to add to the final price of the car.

— Shop around for the best financing deal. Compare financing arrangements from several sources besides the dealer. You may be able to arrange cheaper financing on your own. For example, check with banks and credit unions and see what type of financing arrangements they offer. Don't allow yourself to be pressured into accepting a dealer's financing before you've checked elsewhere.

— Don't sign anything until you're certain you've got the deal you want. And then, make sure you read and understand every document associated with the transaction. If the documents do not reflect the deal you've agreed upon, insist on getting the necessary changes written into the contract before you sign.

— Choose a fuel-efficient car. You can make a sweet deal even sweeter by purchasing a fuel-efficient car that costs less to operate. You can get a copy of "Fuel Economy Guide", published by the Department of Energy, to help you choose a fuel-efficient vehicle. The "Guide" is designed to help consumers compare the fuel economy of similarly sized cars, light duty trucks and vans, and special purpose vehicles. By using the Guide, you can estimate the average yearly fuel cost for any vehicle. To get a free copy of the "Fuel Economy Guide", write to the Consumer Information Center, Pueblo, CO 81009.

Buy A Used Car Cheaper

Sure, it's nice to cruise around town in a new car... if you can keep from thinking about the payments, that is. These days the average cost of a new car is closing in on $20,000. That means that the average car payment is several hundred dollars per month. Kick in the high cost of insurance and the pleasure you feel behind the wheel can soon take a back seat to budget headaches.

Rising new car costs and the high cost of financing are leading more and more Americans to a cheaper alternative—used cars. True, with a used car you forfeit that new car smell and in many cases a new car warranty, but you also avoid oppressive monthly payments and sky-high insurance premiums. If you know what to look for, buying a good used car can be one of the best deals you'll ever make.

Here are some buying guidelines from the U.S. Office of

Consumer Affairs and other consumer agencies, that could help you find a good quality used car, cheap:

— Do your homework. With a few hours of research you can find out how much you should pay for the car you want. You can check newspaper ads and used car guides, such as the "N.A.D.A. Official Used Car Guide" at your local library to get an idea of a fair price. Then compare the seller's asking price with the average retail price listed in the guides. Unless the car is in mint condition, don't pay more than your sources indicate. And remember, prices, especially on used cars, are always negotiable.

— Shop during daylight hours. Twilight or the cover of darkness can hide some visual problems you should know about before you buy a car. Daylight is also a better and safer time to take the car for a test drive. Your inspection and test drive should include a check of all the lights, air conditioner (if equipped), heater and other parts of the electrical system. Also check for exterior rust, scuffed and worn interior and other visual signs of wear. And be sure to listen for any noises that might indicate you're test driving a clunker.

— Have a mechanic you trust inspect the car. A thorough inspection by a competent mechanic is especially important if the car is being sold "as is." Your own inspection may or may not reveal performance or safety problems. Your mechanic can tell you whether or not the car is in good running condition and whether or not it's likely to stay that way.

— Contact the previous owner for information about the car. Ask about the car's performance history. Also find out what repairs, if any, have been made, and whether or not the car has ever been in an accident.

— Get a copy of the original manufacturer's warranty. Ask the previous owner or the vehicle's manufacturer for all warranty information. The original warranty still may be in effect and transferable to you.

— Call the National Transportation Safety Administration's Auto Safety Hotline, (800) 424-9393 to get recall information on the car. Authorized dealers of the make of vehicle you're considering must do recall repair work free even if the new car warranty has expired and regardless of how old the car is (see "How to Get Your Car Repaired Free" later in this chapter).

You also can find out whether or not there is a pattern of repeated complaints on a certain vehicle model by contacting the Center for Auto Safety, 2001 S. Street, N.W., Suite 410, Washington, DC 20009. The Center monitors auto defects and can provide you with information upon request if you include the vehicle make, model and year and a SASE.

— Check for the mandatory "Buyer's Guide" sticker. If you're buying from a dealer, the Buyer's Guide sticker, which provides warranty (if any is offered) and other information, should be affixed to the window of the car. If the buyer's guide is not available, walk away from the deal.

— Read and understand all documents before you sign on the dotted line. Go over each document carefully and if there are changes you want, get them written into the contract. The rule to follow is "don't sign anything you don't understand."

— Find out about your rights. Contact your local or state consumer protection office (see Appendix) for information about your rights when buying a used car. Some state laws extend extra protection to consumers who buy used cars.

— Keep good records. You should save everything related to the transaction, including a copy of the bill of sale. Should problems arise later, your records could prove invaluable.

The Federal Trade Commission (FTC) offers a free publication on buying a used car. To get a copy write to the FTC, Public Reference Section, 6th and Pennsylvania Avenue, N.W., Room 130, Washington, DC 20580; or call (202) 326-2222.

Car Buying Services To The Rescue

If you hate to negotiate and haggle with salespeople, shopping for a new car can be a very unpleasant and costly experience. In fact, it can be a real battle. And if you go into that battle unprepared, you're almost certain to come out a loser. Sure, you'll drive away in a new car, but you're likely to pay a good deal more than you have to.

Of course there are ways you can deal effectively and successfully when buying a new car. As discussed earlier in this chapter, the better prepared you are, the better your chances of getting a good deal. If you know what type of car you want and how much you should pay to get it you can usually negotiate with a salesperson on an equal footing. But if you prefer to avoid all the research and subsequent negotiating, you might look into hiring a new car buying service "to do battle" for you.

Car buying services aren't cheap. Generally you can expect to pay $150 and up depending on the make and model car you want. But you could still come out ahead if the service negotiates a deal hundreds of dollars cheaper than you could do yourself. Some services negotiate with a dealer and get the best price on the car you want, order it from the manufacturer and even arrange for delivery, allowing you to avoid the battle altogether. Others solicit competitive bids from several area dealerships on the car you want, allowing you to choose among the offers. Armed with the low bid, you can visit the dealer and make the deal yourself. The fee you pay depends on the service(s) rendered.

There are hundreds of new car buying services across the country. You can find them listed in the Yellow Pages under "Automobile Brokers," "Automobile Shopping Services," and so on. Some credit unions and motor clubs also offer new car pricing and buying services. If you don't feel competent enough to negotiate the best possible deal yourself, you may be able to avoid the hassle and save yourself some money to boot by using such a service.

Here are several national car-buying services you might contact:

— Auto Advisor, 3123 Fairview Avenue
　 E.,Seattle, WA 98102; (800) 326-1976.

— Automobile Consumer Services, 6355 Corbly

Road, Suite 33, Cincinnati, OH 45230; (800) 223-4882.

— Car Bargains, 733 15th Street, N.W., Suite 820, Washington, DC 20005; (800) 475-7283.

— Car/Puter, 1500 Cordova Road, Suite 309, Fort Lauderdale, FL 33316; (800) 221-4001.

— Nationwide Auto Brokers, 17517 W. 10 Mile Road, Southfield, MI 48075; (800) 521-7257.

— USAA Auto Acquisitions Services, USAA Building, D-3-E, San Antonio, TX 78288; (800) 531-8905.

Car Leasing Lessons

If you think buying a new car outright is beyond your means, you may want to consider leasing. According to industry insiders, more and more people are leasing new cars. In fact, more than 25 percent of the consumers who got new cars in 1994 chose leasing rather than outright purchase. Many of those consumers chose leasing because of the manageable low monthly payments.

While it's true that vehicle lease payments are typically a good deal lower than conventional auto loan payments, there are other "hidden" costs that could make leasing a new car more expensive than buying outright. In order to come out ahead on a leasing arrangement, you'll need to consider more than monthly payments. Here are some suggestions for getting the best deal on leasing a new car:

— Shop around for the best leasing deal. Newspaper ads and other promotions can lead you to dealers who offer attractive leasing deals. Compare each offer carefully and be alert— enticing low monthly payments may be available only if you make a large down payment or a balloon payment at the end of the lease.

— Find out the vehicle's "capitalized" cost and compare that with the list price. In leasing terminology, capitalized cost is the total cost of leasing a vehicle plus license, registration fees, taxes and insurance, less any down payment. You're not getting a good deal if under a leasing arrangement your capitalized cost amounts to more than you would have financed to buy the car outright. If a dealer refuses to provide you with enough information to figure the capitalization cost, find another leasing company.

— Think twice about an open-end lease. Such leases require the consumer to pay the difference if the vehicle is worth less at the end of the lease than was estimated originally.

— Ask questions about the deal and don't sign anything you don't understand. The Consumer Leasing Act requires auto leasing companies to give you pertinent information in writing before you sign a contract. Read the documents given to you by the leasing company carefully. According to the Office of Consumer Affairs some of the most important information to look for includes;

1) up-front costs, such as security deposits, down
   payments, advanced payments and taxes;

2) the terms of the payment plan;

3) termination costs, such as excess mileage
   penalties, charges for excessive wear and tear,
   and disposition charges; and

4) penalties (amount you would be required to pay)
   for early termination or default.

— Find out what it will cost you to purchase the car at the end
of the lease. If you're leasing with the intention of buying, make
sure the purchase option is clearly defined in advance.

— Consider having gap insurance included in the leasing
arrangement. Gap insurance covers the cost of replacing the
vehicle if it is stolen or destroyed. With this type of insurance,
you're covered for the difference between the value of the leased
vehicle and the amount you still owe in payments. Some leasing
companies provide gap insurance free. If not, consider asking
the leasing company to include it in the terms of the agreement.
At most, you shouldn't pay much more than $200 for such cov-
erage.

For additional information on car leasing, you can order a
free publication from the Federal Trade Commission (FTC). Write
to the FTC, Public Reference Section, 6th and Pennsylvania
Avenue, N.W., Room 130, Washington, DC 20580.

How To Get Your Car Repaired For Free

Anyone who's ever owned a car has had to pay for some sort of repairs. That's to be expected. If you put a lot of mileage on a vehicle, sooner or later it'll need a new part or two. Repairs associated with use are often unavoidable and costly (if they aren't covered by a new car warranty). But other major repairs, also unavoidable, don't have to cost you a penny. That's right, in many instances, you can have your car fixed free. Here's how:

* Secret Warranties

Car manufacturers and dealers have been in on a "little secret" whereby many car owners have spent hundreds, even thousands of dollars on repairs they could have had done absolutely free. The secret involves something called, quite appropriately, "secret warranties." These warranties refer to manufacturer defects in cars, light trucks and vans, which aren't usually made known to the public. The defects are inherent, that is, they're the result of a breakdown in the manufacturing process and are with some vehicles when they roll off the assembly line.

Vehicle manufacturers own up to these defects in notices or service bulletins sent to dealer service departments. The bulletins notify the dealers of the defects and describe how to make the necessary repairs. Federal law also requires that service bulletins describing manufacturing defects be sent to the U.S. Department of Transportation's National Highway Traffic Safety Administration (NHTSA). However, federal law does not require that anyone else be notified of the manufacturing problems. So, as a rule, neither the manufacturers nor the dealers notify car owners that an inherent defect may exist in their vehicles.

All too often, manufacturing flaws are not discovered until new vehicle warranties have expired. And the car owners are unaware that the problems they're having with their vehicles are caused by manufacturing defects. As a result, many car owners are paying for costly repairs they're actually entitled to have done free of charge— even after a new car warranty has expired.

States such as California, Connecticut, Virginia and Wisconsin have recently adopted measures to eliminate secret warranties. The "anti-secret warranty" measures make it mandatory for vehicle manufacturers to notify owners directly of manufacturing flaws and the necessary repairs. If you're experiencing inherent problems with a car you bought new, and if you live in a state that has enacted an anti-secret warranty measure, contact one of your state representatives and request a copy of the bill. Then, take advantage of the bill's provisions to get a copy of a secret warranty that may apply to your car. If you're uncertain as to whether or not your state has enacted such legislation, contact a state representative for information.

If your state hasn't enacted an anti-secret warranty measure, you may be able to uncover a secret warranty applying to your vehicle by contacting NHTSA. As noted earlier, under federal law the NHTSA receives copies of all vehicle manufacturer service bulletins. The Administration's Technical Reference Division has extensive files which include make and model of vehicles and the specific problems acknowledged in manufacturer's service bulletins. If there are any secret warranties that are applicable to your vehicle, you can acquire copies of them, free of charge from the TRD. Contact the Technical Reference Division, National Highway Traffic Safety Administration, 400 7th St., SW, Washington, DC 20590.

Once you have proof that one or more secret warranties apply to the problem(s) you're experiencing with your vehicle, contact a dealer. You'll need to provide the dealer with the applicable service bulletin number(s). If the dealer isn't responsive, contact the vehicle manufacturer's customer service department. You should be able to find the addresses and phone numbers for all auto manufacturers in reference material available at your local library.

Safety Recalls

Under the National Traffic and Motor Vehicle Safety Act of 1966, the NHTSA oversees the federal government's vehicle safety recall program. The recall program involves safety-related manufacturing defects and design flaws. Vehicles that are recalled under this program are repaired at no cost to the owners.

Federal law requires that vehicle manufacturers notify registered owners of vehicles affected by safety recalls by first-class mail. According to the NHTSA, about one third of the vehicle owners whose cars are eligible for free repairs don't have them made. In many cases, these car owners simply ignore the safety recall notices they receive. Some car owners aren't aware of applicable safety recalls because they purchased their cars used from previous owners who may have received notices but did nothing about them. Other car owners fail to get the free repair work done because they never receive the notices. Whatever the reason, the owners end up paying for repairs they could have gotten done free of charge.

Here's how you can take advantage of government mandated vehicle safety recalls and free repairs:

— When buying a used car, check with the previous owner or the NHTSA and find out whether or not a safety recall is in effect. If a recall has been issued, take your vehicle to the service department of a new car dealer who sells the make of vehicle subject to the recall. The dealer's service then will make the mandated repairs free of charge.

— If a problem develops in a new car after its warranty expires, contact the NHTSA to see if a safety recall has been announced. If so, there's still a good chance you can get the repairs done for free.

— Regardless of whether a car is used or new, it's a good idea to check at least once a year to see if a safety recall has been announced for your particular make and model. Don't count on receiving a vehicle safety recall notice in the mail. Sometimes the notification system breaks down, leaving car owners in the dark. Contact the NHTSA to keep up-to-date on recall notices.

— Contact the dealership that sold you the new car and ask if any recall notices are applicable. You also can get the information by calling NHTSA's toll free hotline, (800) 424-9393. If there has been a safety recall that may pertain to your car, NHTSA will send you a "request for information" card. The card is preaddressed with the name and address of your vehicle's manufacturer. You should provide all the information requested including the vehicle's identification number (VIN). Upon receipt of your information card, the manufacturer will let you know whether or not the recall applies to your vehicle. If the car is used, the manufacturer can tell you whether or not the repair has already been made.

Emission Recalls

Besides safety recalls, the government also mandates recalls and free repairs for inherent emission problems. Under the National Clean Air Act, emission recalls are designed to correct manufacturer flaws in vehicles that contribute to air pollution problems. Correcting emission problems usually corrects performance problems— hard starting, hesitation, misfiring, rough idling, lack of power, pinging, and so on— as well.

The Environmental Protection Agency (EPA) oversees the emission recall program. You can contact the EPA to find out whether or not your vehicle is included in an emissions recall. Contact the Manufacturing Operations Division, Environmental Protection Agency, 401 M. Street, SW, Washington, DC 20460; (202) 260-2479. You also may be able to get the information from a new car dealer who sells your make of vehicle, or you can write to the customer service department of the vehicle's manufacturer. If you find that your car is affected by an exhaust emissions recall, take your vehicle to a new car dealer who sells your make and model and get the necessary repairs done free.

— Manufacturer Goodwill Programs

All car manufacturers have "goodwill" programs or policies that provide car owners with free or partially free repairs to correct manufacturer defects after new vehicle warranties have expired. Generally, manufacturers live up to the intent of their goodwill policies whenever car owners present proof (typically, a service bulletin) that inherent defects are present and that repairs are necessary.

In the case of a vehicle recalled under the safety recall program, the offer of a free repair remains in effect for eight years after the recall is announced. If you learn that your car has been recalled, but the time allowed for the free repair has elapsed, you still may be able to take advantage of the manufacturer's goodwill policy. The manufacturer may pay for all or part of the necessary repair. If you fall into this category, it's best to contact you car's manufacturer customer service department to find out whether or not its goodwill policy covers expired recalls. If it does, you may be able to get your car fixed free or at a very low cost. Check your local library for a listing of addresses and phone numbers for all vehicle manufacturers.

Maintenance And Repair Money-Savers

According to the U.S. Department of Transportation, American car-owners spend about $100 billion a year on auto repair. That's a bundle of money, and what makes it worse is that industry experts estimate that at least 40 percent of that money is spent on unnecessary repairs and related costs. That's around $40 billion a year!

You don't have to be a part of that rip-off. The most important step you can take to avoid unnecessary repairs and save money on needed repairs is to find a competent, reputable mechanic. And the time to do that is "before" you need repairs. Here are some insider guidelines for doing just that:

— Find a reliable repair shop before you need one. You'll be better able to make money-saving decisions if you aren't rushed or in a panic. Get recommendations from your family and friends or an independent consumer rating organization. Also check out the repair shop's complaint record with your state or local consumer protection office or Better Business Bureau.

— Choose a repair shop that employs professionally trained mechanics. Look for mechanics who have trade school diplomas, advanced coursework certificates, and/or Automotive Service Excellence (ASE) certification. Such credentials and certification is an indication that trained and experienced people will work on your car.

The National Institute for Automotive Service Excellence conducts the only "industry-wide" national certification program for automotive technicians. The Institute, an independent non-profit organization, confers ASE certification on individuals who have successfully completed a series of standardized specialty exams. For more information about the ASE certification program, contact the National Institute for Automotive Excellence, 13505 Dulles Technology Drive, Herndon, VA 22071.

— Find out all the shop's polices before you agree to have any work done. The shop's labor rates, guarantees, methods of payment and so on should be clearly posted and/or explained to your satisfaction. If they aren't, find another shop.

— When you take the car in for repair, describe the symptoms. Don't tell the mechanic what you think is wrong with your car. Your diagnosis may be way off the mark, leading the mechanic to spend more time, and you, more money, diagnosing and correcting the real problem. Remember, you're paying the mechanic to diagnose and correct the problem(s).

— Get more than one estimate. You may find a competent mechanic who will do the job for much less than the original estimate. Contact at least three shops and be sure to get all estimates in writing. And request that each estimate be itemized by labor costs, parts cost, etc.

— Make sure the mechanic understands that no work can begin without your authorization. And don't authorize any work unless you receive a written estimate. The estimate also should include the shop's agreement that no work beyond that specified in the estimate will be undertaken without your authorization. If the problem can't be diagnosed right away, insist that the shop contact you for your authorization once the problem has been found.

— Find out whether or not the repair is covered under warranty. If so, follow the warranty instructions exactly. Keep in mindthat some car manufacturers might be willing to repair certain problems without charge even though the warranty has expired. If you're not sure your vehicle's problem falls into such a category, contact the manufacturer's regional representative or the dealer's service department for information.

— Take your car for a test drive before you pay for any expensive repairs. If possible, take along a knowledgeable friend or associate who can help you determine whether or not the car is running right. If the problem hasn't been corrected, don't pay the repair bill.

— Don't pay for services you did not receive. Read the repair bill carefully and make sure you're are being charged for only those repairs you authorized. Also make sure you get the repair warranty. The warranty should be in writing and it should specify how long the work and parts are guaranteed. Also be sure you keep copies of all paperwork.

Many states, cities and counties have special laws dealing with vehicle repairs. You can contact your state or local consumer protection office (see Appendix) for information about the laws in your state.

Cheap Driving Tips

Getting necessary repairs done right is one way to save money as a car owner. Another way is to get every mile you can for each dollar you spend on gasoline. Here are eight fuel-efficient suggestions:

1) Pump your own. Depending on where you fill up, you can save from 15 to 20 cents per gallon by pumping your own gasoline.

2) Use the lowest octane called for in your owner's manual. High-octane fuel is expensive, and in many cases unnecessary. Most of today's vehicles operate efficiently on lower octane

gasoline. Follow the guidelines in your owner's manual.

3) Keep your tires inflated to their proper pressure. Insufficient tire pressure, along with poor alignment, can cost you almost two extra miles per gallon of gasoline.

4) Keep your car's engine tuned. You can improve the mileage in older cars by 15% to 20% by paying keeping the engine tuned properly.

5) Avoid sudden accelerations whenever possible. Excessive stop and go driving can reduce your car's fuel efficiency.

6) Lighten up. The more weight your car carries, the more gas it consumes. Don't haul any unnecessary heavy items in your car's trunk.

7) Use the air conditioner sparingly. Air conditioning lowers fuel efficiency, especially in city driving. Whenever possible, use the air vents to keep cool.

8) Avoid unnecessary engine idle. If you have to wait more than one minute, turn off the motor. You'll use more gasoline by allowing your engine to idle than by restarting.

Learn The Lemon Law

Most states have enacted new car "lemon laws" that protect car owners from getting stuck with a lemon. While the laws may vary from state to state, they generally allow a new car owner a refund or replacement when a new vehicle has a substantial problem that isn't fixed within a reasonable number of attempts. Many lemon laws specify "a reasonable number" of repair attempts as four. A refund or replacement also may be in order if a problem has kept a vehicle out of service for thirty days within the first 12,000 miles/12 months.

If you think you've been sold a lemon, try the following:

— Contact your state or local consumer protection office (see the Appendix) and request information on the lemon laws in your state. Also find out the steps you must take to resolve the matter.

— Provide the dealer with a written list of symptoms each time you bring your car in for repairs. Keep copies of this list for your records.

— Get copies of all repair orders showing the reported problems, the repairs performed, and the dates that the car was in the shop for repairs.

— Contact both the dealer and the manufacturer to report the problem. In some states, consumers are required to do so to give the manufacturer an opportunity to fix the problem. You can find an address for your car's manufacturer in your new car owner's manual.

If you take all the above steps and the problem still doesn't get resolved, you might have the option of participating in an arbitration program. Such a program may be offered by the manufacturer or by your state. Your state or local consumer protection office can provide more information.

Ten Tips For Cheaper Auto Insurance

1) Comparison Shop

It's a recurring theme among savvy shoppers: shop around and compare service and prices before you sign on the dotted line. And it's an important theme to put into practice when choosing automobile insurance coverage on a new or used car. That's because rates for the same coverage can vary by hundreds of dollars among insurers. Services provided also can be vastly different.

There are several ways to go about finding the lowest rates and the best service. You can contact your state insurance department (see the Appendix), check consumer guides, and talk with several insurance agents and companies. The information you gather will give you an idea of the coverages and price ranges available. You also should find out about the services each company offers and how much you'll have to pay for those services. Then, narrow your choices to three or four companies and request price quotes. Choose the insurer that offers the most reasonable rates and quality service.

2) Request Higher Deductibles

Here's the way it works: the lower your deductible, which is the amount of money you'll be required to pay before you make a claim, the higher your premium. On the other hand, if you're willing to pay higher deductibles on collision and comprehensive coverage, you can lower your premium substantially. You may be able to cut your costs by 30% or more simply by asking for higher deductibles.

3) Eliminate Cost Ineffective Coverage On Older Cars

You may want to consider dropping collision and/or comprehensive coverages on a car that's worth less than $1,000. Such coverage is probably not cost effective because of the annual costs and deductibles. For example, it's generally advisable to drop collision coverage when the premium is at least 10% of the car's market value. Any claim you might make is not likely to justify the cost of such coverage.

4) Avoid Duplicate Medical Coverages

If you have a good health insurance policy, you may be able to eliminate duplicate medical coverage in your auto insurance policy. Such medical coverage insures you and your passengers against medical fees incurred because of a car accident. An adequate health insurance policy, however, should already give you this protection. Your passengers also should be protected by their own health insurance and your liability coverage.

By eliminating this duplicate medical coverage in your auto policy, you could lower your personal injury protection cost by 30% to 40%.

5) Buy An "Insurance Friendly" Car

Insurance costs should be a consideration before you buy a new or used car. A "low profile" or conservative car costs substantially less to insure than a high profile sports car that may be expensive to repair and a prime target for thieves. Compare premiums on alternative cars before you buy. One good source of comparison information is the "Highway Loss Data Chart". The Chart is available free by writing to the Insurance Institute for Highway Safety, 1005 North Glebe Road, Arlington, VA 22201.

6) Take Advantage Of Discounts

Most insurers offer a variety of discounts which can result in cheaper coverage for most motorists. For example, some companies offer discounts to individuals who drive fewer than a predetermined number of miles per year. Some coverages offer discounts for safety features such as automatic seat belts and air bags. Some insurers also offer discounts if more than one car is on the same policy. Other discounts also may be available if:

— you've had no accidents in the past three years
— you've had no moving violations in the past three years
— you're over 50 years of age
— your vehicle is equipped with an anti-theft device
— if you have auto and homeowners coverage with the same company
— if you are a nonsmoker

Make sure you check with your insurer about these and other discounts for which you may qualify.

7) Take Advantage Of Discounts For Your Children

You should qualify for a lower premium if your children receive a grade of "B" or higher in an approved driver-training course. You also may be eligible for lower premiums if your children make above average grades in school. Ask your insurer if these discounts are available.

8) Take A Driver's Safety Course
Some insurers reward motorists who complete defensive driving courses with a reduction in premiums. In some states the reduction may be as high as 15%.

9) Participate in A Car Pool

Many insurance companies are now offering lower premiums to motorists who join car pools. The theory is that since you are driving your own vehicle less, you're exposing yourself and your vehicle to less risk.

10) Drive Safely And Defensively

Even if you have a minor accident, your premium is likely to increase by 25%. That's why it pays to be a safe and defensive driver. Safe driving also means obeying the speed limit and other traffic laws. Speeding tickets, drunk-driving tickets, and an otherwise poor driving record could increase your premium by as much as 50%.

For more information on auto insurance coverage, contact the National Insurance Consumer Helpline at (800) 942-4242.

Free Car Safety Booklet

You can get important car-buying information, including safety features, crash test results, and theft ratings for new cars from the Federal Trade Commission's booklet "Buying A Safer Car". To get a free copy of this booklet, write to the Consumer Information Center, P.O. Box 100, Pueblo, CO 81002. Ask for "Buying A Safer Car", #501B.

NOTES

_____

_____

_____

_____

_____

_____

_____

_____

C H A P T E R   6

6

CHEAPIES, FREE GOODIES AND GIVEAWAYS

Health Care Cost Cutters

Americans are spending over $700 billion a year on health care. That's enough to make all but the wealthiest people sick. For many people, with little or no insurance, a routine trip to the doctor's office or a brief stay in a hospital is an expense they can barely afford. And unfortunately, many of these people aren't aware that there are many easy ways to cut health costs without sacrificing quality of care.

The most obvious way to reduce health care costs is to stay healthy. If you don't get sick, you won't need to worry about sky-high medical bills. Certainly you can take steps to reduce your risk of health problems. Proper nutrition and regular exercise can help you stay fit, but nothing can guarantee your continued good health.

Whether you're faced with taking prescription and/or over-the-counter (OTC) drugs, a stay in the hospital, or some other medical treatment, you need to get the best care available at prices you can afford. The good news is that there are many free and low-cost sources of quality health care available. There also are many proven ways to reduce your medical expenses and still get the care you need.

While you may be able to take advantage of many of the suggestions offered in this chapter, keep in mind they are just that— suggestions. You should always consult your doctor or another health care professional before making any decisions about your health care.

Where To Find Cheap And Free Health Care

Everyone wants the best possible health care. The problem is, how to get it without spending your life savings. Fortunately there are several sources of quality health care that everyone can afford. And many of these sources offer this care free of charge. Here are several sources for which you may qualify:

1) Local Free Health Clinics

Here's a source of free health care that may very well be in "your own backyard"— your local health department. Many local health departments offer free or low-cost clinics and screening centers which handle non-emergency health problems. Many offer free prenatal and well-baby clinics as well.

Most of the health services offered by local health departments are available free or on a "sliding-fee-scale" basis. The services offered, eligibility requirements, and fees (if any) vary with each health department. You should contact your local health department to find out what free and low-cost services are provided as well as eligibility requirements, and what times the services are provided.

You also can find out about local health clinics which offer free and low cost services by contacting your state department of public health.

2) Government Medical Programs

The federal government's Medicare health insurance program provides comprehensive "acute-care" coverage for people age 65 and over. About four million people with disabilities and nearly 200,000 people with chronic kidney disease also are covered by Medicare health insurance. The program is funded through social security contributions, premiums and general revenue.

Medicare consists of two parts: Hospital Insurance and Medical Insurance. Medicare-covered services may be provided through fee-for-service arrangements, or by managed care plans, such as HMOs. Some medicare-covered services, such as flu shots for people 65 or older may be free (see "Free Flu Shots" later in this chapter).

Another low-cost medical program is Medicaid. This is a federal/state program which provides medical services to low-income and medically needy people. The services offered and eligibility requirements for the Medicaid program vary from state to state.

You can contact the Medicare Hotline (800) 492-6603 or (800) 638-6833 for information about both Medicare and Medicaid. You also can get referrals and informational publications about Medicare and Medicaid by calling the Hotline.

You also can get free information about Medicare health insurance— how it works and who is eligible for coverage— by writing to: Medicare Publications, Health Care Financing Administration, 6325 Security Boulevard, Baltimore, MD 21207. Request any of the following informational publications:

— "The Medicare Handbook"
— "Medicare and Coordinated Care Plans"
— "Medicare and Other Health Benefits"
— "Guide to Health Insurance for People With Medicare"
— "Medicare Coverage for Second Surgical Opinion"
— "Medicare and Advance Directories"
— "Medicare and Your Physician's Bill"
— "Medicare Savings for Qualified Beneficiaries"
— "Medicare Coverage of Kidney Dialysis and Kidney Transplant Services"
— "Medicare Hospice Benefits"

The above publications also may be obtained from any Social Security office.

3) Emergency Rooms

Let's face it, when confronted with a medical emergency, the last thing you want to think about is how you're going to pay for "services rendered." The good news is that federal Law says you don't have to. Emergency rooms are required by law to provide certain emergency services free of charge. Emergency room personnel must provide an initial screening to assess a patient's condition. Such a screening is designed to eliminate the automatic transfer of patients who are unable to pay.

Free emergency room care includes the initial assessment of a patient's condition, measures taken to prevent death or further disability for patients in imminent danger, as well as any measures necessary to stabilize the patient. Once a patient has been stabilized and a short-term assessment of his/her condition has been made, emergency room doctors can refer the patient to other hospitals or clinics for further treatment.

Keep in mind that emergency rooms are for medical emergencies and not routine health care. Too many people use emergeny rooms for non-urgent medical treatment which can be very costly. So if it isn't a medical emergency, stay away from the emergency room. Otherwise you're likely to pay dearly for whatever treatment you get.

4) Clinical Trial Programs

Each year the finest medical research professionals receive millions of dollars to study causes, treatments and cures to a variety of illnesses and diseases. If you suffer from a health condition which is currently being studied by these medical professionals, you could be eligible for free medical treatment. The free medical treatment is made possible through "clinical trial" programs. You also may be able to take advantage of a clinical trial if your doctor recommends that you undergo an experimental new treatment.

Clinical trials are conducted in various locations throughout the U.S. There are several ways you can find out about what trials are being conducted and whether or not you are eligible to receive free treatment. The National Institutes of Health (NIH) Clinical Center (Bethesda, MD 20892; Phone: (301) 496-2563) is one of the world's leading biomedical research centers, and can provide you with a brochure describing current Clinical Center Programs.

The Division of Research Grants at the National Institutes of Health also can provide you with free information about clinical trials. You can find out about grants awarded to government research institutions, universities or hospitals which deal with current research into your medical concerns. This office also offers a brochure which describes their services. To get the brochure and other information write to the Division of Research Grants at NIH, 5333 Westbard Ave., Room 148, Bethesda, MD 20895; Phone: (301) 496-7543.

The NIH also publishes a catalog which describes all of the ongoing clinical trials that are looking for participants. For a free copy of this catalog, send a postcard to Clinical Center Communications, NIH, Building 10, Room 1C255, 10 Center DRMSC, Bethesda, MD 20892.

You also can get information about clinical trials being conducted in the U.S. and abroad through the National Library of Medicine. Contact the National Library of Medicine, Building 38A, Room 4n421, 8600 Rockville, MD 20894; Phone:(800) 638-8480.

How To Cut Hospital Costs

Under many insurance policies, hospital bills are paid in full. Other policies may pay 90% or more of a patient's hospital costs. For people covered under such policies, quality of care, not price, is the major concern. However, people with little or no insurance, or people whose policies require them to pay 20% of hospital costs must give more consideration to prices.

Here are some cost-cutting suggestions:

1) Have necessary tests done by outside labs. You can reduce the costs of preadmission tests, such as EKGs, blood tests, urinalysis and chest X-rays done by an outside lab or on a hospital outpatient basis. Ask your doctor if the hospital will accept the results of testing done in facilities other than the hospital. If it will, you'll save on the cost of the tests and you'll not have to pay for a day or two spent in the hospital.

2) Don't pay for unnecessary tests. Check with your doctor to find out whether or not all the entry tests the hospital requires are really necessary. Also find out if the tests were ordered by your

doctor. In some cases, insurance companies may not reimburse you if the tests weren't specifically ordered by your doctor.

3) Find out whether or not your treatment can be done on an out-patient basis. If preadmission testing results from an outside lab are acceptable, the hospital also may agree to treat you as an outpatient, eliminating the expense of a lengthy stay in the hospital. An outpatient clinic also may be acceptable for your treatment. If you need surgery, find out if it is a procedure that can be performed on an outpatient basis. Many surgical procedures, such as uncomplicated hernia repair, cataract removals and lens implants, knee arthroscopy, and some biopsies can often be done in an outpatient clinic.

4) Check out as soon as you can. The rule of thumb here is to arrive late and check out early. That way you won't have to pay for the privilage of sitting around and waiting for a doctor to see you. Check with hospital admissions and find out when the admission day begins and ends. The idea is to keep your hospital stay as brief as possible. Keep reminding yourself that "the shorter the stay, the less you pay."

5) Don't check in on Friday. Hospital labs are usually closed over weekends. That means if you check in on Friday, you'll have to pay for two-and-a-half days of waiting for the lab to reopen on Monday.

6) Get a second opinion. Doctors aren't infallabile. They can mis-diagnose or prescribe the wrong treatment or procedure. Getting a second medical opinion could save you from unnecessary and expensive treatment. It's especially important to get a second opinion when surgery is required. If there is no emergency and

the surgery doesn't have to be performed right away, a second opinion may result in another less expensive medically acceptable choice, such as physical or drug therapy. Your medical insurer also may require a second opinion before you have non-emergency surgery.

If you do get a second opinion, make sure you ask your doctor to forward copies of all your medical records, X-rays and tests to the doctor giving the second opinion. Otherwise, you might have to pay for duplicate tests.

7) Get an itemized hospital bill. Make sure you aren't being overcharged. Check the bill and challenge any overcharges you find, even if your insurance company is paying the bill. Don't pay for days not spent in the hospital or for medication, tests and procedures not performed.

8) Avoid paying for retesting. If a test or procedure is performed improperly, or if the results are lost, don't pay for the retests. You only have to pay the first time the tests were given.

Eight Ways To Cut Drug Costs

If you've already read the first several chapters of this book, you should know that one of the best ways to save on medicines is comparison shopping. Since pharmacies and other drug outlets may charge widely different prices for the same medicines, you should get price quotes from several outlets on the medication you need.

Besides shopping around for the best price, there are several other easy ways you can get cheaper medicine. Here are eight money-saving suggestions:

1) Generic Drugs

Ask your doctor or pharmacist about the availability of generic equivalents the next time you need to fill a prescription. If available, a generic equivalent can cost up to 80 percent less than its brand name counterpart. And don't worry, the disparity in price is not because generics are inferior to brand name drugs. FDA studies have shown that there's no significant difference in effectiveness between brand name and generic drugs. The price difference is largely due to the widespread and expensive marketing brand-name drugs receive. Generic drugs are not heavily advertised.

Your doctor or pharmacist can tell you whether or not a generic equivalent is available and an appropriate substitute for a brand name prescription.

As an example of possible generic drug savings, here are four popular brand-name drugs, and their generic equivalents. The average savings are based on typical drug store prices. Actual savings will vary depending on where you shop.

Prescription	Brand-Name	Generic	Average Generic Drug Savings
Antiobiotic	Keflex	Cephalexin	40%

Diuretic	Lasix	Furosemide	40%
Painkiller	Darvon	Propoxyphene hydrochloride	40%
Painkiller	Tylenol	Acetaminophen	35%
Tranquilizer	Valium	Diazepam	50%

2) Mail Order Pharmacies

Mail order pharmacies often offer greater savings on both prescription and over-the-counter medications than you'll find at local drugstores. What's more, you can order through the mail and have your medications delivered right to your door. Granted, delivery may take up to two weeks (usually just a few days), but the lower prices, convenient ordering-by-phone, and home delivery service can more than make up for the wait. Unless, of course, you need the medicine right away.

Generally, you can expect to save 35 percent and more on some prescription drugs, OTC medications and other health-related products when you buy from a mail order pharmacy. You can get discount prices on medication for long-term care maintenance of chronic conditions, such as heart disease, diabetes and hypertension.

You'll need to send a copy of your prescription, as well as authorization from your doctor, before a mail order pharmacy will sell you medications. Some pharmacies also require that their customers belong to membership groups. You may be able to join such a membership group through your employer, union or health insurance plan. There are, however, many mail-order pharmacies that offer disounts to everyone. It's a good idea to include mail-order pharmacies on your comparison shopping list when you're looking for a cheaper prescription and/or OTC drug outlet.

Listed below are several mail-order pharmacies which will send you product catalogs and provide price quotes upon request. Keep in mind, you should always consult your doctor before ordering any medication through a mail-order pharmacy.

— Action Mail Order Drug Company, P.O. Box 787 Waterville, Maine, 04903-0787; (800) 452-1976; Fax: (207) 872-6130. Call or write for a free catalog listing OTC medicines, vitamins and minerals, and other health related products.

— AARP Pharmacy Service, 144 Freeman's Bridge Road, P.O. Box 2211, Schenectady, NY 12309; (800) 456-2279; (800) 456-2226 (price quotes). Members of the American Association of Retired Persons (AARP) can take advantage of discounts by mail by ordering from the AARP Pharmacy Service. You must be at least 50 years old and pay a $5.00 annual fee to qualify for membership. Call or write to request a free catalog and/or pre-scription price quotes.

— America's Pharmacy, P.O. Box 10490, Des Moines, IA 50306-0490; (515) 287-6872. Call or write to request a free catalog.

— Family Pharmaceuticals, (800) 922-3444. Anyone can order prescription and OTC medications through this mail-order house.

— Medi-Mail, P.O. Box 98520, Las Vegas, NV 89193-8520; (800) 331-1458. Call or write for a free listing of products and services and/or a price list of prescription and OTC medications.

— Pharmail Corporation, P.O. Box 1466, Champlain, NY 12919; (800) 237-8927. Call or write for a free price list of common medications and/or a price quote on an OTC or prescription drug.

3) Hospital Pharmacies

You can save a substantial amount of money by purchasing drugs at a hospital pharmacy. In some cases you can save as much as 40 percent on certain drugs. That's because hospitals frequently receive discounts on drugs and in turn pass those savings on to qualified patients.

You may be able to take advantage of these discounts if your doctor is affiliated with a hospital or you are being treated at a hospital clinic.   Be sure to compare prices between the hospital's pharmacy and other outlets. You may be surprised at the potential savings.

4) Senior Citizen Discounts

Many drugstores and pharmacies give senior citizens a discount of 10%. The discount may not be posted so it's a good idea (if you qualify) to ask whether or not the discount is available.

5) Drug Manufacturer Giveaways

Many major drug manufacturers offer giveaway programs that provide certain patients with free drugs. In most cases, patients who qualify for these programs are low-income people without insurance who can not afford to pay for the medication themselves. The programs vary from manufacturer to manufacturer with one or more drugs available.

You can not apply to any of these manufacturer aid programs directly. The drug companies will only accept applications from physicians. Find out whether or not your doctor is aware of these programs. If not, ask him/her to contact the Pharmaceutical Manufacturers Association (PMA), 1100, 15th Street NW., Washington, DC 20005; (202) 835-3400 and request its guide to these aid programs. Remember, the PMA will not respond to individual patient inquiries about these programs. The information is available only through a physician. You also can have your doctor apply directly with the manufacturer(s).

6) Sample Drugs

You may be able to get free medication by using samples obtained from your doctor. Most doctors receive numerous sample drugs from drug manufacturers. The samples help doctors evaluate treatment options for their patients. This is often a cheap way to test a new prescription to see how it works for you. Ask your doctor if samples of a prescribed drug are available. If a sample is available, your doctor may give it to you free of charge.

7) Follow Doctor's Orders

Regardless of where you get your prescription medication, always make sure to take it as directed. If your doctor instructs you to take the entire prescription, that's exactly what you should do— even if you start feeling better before you've taken all the medication. You risk a relapse if you stop taking the medication before the prescription has run its course. In that event, it's likely that you'll need to buy more medicine. It's cheaper to follow directions the first time.

8) Watch Out For Adverse Drug Interaction

Make sure your doctor and pharmacist are aware of all the drugs you are taking. That's because some drugs don't mix well together. Some cancel each other's effectiveness, while others may be dangerous when taken together. It's especially important when you're taking both prescription and OTC drugs to ask your doctor or pharmacist if the two can be taken together safely. Otherwise you could be risking your health and wasting your money.

9) Buy In Bulk

If your prescription calls for long-term maintenance of conditions such as diabetes and hypertension, you may want to consider buying your medication in bulk. You'll get bulk-purchase discounts and you'll have fewer copayments to make if you buy a two or three months supply at one time.

Home Medical Tests Can Save You A Bundle

During the past several years "home versions" of expensive medical tests have become available to most people. Home tests are available for monitoring or screening certain conditions, including pregnancy, diabetes, high blood pressure, and occult blood in the stool (an early warning sign of colorectal cancer). A relatively new urinary profile test allows a patient to test his/her general health at home, as well.

Obviously, you shouldn't use these tests without first consulting with your doctor. Your doctor can tell you what type of home testing is appropriate for your condition, how often you should do the testing, and how to interpret and respond to the results. You also should keep in mind that home testing will not eliminate the need for regular medical checkups with your physician. They can, if used properly, help you avoid some visits to the doctor's office, however. They also can provide early warning of a serious health problem.

You can find home health testing kits at most drugstores and discount supply houses. Prices will vary (see below), depending upon the type of test you buy and where you buy it. Generally, you can expect to pay considerably less for a home health testing kit than you would if you have the test done in a lab. What's more, if your doctor prescribes a home test, the cost of the kit may be covered by your health insurance policy.

Here are several of the most commonly used home health testing kits and what you might expect to pay for them:

— Ovulation: $30 to $50.

— Pregnancy: $10 to $15.

— Urinary Tract Infection: $10 to $15.

— Blood Pressure: $40 to $100 or more for an automatic electronic machine; $20 to $30 for a manual home testing kit.

— Blood glucose monitor: $40 to $70 for 50 chemically treated strips; $60 to $200 for an electronic monitor.

— Fecal Occult Blood Test: $10 to $15.

Cheap And Free Home Remedies

There are many medical conditions that respond favorably to tried and true home remedies which have been around for generations. Besides bringing relief from minor maladies, home remedies are cheap when compared with over-the-counter products. In fact, you probably already have many "healing" ingredients, such as baking soda, honey, tea, herbs, spices, and vinegar, in your cupboards at home. If you know how to use them to alleviate minor aches, pains and other discomforts, you may be able to save yourself an expensive trip to the drugstore.

Of course, no home remedy is intended to take the place of conventional medical treatment. Before you try any new treatment consult your doctor for his/her advice.

While a lengthy list of home remedies is beyond the scope of this book, here are a few that could provide some relief as well as save you some money.

— Backache: There are actually many home remedies that may help ease a backache. For example, while lying on your back on the floor, allow your feet and calves to rest on a low box or chair so that your knees form a right angle. Place a small, flat pillow under your neck and relax in this position for several minutes. Other temporary remedies include the application of ice if the pain results from a spasm or a sudden strain. Follow the ice treatment with moist heat. Keep in mind, if your backache persists, or is accompanied by other symptoms, such as fever, numbness, or abdominal pain, you should see your doctor as soon as possible.

— Common Cold: Besides getting plenty of rest, there are several home remedies that can help alleviate the misery associated with colds. For example, try eating spicy foods to make your nose and eyes run. This will help clear congestion. Hot peppers and cloves work especially well as expectorants to help you cough up mucus and keep your lungs clear.

Studies indicate that Vitamin C may help bring some relief from the incessant coughing and sneezing that accompanies some colds. Vitamin C also may help shorten the duration of a cold. So try drinking lots of juice. Orange and grapefruit juice are especially good sources of Vitamin C.

You can relieve the irritation caused by a sore throat by gargling saltwater. For best results, fill a glass with warm water and add one teaspoon of salt. Gargle the mixture whenever your throat seems most irritated.

To get a good night's sleep, try drinking a cup of herbal tea just before bedtime. Hops and valerian herb teas work especially well as natural tranquilizers. A teaspoon of honey added to the tea may help increase its sedative effect.

— **Cold Sores:** Some people swear by the "freeze-dry" method of conquering cold sores. It's an old remedy that involves applying an ice pack on a fresh cold sore for about 10 minutes, several times a day. Applying a wet, hot tea bag on a cold sore also can sometimes work wonders. Make sure you dry the area thoroughly following this treatment. In fact, the most important thing to do when a cold sore appears is to keep it clean and dry. One way to do that is to cover the sore with petroleum jelly, which will keep the area protected.

— **Headaches:** Some experts believe that nearly 90 percent of all headaches are caused by tension. With that in mind, try to relax the next time you have a headache. Simple relaxation exercises can help alleviate your misery. For example, let your head drop slightly forward, then rotate it slowly, first in one direction, then in the other. You also might try tensing all the muscles in your shoulders, neck, face, and jaw. Maintain the tension for about thirty seconds, and then release it suddenly.

For some people, other relaxation techniques, such as yoga and meditation, can bring release from a tension headache. Deep breathing exercises also can relieve tension and lessen the severity of a headache.

Of course, if your headache persists, see a doctor as soon as possible.

— Heartburn: For some people, baking soda makes an effective (and inexpensive) antacid. Baking soda is not a good remedy for people with hypertension, however, because it's loaded with sodium. In lieu of baking soda, you might try an herbal remedy such as gingerroot. For best results, take it in capsule form just after you eat. While no one knows for sure why it works, many experts believe that gingerroot somehow absorbs the acid which causes heartburn.

— Insomnia: There are several home remedies that can help keep you from tossing and turning all night. For some people, a warm bath just before bedtime does the trick. It helps them relax and put aside all the troubles of the day. You might even try taking a casual stroll around the block before you take your bath. The key is unwinding before you get in bed.

A light snack before bedtime also can help you get a good night's sleep. Foods that contain carbohydrates, such as cereal, rice cakes, and muffins, work especially well because they help stimulate the body's natural tranquilizers.

— Motion Sickness: Ginger root is an effective anti-motion sickness remedy that prevents nausea and doesn't cause drowsiness. Taken in capsule form at least ten minutes prior to departure, ginger root works as well as, or better than, over-the-counter anti-motion sickness medications.

— Sunburn: It may leave you smelling like a salad, but vinegar can take away most of the sting of a newly acquired sunburn. It's a fast-acting and cheap remedy. A mixture of skim milk and cold water applied as a compress to scorched skin also can bring relief.

Free Flu Shots

You could be eligible to get a free flu shot and avoid a viral infection that can lead to a much more serious illness such as pneumonia or bronchitis. Medicare may pay for the flu shot.

If you're covered by Medicare, you won't have to pay the usual co-insurance or deductible amounts. Medicare will pay those amounts, as well as an amount for the vaccine and the person who gives you the shot. If the person giving you the shot accepts the Medicare payment as payment in full, the shot will be free.

Medicare Health Insurance provides comprehensive acute-care coverage for more than 35 million people age 65 and over. The program also provides coverage for almost four million disabled people and about 200,000 people with chronic kidney disease who need dialysis or kidney transplants.

So if you are covered by Medicare, it's a good idea to take advantage of this service and get a free flu shot. The Public Health Service recommends that you get a flu shot every year if you are 65 or older, even if you are generally healthy.

Medicare will pay for the shot anywhere flu shots are administered, as long as the provider is complying with Medicare rules in your state.

How To Get A Free Copy Of Your Medical Information File

The Medical Information Bureau (MIB) is a data bank used by over 700 insurance companies. Medical (and some non-medical) information is collected from insurers and, with your permission, shared when you apply for individual life, health, or disability insurance. You might want to obtain a copy of your MIB report (if one exists) and make sure the information it contains is correct. You can verify the report's accuracy and completeness by showing it to and discussing it with your doctor. To get a free copy of your medical information file, write to the Medical Information Bureau, P.O. Box 105, Essex Station, Boston, MA 02112.

If the originating insurance company feels there is sensitive medical information recorded in your file, the company may require the MIB to send your medical record only to your doctor.

You can get more information on how to obtain your own medical records by sending for a free brochure titled, "Your Health Information Belongs To You". The brochure is available upon request from the American Medical Record Association, 919 North Michigan Avenue, Suite 1400, Chicago, IL 60601. Include a SASE with your request.

This Free Information Can Help You Choose The Right Doctor

If you want to find out whether or not a doctor is board-certified, the information is just a toll-free call away. Call the American Board of Medical Specialties at (800) 776-2378 between 9 a.m. and 6 p.m. (Eastern time) Monday through Friday. Operators will tell you whether or not the doctor in question is board-certified. Other information provided includes the year the doctor was certified and by which certification board.

Dental Clinics Can Save You Hundreds of Dollars On Dental Work

Check with a local or a nearby university and find out whether or not it has a dentistry school. If it does, you may be able to get expert dental work at a fraction of the price you'd pay a private dental practice. That's because university dental students need to practice on real patients. That's not as painful as it sounds because all dental work done is overseen by faculty who are eminently qualified in their field. You'll get the professional dental care you need for about half the price you'd pay a dentist in private practice.

Check your phone directory for dentistry school listings.

These Hotlines Can Provide Free And Low-Cost Medical Information

These agencies, foundations, and other organizations can provide you with free and low-cost help for many of your most pressing health problems. They can provide you with helpful information, answer your questions and provide medical referrals.

— Agency for Health Care Policy and Research (AHCPR), P.O. Box 8547, Silver Spring, MD 20907; Phone: (800) 358-9295. The AHCPR, a division of the U.S. Department of Health and Human Services, also can provide written reports on specific medical conditions. The reports are known as practice guidelines and are available free of charge.

— Alzheimer's Association, 919 N. Michigan Avenue, Suite 1000, Chicago, IL 60611; Phone: (800) 621-0379; (800) 272-3900 (in Illinois). Provides information on printed material available from the association. Also makes referrals to local Alzheimer's chapters and support groups.

— Alzheimer's Disease Education and Referral Center, P.O. Box 8520, Silver Spring, MD 20907-8250; Phone: (800) 438-4380. The Center, which is a service of the National Institute on Aging, distributes information on Alzheimer's Disease, current research activities, and on services available to patients and family members.

— American Cancer Society, 1599 Clifton Road NE, Atlanta, GA 30329; Phone: (800) ACS-2345. Makes referrals to local chapters which offer support services. Provides publications and general information about cancer and how to cope with cancer.

— American Diabetes Association, P.O. Box 25757, 1660 Duke Street, Alexandria, VA 22314; (800) 232-3472. Offers printed material and referrals for information on local support groups.

— American Heart Association, 7272 Greenville Avenue, Dallas, TX 75231; (800) 242-1793.

— American Lung Association, 1740 Broadway, New York, NY 10019; Phone: (800) 586-4872.

— American Parkinson's Disease Association, 60 Bay Street, Suite 401, Staten Island, NY 10301; Phone: (800) 223-2732.

— American Speech-Language- Hearing Association, Consumer Affairs Division, 10810 Rockville Pike, Rockville, MD 20852; Phone: (800) 638-8255. Provides information on hearing aids and on certified audiologists and pathologists.

— Arthritis Foundation, 2045 Peachtree Road, N.E., Atlanta, GA 30326; (800) 283-7800. Provides general information, printed material, and referrals to local support groups.

— Asthma and Allergy Foundation of America, 1125 15th Street N.W., Suite 502, Washington, DC 20005; Patient Information Line: (800) 7-ASTHMA. Provides general information, as well as printed material, videos and referrals.

— Cancer Information Clearinghouse, National Cancer Institute, Building 31, Room 10a30, Bethesda, MD 30014; Phone: (800)

4- CANCER; (800) 524- 1234 in Hawaii. Provides information on state-of-the-art cancer treatments and clinical trials and answers questions about cancer. Also provides free publications, including a booklet titled "What Are Clinical Trials All About?", and a research report, "Bone Marrow Transplantation."

— CDC National AIDS Hotline, 215 Park Avenue South, Suite 714, New York, NY 10003; Phone: (800) 342-AIDS. Provides recorded information concerning the prevention and spread of AIDS.

— CDC Sexually Transmitted Disease (STD) Hotline; Phone: (800) 227-8922. Provides useful information and confidential referrals for treatment.

— Chronic Fatigue and Immune Dysfunction Syndrome (CFIDS): CFIDS Association of America, P.O. Box 220398, Charlotte, NC 28222-0398 (include a SAE and 52 cents postage for information); Phone: (800) 442-3437.

— The Health Information Center of the U.S Public Health Service; (800) 336-4797. The Center can provide printed guidelines on specific medical conditions, as well as make referrals to other health care resources.

— Impotence Institute of America Hotline; (800) 669-1603. Provides literature, physician referrals and information about local support groups.

— Lupus Foundation of America, 4 Research Place, Suite 180, Rockville, MD 20850; Phone: (800) 558-0121.

— Medical Alert Foundation International, P.O. Box 1009, Turlock, CA 95081; Phone: (800) 344-3266; (800) ID-ALERT.

— National Center for Nutrition and Dietetics Hotline; (800) 366-1665. Provides general information on nutrition, literature, and answers questions on healthful eating habits.

— National Clearinghouse for Alcohol and Drug Information, 11426-28 Rockville Pike, Suite 200, Rockville, MD 20852: Phone: (800) 729-6686. Provides a variety of government publications on alcohol and drugs

— National Council on Alcoholism and Drug Dependence, Inc., 12 West 21st Street, New York, NY 10010; Phone: (800) NCA-CALL.

— National Health Information Center, P.O. Box 1133, Washington, DC 20013; Phone: (800) 336-4797; (301) 565-4167 in MD. Provides phone numbers for hundreds of health-related organizations. Also offers a variety of informational publications.

— National Institute on Aging, Public Information Office, Building 31, Room 5C27, Bethesda, MD 20892; (301) 496-1752. The Institute provides information on a variety of aging-related topics, including disabling conditions, community resources, and support groups.

— National Kidney Foundation, Inc., 30 East 33rd Street, 11th Floor, New York, NY 10016; Phone: (800) 622-9010. Provides general information, as well as referrals.

— National Multiple Sclerosis Society, 733 Third Avenue, 6th Floor, New York, NY 10017; Phone: (800) 227-3166. Provides information upon request.

— National Stroke Association, 8480 East Orchard Road, Suite 1000, Englewood, CO 80111; Phone: (800) 787-6537. Provides printed material, as well as referrals.

— Project Inform, (800) 822-7422. Provides information about clinical trials, new drugs and drug reimbursement programs to patients who are HIV-positive or who have AIDS.

Free Drug Savings And Safety Information

The following sources can provide free information booklets on cutting drug costs and using them safely:

— AARP: For a free copy of "Getting the Most From Your Medication," write to: AARP Fulfillment, 601 E St. N.W., Washington, DC 20049.

— Food and Drug Administration: Offers free brochures titled, "Some Things You Should Know About Prescription Drugs" and "Food and Drug Interactions: Know The Right Way To Take Your Medicines." For a free copy of each booklet, write to Leonard Genova, 900 Madison Avenue, Baltimore, MD 21201.

— National Council on Patient Information and Education (NCPIE): Offers a free copy of "Get the Answers About Your Medicines". To get a copy, send a #10 SASE to NCPIE, 666 11th St. N.W., Suite 810, Washington, DC 20001.

— National Institute on Drug Abuse (NIDA): To get a free copy of "Using Your Medicines Wisely," write to the NIDA, Information Services, P.O. Box 2345, Rockville, MD 20847-2345; or call (800) 729-6686.

Free Health Care Advice From The Government

The federal government produces hundreds of informational brochures and booklets covering a variety of consumer topics, including health matters. Many of the booklets are free, while others may cost as little as 50 cents. You can order booklets on nutrition, prescription and OTC drugs, medical treatments, exercise, and more. See chapter 10, "Government Goodies", for information on how to order the most current "Consumer Information Catalog" which lists available booklets you can get free or at a low cost.

NOTES

_____

_____

_____

_____

_____

_____

C H A P T E R   7

CHEAPIES, FREE GOODIES AND GIVEAWAYS

Traveling Cheaply

Planning a vacation can be a frustrating experience, especially if you're on a tight travel budget. How do you get where you want to go, and stay there as long as possible without spending your life savings? Should you travel by air or hit the open road behind the wheel of your own car? Will you stay in a hotel, motel, or a tent? Should you pay someone to plan and arrange your trip for you? Answering these and other practical travel questions can take a lot of the pleasure out of planning your "great getaway." Unless, of course, you're a savvy consumer and know how to get from here to there as cheaply as possible.

Traveling cheaply doesn't mean stopping long enough in

each state only to have your picture taken beneath a "Welcome to" sign. There are many ways you can cut costs without cutting out enjoyment and comfort. What follows are some travel industry insider suggestions and tips for traveling cheaply without sacrificing the pleasure of your dream vacation.

Air Travel Cheapies

Ten Ways To Get The Lowest Air Fare

Finding the lowest air fare to your intended destination can be more of an adventure than the flight itself. With the airlines in intense competition for your travel dollars, you're likely to encounter special promotions offering discount fares, fare wars, and other enticements to get your business. It's enough to make even the most seasoned traveler dizzy.

So, how do you sort through all the offers to get the cheapest air fare possible? You could call each airline and ask about the fares they charge. You also can scan newspaper ads where airlines advertise many of the discount plans that apply to your area. You can have a good travel agent do the searching for you. And you can use any of the following ten airline industry insider tips to help you get the best deals on air fare:

1) Take advantage of fare wars. Major airlines are in stiff competition for your business and offering "discount sale" tickets is one way they try to get it. To take advantage of such discounts, you may be required to book at least two weeks in advance, stay over a Saturday night or meet some other qualifications. If you

do, you could save 30% or more off regular non-discount air fare.

You also can get a real bargain, even if you bought your ticket before a discount was offered. That's because you're allowed to exchange a ticket for the cheaper fare (to the same destination). You'll be required to pay a fee of $25 to $35 to exchange your ticket for a cheaper fare, but the savings can still be considerable.

Make sure your travel agent knows you're interested in fare war tickets. That way you'll be on the top of the list to get a reduced fare when an air fare war begins.

2) Whenever possible, travel on Tuesday, Wednesday and Saturday. Because fewer people fly on those days, most airlines lower their prices in an effort to fill seats. The toughest times to get discounts are Friday afternoons and Monday mornings. Business travelers fill most seats during those times, so there are fewer discounts available.

3) Stay over on a Saturday night. Most major airlines frequently require Saturday night stays. That's because they don't want business-travelers, who typically return home for the weekend, buying up all the cheap seats. In many cases, there's a marked difference in price between staying over Saturday night and not staying over. If you don't choose to stay over on a Saturday, your round-trip air fare is likely to be much higher than it would be if you do stay over.

4) Fly low fare airlines.

Within the past couple of years, many small airlines have started up service in various parts of the country. While these small airlines offer little in the way of frills— you may not get a meal or see a movie— their fares can be considerably lower than the regular fares charged by major airlines. If you don't mind a "back to basics" flight, low fare airlines offer some great travel bargains.

Here are several of the new low fare airlines, offering some of the cheapest rates for air travel:

— Carnival Airlines, (800) 824-7386. Flies from New York area airports to several cities in Florida and Puerto Rico. Also offers flights between Miami and Los Angeles.

— Kiwi International Airlines, (800) 538-5494. This Newark, New Jersey-based airline connects New York with several major cities, including Chicago, Atlanta, Orlando and Tampa. Kiwi also offers flights between some of those cities.

— Midway Airlines, (800) 446-4392. Based at Chicago's Midway airport, this low-fare airline offers flights between Chicago and New York, Philadelphia, Washington, D.C., and other major U.S. cities.

— Morris Air, (800) 446-7747. Based in Salt Lake City, Utah, Morris Air offers low-fare flights primarily in the Western United States.

— Reno Air, (800) 736-6246. Reno Air offers flights departing from Reno, Nevada and San Jose, California to several major cities in California and the Northwest.

— Southwest Airlines, (800) 435-9742. Despite being one of the largest airlines in the U.S., Southwest offers fares as low as many of the smaller low-fare airlines. Flights are in the Midwest, West, and Southwest.

— Tower Air, (800) 221-2500. Offers daily flights between New York and Los Angeles and Miami as well as flights between New York and San Francisco, Orlando and San Juan.

5) Be flexible in your travel plans. If your travel plans aren't cast in stone and you can leave on a moment's notice, you're likely to get some of the lowest fares available. Obviously, this type of travel isn't for everyone, but for the person who isn't "locked in" to one airline or one specific departure date, discount airfare is usually available.

If possible, give yourself a span of several days for your departure. Then, get a good travel agent to "shop around" (by computer) for the best deal. The agent's computer search will track down an airline's lowest fares to your destination. Make sure the search includes all the airports near where you will be departing and your destination. You may get considerable savings by departing from or arriving at an alternative airport nearby.

6) Use a consolidator. Consolidators buy blocks of airline tickets at wholesale prices, then resell them to consumers, travel agents and travel brokers at prices that are often significantly less than regular air fare. Unless they are competing with an airline's fare

war, consolidators can usually save you over 20% on the price of a ticket. On some international flights, you can save as much as 50% off regular fare by purchasing from a consolidator.

While generally much cheaper than regular fare, consolidator tickets usually come with some restrictions. For example, you won't be able to get an advance seat assignment or order a special meal. You also may not be able to get frequent-flier credit, and refunds are extremely hard to get. You should ask about these and other possible restrictions before you buy.

To locate consolidator tickets, check the travel sections in Sunday newspapers such as the New York Times (available at most public libraries). Many discount agencies advertise their fares in the back of travel sections in small ads that list destinations and ticket prices. You also may be able to purchase consolidator fare through a reputable travel agent.

If you do buy a ticket through a consolidator, be sure to pay with a credit card. That way, if there's a problem, you'll retain your right to withhold payment.

7) Enroll in a frequent flier program. There's no charge to join these money-saving programs which are offered by virtually all major airlines (see "Join a Frequent Flier Program..." later in this chapter). Being a member of a frequent flier program entitles you to free trips, upgrades, and other awards. The benefits are based on how often you fly on a particular airline or by using specified hotels, rental cars, credit cards, and so on.

8) Take advantage of all senior citizen discounts. If you're 62 or older, you can usually get a 10% senior discount off advertised

airfare (except for short-term discount fares) when you fly with most airlines. Airlines also offer special discounts to seniors on many flights, excluding short hauls. These discounts are available through the purchase of "senior coupons," and must be reserved two weeks in advance. You should ask about any restrictions that might apply with a senior coupon before you buy.

9) Fly as an air courier. You can save 50% to 80% on your airfare— especially when flying overseas— by flying as an air courier. There's some work involved, since air couriers deliver documents and other air shipments to worldwide destinations. As a courier, you'd be responsible for delivering such a shipment to its intended destination. In return, you would receive a reduction in airfare.

Admittedly, your responsibility as a courier might not make flying as relaxing as it would be if you were a regular passenger. And you have to have some interest in going to destinations not necessarily of your own choosing. You'll have to register (for a small fee) with a courier company. Your regular work schedule also must be flexible enough to allow you to take advantage of courier flights as often as possible. You won't be able to get tickets for two, and you'll have to travel with little or no luggage. However, if you can fly as an air courier, you could end up getting some of the lowest airfares around.

You can find out more about air courier travel in "The Insider's Guide to Air Courier Bargains", by Kelly Monaghan (Inwood Training Publications, Box 438, New York, NY 10034; $16.95— includes postage and handling).

10) Comparison Shop. As with any other purchase, comparison shopping offers you the best opportunity to find the best deals on air fare. Differences in air fares can be substantial from airline to airline, and if you have the time to invest and perseverance you should be able to find the lowest fare to your destination.

The best advice is to plan as far ahead as possible. Many airlines set aside only a few seats on each flight at discount rates. The best bargains sell out quickly, so you'll have to be ready for them as soon as they're available.

Join A Frequent Flier Program For Cheaper Air Travel

If there's a lot of air travel in your future, you should consider joining a frequent flier program. These programs, offered by most major U.S. airlines, allow frequent fliers to earn free trips, upgrades (from coach to first class), or other awards. The benefits you receive are based on how much mileage you accumulate on a particular airline.

Even if you don't fly often—or at all, you still can reap benefits from a frequent flier program. Many frequent flyer programs allow you to earn credit mileage by using specified hotels, rental cars, or credit cards. In fact, virtually every major airline is affiliated with a credit card issuer. These programs generally offer one frequent-flier mile per dollar charged on a participating Visa or MasterCard.

Some frequent-flier programs also offer mileage credit if you stay in hotels or rent cars from participating companies. You also can accumulate miles by signing up with a long distance phone company, such as MCI, AT&T and Sprint, that is linked up with a major airline's frequent flier program. You'll get credit just by making a long distance call.

There's no charge for becoming a member in a frequent flier program. You just find one that suits your needs and enroll. To do that, you should check out the frequent flier programs offered by a number of airlines. Here are some things to consider when looking for a program.

— Does the airline offer regular flights to destinations where you're likely to want to go?

— Does the airline have "tie-ins" with other carriers, especially those flying international routes? Do commuter-carrier "partners" provide some of the airline's service? If yes in both cases, find out whether or not you earn credits and can use awards on the other airlines.

— How many miles, or trips, does the airline require before honoring particular awards? Most airlines now require you to fly from 20,000 to 25,000 miles before you can redeem your mileage for a free round-trip domestic coach ticket. Some airlines also limit that mileage to off-peak travel time (the beginning of September through the middle of November).

— Does the airline have a minimum award per flight? For example, some frequent flyer programs offer awards if your flight is at least 500 miles. In that case, if your flight is less than 500 miles, you are not eligible for an award.

— Is there a deadline for using accumulated frequent flyer miles?

Many airlines now have a three-year expiration on accumulated mileage.

— Are there any "blackout periods" during which the airline will not honor awards? If so, find out the number and length of these blackouts. On some airlines, the Thanksgiving blackout period may last a week.

— Will the airline give credit for mileage flown before you become a member? The best advice here is to become a member before you travel. This is especially important if you plan on doing a lot of traveling by air. In most cases, airlines won't allow credit for mileage flown before you became a member. By comparing the programs offered by several airlines, you can select one that best suits your needs. Once you do, take full advantage of all the awards offered to rack up mileage on your way to a free ticket, upgrades, room discounts and more travel savings.

Volunteer To Be "Bumped" And Fly For Free

What happens when an airline sells more tickets than it has seats available on a scheduled flight? That's not a silly question, because it happens on a regular basis. And knowing the answer could enable you to fly to your destination free of charge.

Most airlines overbook their flights to avoid getting stuck with empty seats due to "no-shows." Overbooking is an essential safeguard for airlines because the average no-show rate on most flights is 10% to 15%. However, when an oversale occurs and there are more passengers than available seats, some passengers must stay behind. These travelers are, in effect, "bumped" from the flight. When that happens, Department of Transportation (DOT) regulations require the airlines to provide these passengers with compensation.

Few travelers are forced to give up their seats involuntarily. That's because DOT regulations require airlines to look for travelers who are willing to give up their seats voluntarily in exchange for compensation before bumping anyone involuntarily. In other words, if you're in no particular hurry to get to your destination you can give your ticket back to the airline in exchange for compensation and a later flight. In fact, some savvy travelers actually look for flights that have a good chance of being overbooked so they can volunteer to give up their seats.

How much compensation you get by voluntarily giving up your seat depends on the airline and on your skill as a negotiator. Typically you'll get a free trip or vouchers. You also may be able to negotiate for a mutually acceptable amount of cash. If you get bumped involuntarily, the amount of compensation you get depends on your destination and the length of time you're delayed. If the airline gets you to your final destination within an hour of your original scheduled arrival, no compensation is required. However, if the airline cannot get you to your destination within an hour, DOT's denied boarding compensation rules require:

— a payment equal to your one-way fare to your final destination, up to $200, if the airline can't get you to your destination between one and two hours after your original arrival time (between one and four hours on international flights)

— payment up to $400 if your substitute flight gets you to your destination more than two hours later than your original arrival time (four hours on international flights.).

You'll also get to keep your original ticket for use on a future flight. In essence, the denied boarding compensation is a payment for your inconvenience.

Here are some travel industry insider tips for taking advantage of airline overbooking and becoming a voluntary "bumpee":

— Find out whether or not a flight is a near sell-out before you make a reservation. If the flight is almost sold out, make a reservation.

— Consider making reservations on Friday evening, Sunday evening and/or Monday morning flights. Flights during those times are often overbooked. Holiday weekends also are good times to take advantage of overbooking.

— Unless you prefer to be bumped involuntarily, you should be one of the first to check-in when the departure gate opens. Passengers are involuntarily bumped on the basis of check-in order— the last to check-in are the first to be bumped. If you're at the head of the line, you'll have a better chance to give up your seat voluntarily and negotiate your compensation.

— Before you volunteer to give up your seat, find out what compensation the airline is offering.

Lodging Cheapies

How To Get The Best Deal On A Hotel Room

By investing a little bit of time and effort, any traveler can find acceptable lodging at discount prices. In fact, you should never have to pay "full price" for a hotel room. That's because most hotels routinely offer a variety of discounts of up to 50% off their regular room rates. Here are several insider tips on how to find those discounts:

— Call individual hotels to get the cheapest rates. First, call a hotel chain's toll-free number and find out the rate on the type of room you need. Keep in mind that hotels aren't going to volunteer information about special rates— you have to ask. For example, if you plan to stay over a weekend, ask about a weekend special. Also ask whether or not the hotel offers other discounts or packages.

Once you have this information, call the hotel directly and ask the same questions. Compare answers. In many cases, a hotel's toll-free national reservation line and its individual hotels are far apart on price. Individual hotels also may lower prices if business is slow or have special promotions that the national reservation operators know nothing about. Look for the lowest rate on the accommodations you need.

— Ask about group or organization discounts. Most hotels offer standard discounts of 10% to 20% off their regular rates to business or corporate employees, automobile club members, and-military or government workers.

— Take advantage of senior citizen discounts. If you're 62 or older you qualify to receive discounts of 10% to 30% at most hotels. The discount may be even greater if you make your reservations in advance or if you are a member of the American Association of Retired Persons (AARP).

— Reserve early. If you can reserve your room two to three weeks in advance, you may be able to get a discount of up to 50% off regular rates. However, some hotels will require prepayment which may not be refundable in the event you decide to cancel your reservation.

— Make your reservations through a hotel broker. A hotel broker or reservation service can be one of the best sources for room discounts. By purchasing blocks of hotel rooms in most major U.S. cities, brokers are able to resell them at discounts of 50% and more off typical rates. To make a reservation, contact a broker who serves a city you're planning to visit. Ask about available hotels and rates. If you find a good deal, make a reservation. You can find a broker who handles hotels in the city you're planning to visit by calling the city's Chamber of Commerce, visitor's bureau, or department of tourism.

Here are several such reservation services:

* Capitol Reservations, (800) 847-4832. Handles listings for hotels in Washington, DC.

* Central Reservation Service Corporation, (800)

548-3311, or (800) 950-0232. Offers discounts on hotel rooms in several large U.S. cities.

* Hot Rooms, (800) 468-3500. Chicago lodgings only.

* Hotel Reservations Network, (800) 964-6835. This discount broker has listings of lodgings in more than 20 U.S. cities.

* Quickbook, (800) 789-9887. Covers hotels in more than 20 major American cities.

* RMC Travel Centre, (800) 782-2674.

* San Francisco Reservations, (800) 677-1550.

* U.S. Tour Operators Association, 211 E. 51st Street, Suite 12B, New York, NY 10022.

— Check Out Half Price Programs. Half Price programs offer travelers one of the best opportunities to save up to 50% on lodgings. To get such discounts, you'll be required to pay a $30 to $100 annual membership fee. In exchange, you'll receive an ID card and a directory that lists hotels throughout the U.S. that are participating in the program. These hotels are usually medium to budget priced.

You should be able to use the information from the directory to call a hotel directly and inquire about a half-price room. Generally, if the hotel doesn't expect to be more than 80% full at the time of your potential stay, you'll receive up to 50% off the hotel's regular rates. Reservations must be made in advance.

Here are several of the most popular half-price programs:

* America at 50% Discount, (800) 248-2783. Membership fee is $49.95 the first year.

* Encore, (800) 638-8976. Offers a list of 3,000 participating hotels. Annual fee is $49.

* Entertainment National Hotel and Dining Directory, (800) 445-4137. The directory costs $37.95.

* Entertainment Publications, (800) 477-3234. Annual fee is $30 and up.

* Great American Traveler, (800) 548-2812. Offers discounts of up to 50% at more than 2,000 hotels. Annual fee is $49.95.

* ITC-50, (800) 342-0558. Annual fee is $36.

* The Privilege Card, (800) 359-0066. Offers discounts of up to 50% at more than 2,500 hotels. Annual fee is $49.95.

— Look For Wholesale Savings. If you'd rather not get involved with travel agents, clubs, or a time-consuming search, you can contact a wholesale agency, such as The Room Exchange, and book accommodations for 20% to 50% off regular rates at thousands of hotels. You can contact the Room Exchange by calling (800) 846-7000 [212-760-1000, in New York City], and inquire about room availability and rates.

— Book overseas trips through your airline. If you're planning a trip overseas, your airline may offer a discount of up to 50% on accommodations at many European hotels. American Airlines, (800) 832-8383; TWA, (800) 438- 2929; and British Airways, (800) 247-9297.

— Pick the right package. A travel package deal can include hotel, land and/or air transportation, sightseeing tours and other travel services all for one low price. Such packages can be a good deal, if you know exactly what you're getting. Before making a reservation, find out exactly what travel services are included and how much the components of the package would cost separately. You may not be getting a bargain after all.

The U.S. Tour Operators Association (211 E. 51st Street, Suite 12 B, New York, NY 10022) offers "The Worldwide Tour and Vacation Package Planner", a free directory with listings. The directory is available upon request.

— Check Out The Savings At A YMCA. Some travelers scoff at the mere suggestion of staying overnight at a Y, but the truth is YMCA lodging is one of the best travel deals available. While you won't get all the amenities that go with a pricey hotel room, you will get clean, comfortable and safe accommodations at some of the cheapest rates around. For example, single room rates average around $20 a night; double room accommodations from $30 to $40.

YMCA lodging is available at over 40 lodging centers in 39

cities in the United States, as well as in around 50 lodging centers in over 25 foreign countries. To find out more about YMCA lodging, and to get a complete listing of YMCA accommodations, you can order a copy of "The Y's Way International Directory." Write to: The Y's Way, 224 East 47th Street, New York, NY 10017, Include a SASE with your request.

— Always pay by credit card. That way you maintain your right to withhold payment if something goes wrong. If you pay by check, the hotel already has your money, leaving you virtually powerless to challenge a charge you disagree with.

Budget Motels Can Save You 50% Or More

Don't let the popular misconception of motels being "cheap" and "seedy" keep you from getting one of the best bargains in lodging. The truth is, there's very little difference between a nice hotel room and a budget motel room— except, of course, price. Both typically offer enough space for a comfortable bed, clean bathroom with tub and shower, color TV, desk, chair and dresser. The main difference is that you might end up paying twice as much for those accommodations in a typical big-city hotel as you would in a budget motel. And price is just one reason why budget motels are the "fastest growing segment" of the travel lodging industry.

Budget motels are typically located away from downtown areas along or near freeways or Interstate Highways, making them convenient and economical choices if you travel by automobile. Average prices range from $25 to $35 for a single occupancy overnight and from $40 to $50 for two persons overnight.

Of course, prices will vary depending on the motel chain and may even be lower due to special discounts offered from time to time.

The best way to find out exactly how much you'll pay is to contact the motel of your choice and ask for a price quote. Once you get a quote you like, ask for a mailed confirmation that the price is guaranteed. Be sure to inquire about the lowest rates and also inquire about discounts. Many motel chains offer discounts to senior citizens, families, automobile club members, military personnel, and other group or promotional discounts.

Listed below are the addresses and toll-free reservation numbers for several of the most popular budget motels through-out the United States. While the reservation operators will be able to provide some information about rates and discounts, you should contact the motels in writing for detailed information about accommodations and rates.

— BEST INNS OF AMERICA, P.O. Box 1719, Marion, IL 62959; (800) 555-1212.

— BEST WESTERN, INC., Best Western Way, P.O. Box 10203, 6201 N. 24th Parkway, Phoenix, AZ 85064; (800) 528-1234; (800) 528-2222 (Telecommunication device [TDD]).

— BUDGET HOST INNS, Box 14341, Arlington, TX 76094; (800) 283-4678.

— BUDGETEL INNS, 250 W. Wisconsin Avenue, Milwaukee, WI 53202; (800) 428-3438.
— CLARION, Choice Hotels International, 10750 Columbia

Pike, Silver Spring, MD 20901; (800) 221-2222.

— COMFORT INN, Choice Hotels International, 10750 Columbia Pike, Silver Spring, MD 20901; (800) 221-2222

— CROSS COUNTRY INNS, 6077 Frantz Road, Dublin, OH 43017; (800) 621-1429.

— DAYS INN, 339 Jefferson Road, Parsippany, NJ 07054; (800) 329-7466.

— EXCEL INNS, Excel Inns of America, 4706 E. Washington Avenue, Madison, WI 53704; (800) 356-8013.

— E-Z 8 MOTELS, 2484 Hotel Circle Place, San Diego, CA 92108; (800) 326-6835.

— FRIENDSHIP INNS, Choice Hotels International, 10750 Columbia Pike, Silver Spring, MD 20901; (800) 424-4777.

— INDEPENDENT MOTELS OF AMERICA, P.O. Box 202, Winner, SD 57580; (800) 341-8000.

— MOTEL 6, 14651 Dallas Parkway, Dallas, TX 75240; (214) 386-6161 (information); (505) 891-6161 (reservations).

— RED ROOF INNS, 4355 Davidson Road, Hilliard, OH 43026; (800) 843-7663.

— RODEWAY INNS, Choice Hotels International, 10750, Columbia Pike, Silver Spring, MD 20901; (800) 424-4777.
— SUPER 8 MOTELS, INC., 1910 Eighth Avenue, N.E., Box

4090, Aberdeen, SD 57402; (800) 800-8000; (800) 533-6634 (TDD).

— TRAVELODGE, Trusthouse Forte Hotels, INC., 1973 FriendshipDrive, El Cajon, CA 92920; (800) 578-7878.

College Dorms Offer Cheap Lodging

Many travelers are finding that college dorms make excellent choices for overnight lodging. Dorm rooms are clean, comfortable and inexpensive. Several colleges across the country are now providing cheap housing in their dormitories during the summer and other college vacation periods. Prices range from $15 to $30 per night for single occupancy.

When planning your vacation, check for colleges in the area(s) you plan to visit. Then make your reservations by calling the schools directly. Ask about the availability of overnight dorm accommodations and rates. If you have children, be sure to ask whether or not they can stay in your room. Some colleges don't allow children to stay overnight in their dorms, even when with their parents.

Join A Travel Club And Cut Vacation Costs By 40%

There are four regional travel clubs in the United States offering access to first class flights and/or excursions at savings of up to 40% off average commercial rates. Membership in one of these clubs requires paying an initiation fee and $70 to $100 in annual dues.

You can get more information about what these regional travel clubs offer and their fees, by contacting any of the following:

— Ambassadair, (800) 225-9919.

— Nomads, (313) 941-8000.

— Ports of Call, (800) 843-6774.

— Sky Cruisers, (813) 536-2267.

Set Sail For 50% Off With A Cruise-Only Travel Agency

If a cruise is your idea of a dream vacation, get your travel budget in hand and contact a cruise-only travel agency. You don't have to pay several thousand dollars for a seven-day cruise. Deep discounts of 50% and more are possible on the cruise of your choice. Of course, you'll have to do some comparison shopping. There are hundreds of cruise-only travel agencies which specialize in getting vacationers on the right cruises at bargain prices. These agencies are able to offer such discounts because they can sell large blocks of tickets for specific cruise lines. With a little searching, you should be able to locate a cruise you can afford.

Listed below are several cruise-only travel agencies which offer discounts of 20% to 60% off list prices on cruise packages. To find a cruise-only agency near you, write to the National Association of Cruise Only Agencies, 3191 Coral Way, Suite 630, Miami, FL 33145. Include a SASE with your request.

— Cruises of Distinction, (800) 624-3445. Offers discount voyages and last minute cruise bargains.

— Cruise Headquarters, 4225 Executive Square #1200, La Jolla, CA 92037 ; (800) 424-6111. Offers land and sea packages.

— The Cruise Line, Miami, FL; (800) 777-0707. Offers discounts on cruise vacations. Also publishes a free magazine "World of Cruising" which features cruise deals.

— Cruise Pro, 99 Long Court, Suite 200, Thousand Oaks, CA 91360; (800) 222-7447; (800) 258-7447 (in CA).

— Cruises Only, 1801 East Colonial Drive, Orlando, FL 32803: (800) 683-7447.

— Family Cruise Club, Las Angeles, CA; (800) 242-9000. Offers discounts on family cruises.

— Landry & Kling East, Inc., Gables Waterway 1, 1309 S. Dixie Highway, Suite 1207, Coral Gables, FL 33146; (800) 223-2026. Specializes in group, luxury and extended cruises.

— Spur of the Moment, (800) 343-1991. Specializes in

discount cruises and last minute bargains.

— Worldwide Cruises, (800) 882-9000; Offers deep discounts on cruise vacations.

Freighters Offer Yet Another Cheap Way To Cruise

They're not as romantic as the regular cruise lines, but freighters definitely offer bargain rates on cruises. If your itinerary is flexible, and you don't mind "roughing it"— no casinos, spas, floor shows, or gourmet cuisine— you may be able to book passage on a freighter for considerably less than you'd pay on a traditional cruise ship.

Most freighters don't accept passengers, but those that do offer average rates of $80 to $100 per day per person. Compare that with the average cruise cost of $160 to $220 a day per person. Of course, a cruise on a freighter might last several weeks, so the price tag can still be fairly hefty.

Cruising on a freighter is not for everyone, but if you want a true get-away at a bargain price, it just may be the ticket. Here are several companies that book passage on freighters:

— Bergen Line, (800) 323-7436.

— Freighter World Cruises, (818) 449-3106.

— Ivaran Lines, (800) 666-9333.

— TravLtips Cruise & Freighter Travel Association, (800) 872-8584.

Seniors Get Discounts on AMTRAK Travel

If you're over 65, you can ride the rails of AMTRAK at a reduced rate. AMTRAK offers a senior citizen discount of 25% on one-way tickets. It's a cheap and interesting way to travel. For more information, call AMTRAK at (800) 872-7245.

Travel Abroad For Free

If you qualify for the U.S. Speakers Program, the government will pick up the tab for your overseas travel. The Speakers Program is looking for experts on a number of topics to travel abroad and participate in seminars, colloquia and symposia. Experts are needed to cover topics in arts and humanities, economics, science and technology, international political relations, and social and political processes.

You can find out whether or not you qualify for the Speakers Program by contacting U.S. Speakers, Office of Program Coordination and Development, U.S. Information Agency, 301 4th Street, SW, Room 550, Washington, DC 20547.

Free Travel Information

All 50 states offer free travel information including free maps, travel and lodging guides, and camping guides. To get this free information, call any of the numbers listed below.

* Alabama: (800) 252-2262
* Alaska: (907) 465-2010
* Arizona: (602) 542-8676
* Arkansas: (800) 628-8725
* California: (800) 862-2543
* Colorado: (800) 265-6723
* Connecticut: (800) 282-6863
* Delaware: (800) 441-8846
* District of Columbia: (202) 789-7000
* Florida: (904) 487-1462
* Georgia: (404) 656-3590
* Hawaii: (808) 923-1811
* Idaho: (800) 635-7820
* Illinois: (800) 223-0121
* Indiana: (317) 232-8860
* Iowa: (800) 345-4692
* Kansas: (913) 296-2009
* Kentucky: (800) 225-8747
* Louisiana: (800) 334-8626
* Maine: (800) 553-9595
* Maryland: (800) 543-1036
* Massachusetts: (617) 727-3201
* Michigan: (800) 543-2937
* Minnesota: (800) 657-3700
* Mississippi: (800) 927-6368

* Missouri: (800) 877-1234
* Montana: (800) 541-1447
* Nebraska: (800) 228-4307
* Nevada: (800) 237-0774
* New Hampshire: (603) 271-2343
* New Jersey: (800) 537-7397
* New Mexico: (800) 545-2040
* New York: (800) 225-5697
* North Carolina: (800) 847-4862
* North Dakota: (800) 435-5063
* Ohio: (800) 282-5393
* Oklahoma: (800) 652-6552
* Oregon: (800) 547-7842
* Pennsylvania: (800) 847-4872
* Rhode Island: (800) 556-2484
* South Carolina: (803) 734-0122
* South Dakota: (800) 732-5682
* Tennessee: (615) 741-2158
* Texas: (800) 452-9292
* Utah: (801) 538-1030
* Vermont: (800) 837-6668
* Virginia: (800) 847-4882
* Washington: (800) 544-1800
* West Virginia: (800) 225-5982
* Wisconsin: (800) 432-8747
* Wyoming: (800) 225-5996

C H A P T E R   8

8

CHEAPIES, FREE GOODIES AND GIVEAWAYS

College Cheapies

First, the bad news: at today's costs, you can expect to pay between $35,000 and $100,000 for a four-year college degree. What's more, the American Council on Education estimates that the cost of public and private colleges will increase by up to 18% within the next two years. Those are frightening figures for anyone trying to come up with enough money to get a college education. Even more so because in today's world, a college degree is generally considered a requirement for the majority of the best-paying jobs.

The good news is that there are hundreds of millions of dollars in financial aid given away free to students every year. Most of that assistance is given in the form of grants and scholarships which do not have to be paid back. In essence the money is a gift to be used to help reduce college costs. And in many cases scholarship and grant money is awarded regardless of financial need or academic achievement.

Many students overlook this potentially rich source of college funding because they aren't aware the funds are available or they don't believe they're eligible to receive them. In fact, even with the hundreds of millions of dollars awarded annually, more than $135 million dollars in scholarship money goes unclaimed every year.

The key to getting your share of this "free money" is finding out who is giving it away and how you can qualify. It will take time and effort on your part. You'll need to do a good deal of research, dig out family and financial records, fill out applications, and meet filing deadlines. You're also likely to encounter some frustration and rejection along the way. But if you persevere, there's a very good chance that you'll qualify for some sort of grant or scholarship that can help reduce your college costs by a substantial amount.

Sources Of Free Money For College

Financial aid for postsecondary education is available from a number of sources, including the federal government, state governments, individual colleges and universities, private organizations, and military education programs. Generally, the aid consists of loans, grants, scholarships and employment opportunities, and may be either need-based or merit-based. While loans are to be paid back, grants and scholarships are not. The money is a gift, free and clear. The only catch is that the money must be used to help pay for your education.

The most common sources for grants and scholarships (money that does not have to be paid back) include:

1) The Federal Government and State Governments.
Both offer a number of grants and scholarships including,

- Federal Pell Grant
- Federal Supplemental Educational Opportunity Grant (FSEOG)
- Federal, Campus-based Work Study Programs
- State Student Incentive Grants (SSIG)
- Robert C. Byrd Honor Scholarship Program (Byrd Program)
- Paul Douglas Teacher Scholarship Program
- National Science Scholarships Program

2) Private Sector funding. This type of funding includes grants and scholarships from sources other than federal or state. Such private financial aid may be available from the following sources:

— Companies and labor unions that have financial aid programs for employees and their family members.

— Foundations, religious organizations, fraternities or sororities, town or city clubs, community organizations and civic groups.

— National Honor Society and National Merit Scholarships which are available to students who maintain high grades.

— Organizations and associations connected with your field of interest, such as the American Medical Association.

3) Military Financial Aid Programs. The U.S. armed forces offer a number of educational programs for students during or after active duty in the military. Some of the programs offered include:

— Reserve Officer Training Corps (ROTC)
— Military Academies
— Montgomery GI Bill

You should contact the financial aid advisor at each school you are considering. The advisor can tell you whether or not the aid programs listed above (and other financial aid programs) are available there and how much the total cost of attendance will be. High school students also can talk with their guidance counselors for information about financial aid in general and for help infinding the most likely sources of money.

How To Apply For Financial Aid

In order to qualify for federal aid, you must submit a financial aid application. You can get a "Free Application for Federal Student Aid (FAFSA)" from your school or from the Federal Student Aid Information Center, P.O. Box 84, Washington, DC

20044. You should send a completed copy to each school that interests you. Applications may be submitted by mail or electronically if the school has electronic application capability.

Some state and college aid programs may require information in addition to that submitted on the FAFSA. Such programs also may require payment of a processing fee. Check with your state scholarship/grant agency (see Appendix) or school financial aid administrator to find out whether or not you need to complete any forms in addition to the FAFSA.

Generally, you should have the following records and information handy when applying for financial aid:

— Your most recent tax return; your parents' tax return if you apply as a dependent student; your spouse's tax return if you're married and your spouse filed a separate return.

— W-2 forms and other records of money you earned over the past year.

— Any records of tax-free income, such as social security, welfare, AFDC or ADC, or veterans benefits.

— Current bank statements; mortgage information; business and farm records; and records of stocks, bonds and other investments.

— Your social security and student drivers license numbers.

— Names and codes of colleges you wish to receive this application.

You should complete and submit the FAFSA as soon after January 1 as possible. Do not sign, date, or mail your application before January 1. The deadline for receipt of the completed FAFSA is May.

1. State and college deadlines may be earlier than the federal deadline, so you should check with your financial aid administrator for the appropriate information.

Be sure to read the instructions carefully when you're filing the FAFSA and/or other financial aid applications. Most mistakes are made because students fail to follow instructions. Be especially careful when completing questions on income, because most mistakes occur on those questions.

Free Money From The Government

When it comes to higher education, Uncle Sam is a good provider. How good? Well, the federal government alone supplies $25 billion a year or about 75 percent of all student aid. Individual states also generally provide various financial assistance programs that can significantly lower college costs for certain students. Much of this assistance, on both the federal and state level, is available through scholarships and grants which do not have to be repaid. In essence, they're gifts to those individuals who qualify. Low-cost Federal loans also are available, but those, like any other loans, must be paid back.

Here are some of the most common sources of "free" federal and state financial aid:

Federal Pell Grants

This is one of the most popular federal student aid programs. Grants are awarded on the basis of financial need. They're given only to undergraduate students who haven't earned a bachelor's or a professional degree. In 1993-94, over 4 million students were awarded Pell Grants of up to $2,300. How much you can get depends on several factors, including your cost of attendance, whether you're a part- or full-time student, whether or not you attend college for a full academic year or less, and your Expected Family Contribution (EFC). The deadline for applying for a Pell Grant is May 1.

If you qualify, A Federal Pell Grant is an excellent source of free financial aid to which other aid may be added.

Federal Campus Based Programs

These federal programs are also need-based. They provide money to colleges to give to needy students through several Campus-based programs, including Federal Supplemental Educational Opportunity Grants (FSEOGs) and the Federal Work-Study Program (FWS). FSEOGs are awarded to undergraduate students who have "exceptional" financial needs or those with the lowest EFCs. The program gives priority to students who receive Federal Pell Grants. And like Pell Grants, FSEOGS don't have to be repaid. If you qualify for an FSEOG, you can get from $100 to $4,000 a year, depending on when you apply, your level of need, and the amount of funding available to the school you're attending. Funding for this program is limited, so it's best that you apply as early as possible.

Under the Federal Work-Study program, college students with financial need are provided with jobs, either on- or off-campus. The program allows students to earn money to help pay college expenses. If you qualify for the FWS program, you'll be paid at least the current minimum hourly wage. You could earn even more, depending on the type of job and the skills required. The number of hours you're allowed to work depends on your class schedule and your overall academic standing.

An important thing to remember is that you can get scholarships and grants from more than one federal program. You can get up-to-date information about all these programs and eligibility requirements by contacting the Federal Student Financial Aid Information Center toll-free at 1-800-4-FED-AID [433-3243] (the Information Center's toll-free TDD number for the hearing-impaired is 1-800-MIS-USED (647-8733). You also can write to the Information Center and request a free copy of "The Student Guide". The Guide provides updated information on all Federal student aid programs. To get a copy of "The Student Guide", write to: Federal Student Aid Information Center, P.O. Box 84, Washington, DC 20044.

State Financial Assistance

Most states allot portions of their state budgets to their own public colleges and universities. The money helps keep tuition costs down for students attending these colleges. Many states also provide financial assistance directly to certain students on a need-based or merit-based basis. A large portion of state aid is in the form of scholarships and grants which do not have to be repaid.

Some of the most common sources of state educational grants and scholarships include the following:

— Merit-based financial aid. Grants and/or scholarships given with this type of aid are based solely on academic achievement, regardless of financial need. A merit-based scholarship may be given to a student who has shown academic excellence in high school or a student who has displayed athletic or artistic excellence. In most cases, merit-based grants and scholarships are awarded on the basis of outstanding academic performance or potential. High school guidance counselors should be able to provide information about merit-based aid available in each state.

— State Student Incentive Grant Program (SSIG). This program is funded jointly by the U.S. Department of Education and individual states. Each state has its own name for this grant program, as well as its own requirements for eligibility, award amounts, and application process.

— Robert C. Byrd Honors Scholarship Program (the Byrd Program). Under this program, students who demonstrate excellent academic achievement and "show promise" of continued excellence, are eligible to receive up to $1,500 per year for up to four years of college education. The award amount you receive depends on your cost of attendance and on the amount of any other aid you may receive. At least 10 Byrd Program scholarships are available in each state. Information on this program is available from the agency in your state responsible for elementary and secondary schools.

— National Science Scholars Program (NSSP). This program is for graduating seniors who have excelled in the physical, life, or computer sciences, mathematics, or engineering. Under the NSSP, scholarships are awarded to two students from each congressional district. These students may receive up to $5,000 a year for up to five years of postsecondary education. Individual award amounts depend on the student's cost of attendance and on the availability of funds. Contact the agency in your state responsible for public elementary and secondary schools for up-to-date information about this program.

— Paul Douglas Teacher Scholarship Program. This program offers financial aid to high school graduates who plan to pursue teaching careers after college. Under this program, individual students may receive up to $5,000 a year (not to exceed $20,000). To be eligible for this scholarship, a student must graduate in the top 10 percent of his/her class, as well as meet any other requirements set by the participating state agency. While the scholarship money awarded does not have to be repaid, recipients generally are required to teach two years for each year of assistance received from this program. Not all states participate in this scholarship program. The higher education agency in your state (see appendix for a state-by-state listing of these agencies, or call 1-800-FED-AID for the address and telephone number of the appropriate state agency) or the agency responsible for public elementary and secondary school education can provide you with more information about this program.

Private Sources of Free Money

There also are thousands of private grants and scholarships available to students with above average academic records, special interests and who meet other qualifications. For example, National Honor Society and National Merit Scholarships are available to students who maintain high grades and otherwise qualify.

Many companies and labor unions also have financial aid programs to help employees, members, or their children pay the cost of postsecondary education. Some trade groups and organizations, such as the American Medical Association (AMA) and the American Bar Association (ABA), offer scholarships to students who plan to pursue careers in the groups' industries. You can locate such groups and organizations in the U.S. Department of Agriculture's "Occupational Outlook Handbook," as well as other directories of associations available at most public libraries.

Private grants and scholarships also are awarded by many foundations, religious organizations, fraternities and sororities, and community organizations and clubs such as 4-H, Jaycees, Chamber of Commerce, American Legion, Elks, Kiwanis, Girl and Boy Scouts, and the YMCA.

Listed at the end of this chapter is a sample of the many grants and scholarships available through private sector funding. You can check available directories at your local library for a more comprehensive listing of this type of financial aid and eligibility requirements.

Military Financial Aid Programs

Another source of financial aid for some students is the military. While this type of financial assistance is not for everyone, the armed forces offers several programs that can help cut college costs significantly. The programs are offered either during or after active military duty— as payment for training or reward for service. Active duty options include pursuing a college degree at a military academy immediately following graduation from high school or enrolling in the Reserve Officers Training Corps (ROTC) program at a civilian school. After service has been completed, former military personnel can take advantage of the Montgomery GI Bill or receive college credit for military training received while on active duty.

Military Academies

Except for the Marine Corps, every branch of the military has its own academy. These are four-year colleges that offer bachelor's degrees and commissions in the military upon graduation. While these academies are highly competitive, they are "tuition-free" to all those students who are admitted. They also provide stipends of $500 a month. The main military academies are: the U.S. Military Academy (West Point, NY); U.S. Naval Academy (Annapolis, MD); and the U.S. Air Force Academy (Colorado Springs, CO).

Two other military academies, the Coast Guard Academy and the Merchant Marine Academy, also offer financial aid in exchange for a student's promise to serve as an officer.

For additional information about specific military academies, you can contact the following:

— Army: Director of Admissions, U.S. Military Academy, West Point, NY 10996-1797.

— Navy: Director of Cadet Guidance, U.S.Naval Academy, Annapolis, MD 21402-5018.

— Air Force: Director of Admissions, U.S. Air Force Academy, Colorado Springs, CO 80840-5651.

— Coast Guard: Office of Admissions, U.S. Coast Guard Academy, 15 Mohegan Avenue, New London, CT 06320.

— Merchant Marine: Office of Admissions, U.S. Merchant Marine Academy, Kings Point, NY 11024.

ROTC

The Reserve Officers' Training Program (ROTC) offers scholarships which cover most of the costs of tuition, fees, and textbooks. The program, offered by the Army, Navy and Air Force, also provides a monthly allowance of $100. If you take advantage of an ROTC scholarship you'll most likely be required to participate in summer training while in college and fulfill your service commitment after you graduate from college.

You can get more information about about ROTC from your local recruiting office. For specific information about Army

ROTC, you can call 1-800-USA-ROTC or write to the Professor of Military Science at a college which hosts ROTC. You also can get information by writing to College Army ROTC, Gold Quest Center, Department PG94, P.O. Box 3279, Warminster, PA 18974-9872.

You also can contact the following for information about Navy and Air Force ROTC scholarship programs:

— Navy ROTC Scholarship Program, P.O. Box 5000, Clifton, NJ 0705-9939; (800) 327-NAVY.

— Air Force ROTC Scholarship Program, Public Affairs Division, Maxwell Air Force Base, Maxwell, AL 36112-6663; (205) 293-2091.

Montgomery GI Bill

The Montgomery GI Bill provides financial support for former military personnel who wish to obtain a college degree after leaving active duty.

Besides the options described above, most branches of the military also offer various tuition assistance programs which enable members to take college courses at civilian colleges during their off-duty hours while on active duty. Military training received while on active duty also can sometimes count toward college credit. In addition, every branch of the military offers training in numerous technical and vocational areas, and military personnel can sometimes receive college credit for this type of training.

You can get more information about education opportunities available through the military at your local armed forces recruiting office.

Seven More Ways To Reduce College Costs

There are several other ways you can reduce colleges costs in addition to receiving scholarships and grants. Here are several suggestions:

1) One of the best and most practical ways of keeping the cost of college down is to enroll in a two-year college and then transfer to a four-year college. In most cases, local community colleges are the least expensive. Tuition is relatively low and the local settings allow most students to live at home and commute to classes. Once a student has achieved an associate's degree or certificate in a two-year college, he/she may choose to transfer to a four-year college and complete the requirements for a bachelor's degree.

Students who choose this option need to take courses in the two-year college that will count toward a bachelor's degree. The courses also should be transferable to a four-year college. Admissions personnel at local community colleges can provide information about required and transferable courses.

2) If possible, you can cut college costs by 20% to 40% by

enrolling in a public school in your own state. Out-of-state students usually pay higher fees to attend a state college or university than "home-state" students. What's more, the tuition costs at public schools are lower than those at private institutions. And, if the school is within commuting distance, you can cut living expenses even more by living at home.

3) Many colleges offer resident advisor programs which enable students to work in residence halls. In exchange for participating in such a program, students receive a cut in tuition costs or a reduction in room and board expenses.

4) Some schools offer cooperative education programs that allow students to alternate between periods of academic study and public or private paid employment. The employment is related to the students' field of study or professional goals. Participating in such a program allows you to earn an income to help pay college expenses and gives you valuable experience in the career you are considering. You may be eligible if you are enrolled at least half-time in a school participating in the cooperative education program. The program is funded through grants to participating schools from the federal government. The National Commission for Cooperative Education (see the information sources at the end of this chapter) can provide you with a directory of participating schools.

5) Reducing the number of credits you need to graduate is another good way to cut college costs. Some schools offer credit for past work experience (paid or volunteer) and home study courses. You also may be able to reduce the number of courses you need to take by passing college level examinations in some subjects. Many colleges recognize programs such as the College-

Level Examination Program (CLEP) and The Advanced Placement Program (APP). You can check with your college's admissions office for more information on these programs.

6) Veterans of the U.S. Armed Forces can reduce college costs considerably by taking advantage of such programs as the Montgomery G.I. Bill noted earlier in this chapter. Disabled veterans are eligible to receive financial assistance to help defray college costs from the Veterans Administration. Dependents of disabled or deceased veterans also may be eligible for such assistance. Contact your local Veterans Administration office for additional information and eligibility requirements.

7) You may be eligible to take advantage of a relatively new program of educational awards. If you're a high school graduate or you have a GED, you may be eligible to receive up to $4,725 a year to help pay for postsecondary education. A new program, National and Community Service, provides full-time educational awards in exchange for service performed either before, during, or after postsecondary education. The money can be used either to pay current college expenses or to repay any federal student loans you may have received. You can get more information on this new program by writing to: The Corporation for National and Community Service, 1100 Vermont Avenue, N.W., Washington, DC 20525; or you can call 1-800-942-2677.

Low-Cost Home Study Colleges

For many people home study (or correspondence study) is the most practical and cheapest way to acquire a postsecondary education. As a home study student, you can work toward a college degree in the comfort of your own home, and maintain your present full-time job. You can avoid high tuition costs, as well as on-campus living expenses. And at many colleges, home-study courses taken from an accredited educational institution are recognized for credit toward graduation should you decide to enroll on campus.

When you enroll in a home-study program, you'll receive lesson materials for study in the mail. Each completed lesson is then mailed back to the school for correction, grading, comment and further assistance by qualified instructors. The exchange provides a personalized student-teacher relationship without the necessity of classroom attendance. In essence, the school comes to you.

Home-study courses can provide you with complete vocational training or prepare you for upgrading in your present job. Some programs consist of a few courses requiring several weeks to complete. Others have over a hundred courses requiring three to four years of study for completion. You can study accounting, business-writing, marketing, photography, electronics, communications, computer programming, and a host of other potentially high-paying career subjects. Some home-study schools also offer both two- and four-year degree programs.

While home-study may not be for everyone, it can be the perfect solution for busy people who can't afford to give up their jobs and enroll on-campus in a college or university. For these people, educational institutions which offer fully accredited home study courses can provide a cheaper way to get college credit or even a degree.

Listed below is a sample list of home study schools which offer a variety of courses. The schools are all fully accredited by the National Home Study Council (NHSC), which has been the nationally recognized accrediting agency for home-study schools for over 65 years. The NHSC also publishes an annual directory of its accredited schools. For a copy of the current directory, write to the National Home Study Council, 1601 18th Street, N.W., Washington, DC 20009.

Home Study Schools

— American Health Information Management Association, 919 North Michigan Avenue, Suite 1400, Chicago, IL 60611; Phone: (312) 787-2672. Offers courses in medical record technology.

— The Barton School, 925 Oak Street, Scranton, PA 18515; Phone: (717) 342-7701. A division of North American Correspondence Schools—National Education Corporation, this school offers courses in medical and dental office assisting.

— California College For Health Sciences, 222 West 24th St., National City, CA 91950; Phone: (619) 477-4800. Offers Associate's, Bachelor's and Master's degree programs in child care, respiratory care, and other health-related fields.

— Cleveland Institute of Electronics, Inc., 1776 East 17th Street, Cleveland, OH 44114; Phone: (800) 243-6446. Offers degree and non-degree courses in electronics engineering, electronics technology, broadcast engineering, electronic communications, and in other areas of electronics.

— Grantham College of Engineering, 34641 Grantham College

Road, P.O. Box 5700, Slidell, Louisiana 70469-5700; Phone: (504) 649-4191. Offers Associate and Bachelor degrees in electronics engineering technology and computer engineering technology.

— International Correspondence Schools (ICS), 925 Oak Street, Scranton, PA 18515; Phone: (717) 342-7701. Offers courses at the postsecondary level in technology, engineering, business, vocational trades, and other areas.

— ICS Center for Degree Studies, 925 Oak Street, Scranton, PA 18515; Phone: (717) 342-7701. Offers specialized degree programs in business, engineering technology, and electronics technology.

— McGraw-Hill Continuing Education Center, 4401 Connecticut Ave., N.W., Washington, DC 20008; Phone: (202) 244-1600. Offers courses in computers, electronics, automotive technology, air conditioning, appliance servicing, home inspection, drafting, small engine repair, bookkeeping, paralegal, desktop publishing, word processing and other areas.

— National College of Appraisal and Property Management, 3597 Parkway Lane, Suite 100, Norcross, GA 30092; Phone: (800) 362-7070. Offers courses in real estate appraisal and property management.

— North American Correspondence Schools, 925 Oak Street, Scranton, PA 18515; Phone: (717) 342-7701. Offers courses in conservation, drafting, legal secretary, and travel.

— NRI Schools, 4401 Connecticut Avenue, N.W., Washington,

DC 20008; Phone: (202) 244-1600. This school is a division of McGraw-Hill Continuing Education and offers courses in air conditioning, writing, microcomputers, electronic communications, bookkeeping, home inspection, paralegal, drafting, word processing, desktop publishing, and other areas.

— Paralegal Institute, Inc., 3602 W. Thomas Road, Suite 9, Drawer 11408, Phoenix, AZ 85061-1408; Phone: (800) 354-1254. Offers courses in legal assistant/paralegal training, Certified Legal Assistant, and Associate degree in Paralegal Studies.

— Peoples College of Independent Studies, 233 Academy Drive,P.O. Box 421768, Kissimmee, FL 34742-1768; Phone: (407) 847-4444.Offers specialized Associate degrees in Travel and Tourism Management, Computer Programming and Electronics Technology.

Private Sector Scholarships And Grants For College Education

Listed below is a sample list from the thousands of private and civic organizations that offer free money in the form of scholarships and grants for postsecondary education. Some of the awards are based on financial need, and some on merit. You can write to the addresses listed below for information and/or applications. Your local library is the best free source for comprehensive directories of the many private sources offering financial assistance for college students.

* AMERICAN COUNCIL OF THE BLIND SCHOLARSHIP: American Council of the Blind, 1010 Vermont Avenue, N.W., Suite 1100, Washington, DC 20005.

Several grants, ranging from $1,000 to $1,800, are awarded to legally blind U.S. citizens for postsecondary education. Contact the "Coordinator of Membership and Student Services" for information.

* AT&T ENGINEERING SCHOLARSHIP PROGRAM: AT&T Bell Laboratories, Crawfords Corner Road, 1E-219, Holmdel, NJ 07733-1988.

* BPW SCHOLARSHIPS: Business and Professional Women's Foundation, 2012 Massachusetts Avenue NW, Washington, DC 20036.

* COMMUNITY SCHOLARSHIP PROGRAM: National Health Service Corps, Health Resources Development Branch, 4350 East-West Highway, 8th Floor, Rockville, MD 20857.

Awards grants to students willing to serve the community in health-related careers.

* DAUGHTERS OF THE AMERICAN REVOLUTION (DAR), AMERICAN HISTORY SCHOLARSHIP: National Society Daughters of the American Revolution, NSDAR Administration Building, 1776 D Street N.W., Washington, DC 20006-5392.

Awards grants of $1,000 to $2,000 based on financial need and class standing to students majoring in American

History.

* DENTAL STUDENT SCHOLARSHIPS: American Fund For Dental Health, 211 E Chicago Avenue Ste 820, Chicago, IL 60611.

* DISABLED AMERICAN VETERANS SCHOLARSHIP PROGRAM: Disabled American Veterans Scholarship Program, P.O. Box 14301, Cincinnati, OH 45250.

* ELKS NATIONAL FOUNDATION MOST VALUABLE STUDENT AWARD: 2750 Lake View Avenue, Chicago, IL 60614.500 scholarships, ranging from $1,000 to $5,000 per year for 4 years, are awarded based on high school class ranking (top 5%), financial need, scholastic achievement and leadership. Contact the "Scholarship Chairperson" in your home state for information.

* JUNIOR/SENIOR SCHOLARSHIPS: Institute of Food Technologies, Scholarship Department, 221 North La Salle Street, Chicago, IL 60601.

Offers scholarships for studies in Food Science and Technology.

* KIWANIS SCHOLARSHIPS: Kiwanis Club of Corsicana, Scholarship Fund, P.O. Box 363, Blooming Grove, TX 76626.

Awards scholarships in all fields of study.

* MINORITY SCHOLARSHIP PROGRAM: American Institute of Certified Public Accountants, 1211 Avenue of the Americas, New York, NY 10036.

Awards grants to Black Americans, American Indians, Asians, and Hispanics to study accounting.

* NATIONAL ASSOCIATION OF AMERICAN BUSINESS CLUBS SCHOLARSHIPS: P.O. Box 1527, High Point, NC 27262.

Offers grants of up to $1,000 per year for students in various health care related fields.

* NATIONAL HONOR SOCIETY SCHOLARSHIPS: National Association of Secondary School Principals, National Honor Society Awards, 1904 Association Drive, Reston, VA 22091.

450 Awards of $1,000 each are given to high school seniors who have been nominated by their local National Honor Societies. Contact the National Honor Society Advisor.

* NATIONAL INDUSTRIES FOR THE BLIND SCHOLARSHIPS: American Council Of The Blind, Scholarship Coordinator, 1155 15th Street, NW Ste 720, Washington, DC 20005.

* NATIONAL INSURANCE INDUSTRY ASSOCIATION AWARD: College of Insurance, 101 Murray Street, New York, NY 10007.

* NATIONAL SOCIETY OF PUBLIC ACCOUNTANTS SCHOLAR-SHIP FOUNDATION: National Society of Public Accountants Scholarship Foundation, 1010 Fairfax Street, Alexandria, VA 22314.

* UNDERGRADUATE SCHOLARSHIPS: Youth Foundation, Inc. 36 West 44th Street, New York, NY 10036.

Over 50 grants, totaling more than $115,000 are award-ed to undergraduate students. The average grant is about $2,000. Contact the Foundation's Vice-president.

Financial Aid Resource List

Department of Education Regional Offices

You can contact any of the DOE regional offices listed below for further information on federal scholarships and grants.

— Region 1: Covers Connecticut, Maine, Massachusetts, New Hampshire, Rhode Island, and Vermont.

Office of Student Financial Assistance, U.S. Department of Education, 5 Post Office Square, Room 510, Boston, MA 02109.

— Region 2: Covers New Jersey and New York.

Office of Student Financial Assistance, U.S. Department of Education, 26 Federal Plaza, Room 3954, New York, NY 10278.

— Region 3: Covers Delaware, District of Columbia, Maryland, Pennsylvania, Virginia, West Virginia.

Office of Student Financial Assistance, U.S. Department of

Education, 3535 Market Street, Room 16200, Philadelphia, PA 19104.

— Region 4: Covers Alabama, Florida, Georgia, Kentucky, Mississippi, North Carolina, South Carolina, and Tennessee.

Office of Student Financial Assistance, U.S. Department of Education, P.O. Box 1692, Atlanta, GA 30301.

— Region 5: Covers Illinois, Indiana, Michigan, Minnesota, Ohio, and Wisconsin.

Office of Student Financial Assistance, U.S. Department of Education, 401 South State Street, Room 700-D, Chicago, IL 60605;

— Region 6: Covers Arkansas, Louisiana, New Mexico, Oklahoma,and Texas.

Office of Student Financial Assistance, U.S. Department of Education, 1200 Main Tower Building, Room 2150, Dallas, TX 75202.

— Region 7: Covers Iowa, Kansas, Missouri and Nebraska.

Office of Student Financial Assistance, U.S. Department of Education, 10220 N. Executive Hills Boulevard, 9th Floor, Kansas City, MO 64153-1367.

— Region 8: Covers Colorado, Montana, North Dakota, South Dakota, Utah, and Wyoming.

Office of Student Financial Assistance, U.S. Department of Education, 1244 Speer Boulevard, Denver, CO 80204-3582.

— Region 9: Covers Arizona, California, Hawaii, and Nevada.

Office of Student Financial Assistance, U.S. Department of Education, 50 United Nations Plaza, San Francisco, CA 94102-4987.

— Region 10: Covers Alaska, Idaho, Oregon, and Washington.

Office of Student Financial Assistance, U.S. Department of Education, 915 Second Avenue, Room 3388, Seattle, WA 98174-1099.

Financial Aid Information And Application Sources

— Federal Aid Information Center, P.O. Box 84, Washington, DC 20044; (800) 4-FED-AID [800-433-3243]. The Information Center can help you complete the federal student financial aid application; locate schools that participate in federal aid programs; determine whether or not you're eligible for federal student aid; receive student aid publications.

— Consumer Information Catalogue, Pueblo, CO 81009; (800)-USA-LEARN. You can write or call to order the free publication, "Preparing Your Child For College: A Resource Book For Parents." The publication provides up-to-date information on how to finance a college education.

— National Commission for Cooperative Education, 360 Huntington Avenue, Boston, MA 02115. You can contact the

Commission for a directory of colleges that participate in federally-funded cooperative education programs.

— Federal Student Aid Programs, P.O. Box 4038, Iowa City, IA 52243-4038. Write to this address if you want a copy of your Student Aid Report (SAR). You also can call 1-(319) 337-5665 to find out whether or not your application for financial aid has been processed or to request additional copies of your SAR.

NOTES

_____

_____

_____

_____

_____

_____

_____

_____

_____

_____

C H A P T E R 9 **9**

CHEAPIES, FREE GOODIES AND GIVEAWAYS

Government Goodies

The government— federal, state, and local— is a veritable goldmine of cheapies and free stuff. Whether you're looking for help with your taxes, technical information, consumer assistance, money for housing or college, or a good buy on personal or real property, there's a government program that can help. As a taxpayer and a consumer, you owe it to yourself to take advantage of government assistance whenever the need arises.

Most of the government goodies described in this chapter are available to the general public free of charge or for a nom-

inal fee. There are thousands of financial and nonfinancial programs and services available. It's up to you to take advantage of
them.

Free Money From The Government

What are your chances of getting federal assistance?
Considering that in 1994 over 1,300 federal financial and nonfinancial assistance programs were available, your chances are
probably a lot better than you think. Billions of dollars in financial assistance, including grants and direct payments and low-
cost loans, are available every year. Generally, this assistance is
available to anyone who meets program eligibility criteria.
Depending on your needs and eligibility, you could receive a
federal grant for a few hundred dollars to $100,000 or more.
And the important thing to remember about grant money is that,
unlike a loan, it doesn't have to be paid back.

Who May Take Advantage of Federal Money
Programs?

There are federal money programs available to assist small
businesses, individual entrepreneurs, homeowners, renters, real
estate investors, artists, college students (see chapter 9, "College
Cheapies"), researchers, farmers, inventors, low-income families, veterans, and other individuals and organizations. The
sheer number and variety of government money programs, while
confusing, offers most people the opportunity to qualify for some

type of grant.

However, before you begin counting your grant money, you'll need to invest a good deal of time and effort in locating appropriate money programs. You'll then need to follow specified application procedures, including the submission of carefully prepared grant proposals. It can be a formidable challenge, but the potential rewards can make all the hard work worthwhile.

How To Locate Federal Money Programs

There are several ways you can get information about government assistance programs. The best source of information is the "Catalog of Federal Domestic Assistance," which is compiled and distributed by the General Services Administration. The catalog, updated twice a year, describes all federal money programs and eligibility requirements. It also offers suggestions on how to follow grant application procedures and on writing grant proposals.

The first place to look for the "Catalog of Federal Domestic Assistance" is in the reference section of your local library. Many state and local government agencies and officials, such as state budget offices, mayors, and city planners also may have copies of the catalog you can study. If you prefer, you also can order a subscription to the catalog by contacting the Superintendent of Documents, U.S. Government Printing Office, Washington, DC 20402; (202) 783-3238.

There's also a federal database containing the information found in the "Catalog of Federal Domestic Assistance." You may request a computerized search of the "Federal Assistance Programs Retrieval System" (FAPRS) from various access locations in your state. To get an up-to-date list of FAPRS access locations in your state, contact the Federal Domestic Assistance Catalog Staff, General Services Administration, Room 101 Reporters Building, 300 7th Street, SW, Washington, DC; (202) 708-5126.

Besides the "Catalog of Federal Domestic Assistance," your local or area library may have other publications which provide information on government money programs. The "Government Assistance Almanac" (J. Robert Dumouchel, Omnigraphics, Inc., Detroit, MI 48226) and "The Action Guide to Government Grants, Loans, and Giveaways" (George Chelekis, Perigee Books, New York, NY) are both excellent sources of information which you may find at your library.

A Few Examples

Here are a few examples of the hundreds of free money and low-cost loan programs available through various federal agencies:

—Housing

"Lower Income Housing Assistance Program"—Section 8 Moderate Rehabilitation.

This is a rent subsidy program designed to help, among others, very-low-income families whose incomes do not exceed 50 percent of the median income for the area; and low-income single persons who are elderly, disabled or handicapped.

Property owners coordinate with the Department of Housing and Urban Development (HUD) and/or local agencies to obtain the subsidies for their renters. For information on this program contact your local department of HUD or write to: Rental Assistance Division, Office of Assisted Housing, HUD, Washington, DC 20410.

"Neighborhood Development Program"

You may benefit from this program if you are a low or moderate-income person living in a neighborhood served by community-based organizations. Funds are made available to private, voluntary, nonprofit community-based organizations to carry out housing and community development activities. The funds may be used to develop new or rehabilitate existing housing. Information on this program and eligibility requirements are available from your local HUD office or by writing to: Office of Technical Assistance, Community and Neighborhood Management Division, HUD, 471 7th Street SW-Room 7218, Washington, DC 20410.

"Rural Housing Preservation Grants"

Eligible beneficiaries of this program may include low-income rural homeowners and rental property owners who require subsidization to improve their housing to minimum code standards. Generally, the funds are to be used for repair or modernization of existing housing. You can get information about this program from your local Farmers Home Administration (FmHA) office, or you can write: Multiple Family Housing Division, FmHA, U.S.D.A., Washington, DC 20250.

"Weatherization Assistance For Low-Income Persons"

Department of Energy (DOE) grants up to $1,700 are awarded to some low-income households. The money may be used to pay for home weatherization projects, such as insulation, storm windows, heating and cooling system modifications, and replacing inefficient furnaces and boilers. For information and eligibility requirements contact the nearest DOE office or write: Weatherization Assistance Programs Division, Conservation and Renewable Energy-DOE, Forrestal Building, Washington, DC 20505.

"Very Low-Income Housing Repair Loans And Grants" ("Section 504")

This program provides grants of $200 to $5,000 to eligible rural homeowner/occupants for repair and/or modernization of their existing homes. To qualify, you must own and occupy a home in a rural area and be 62 years of age or older. Contact your local county FmHA office for information or write: Single-Family Housing Processing Division, FmHA-USDA, Washington, DC 20250.

— Miscellaneous Grant Programs

"Promotion of the Arts— Visual Arts"

This program provides grants in the form of fellowships for visual artists including painters, sculptors, crafts artists, photographers, video artists, printmakers, performance artists, and other qualified artists. Grants to individuals range up to $20,000. For information, write: Visual Arts Program, NEA, 1100 Pennsylvania Ave. NW, Washington, DC 20506.

"Small Business Innovation Research" (SBIR)

The purpose of this program is to stimulate technological innovation. To that end, grants ranging from $26,000 to $220,000 are available to small businesses and individual entrepreneurs. The funds are to be used for research. To get information and eligibility requirements for this program, write: SBIR Coordinator, Office of Grants and Program Systems, Cooperative State Research Service, USDA, Room 323, Aerospace Building, 14th & Independence Avenue SW, AG Box 2243, Washington, DC 20250-2243.

"Forestry Incentives Program"

This program provides direct payments to private individuals and other eligible landowners of private nonindustrial forest land. The money is to be used for tree planting, timber stand improvement, and other specified use. Grants range from $50 to $10,000 per year. For information, contact your local, state, and/or regional Agricultural Stabilization and Conservation Service (ASCS) office or write: ASCS-USDA, P.O. Box 2415, Washington, DC 20013.

"Commodity Supplemental Food Program"

Eligible beneficiaries of this program include infants or children to age six; pregnant, postpartum, or breast-feeding women; or, elderly persons 60 or older. Eligibility requirements also include low-income and/or persons at nutritional risk. For more information about this program, contact local or state human services agencies or write: Supplemental Food Programs Division, FNS-USDA, Alexandria, VA 22302.

The federal money programs listed above are but a small fraction of the programs available to eligible private individuals and other applicants. The thing to keep in mind is that it may take time and perseverance to find a program for which you may qualify. You're likely to encounter a good bit of bureaucratic red tape along the way, as well as a rejection or two. Don't get discouraged. Study the available sources of information and apply to several money programs that appear to fit your circumstances and need. With the number of programs available, there's a good chance you'll find at least one that suits your needs.

Bargains on Government Property

Bargain hunters take note: Uncle Sam is having a sale. As a matter of fact, the federal government is offering for sale to the general public everything from air planes to real estate. Actually, the sale of federal surplus personal and real property has been going on since the Federal Property and Services Act of 1949. Since that time, billions of dollars worth of federal property and goods have been sold to the general public, often at incredibly low prices.

Much of the surplus property is sold through the General Services Administration. The GSA is the federal government's procurement agent for supplies, equipment and vehicles used by various non-military federal agencies. When property is no longer needed or is being replaced, the GSA offers it for sale as "surplus" at public auctions. Other federal agencies, such as the Defense Logistics Agency (part of the Department of Defense) and the U.S. Customs Service also offer federal property for sale.

* Used Federal Personal Property

The GSA is in charge of selling hundreds of millions of dollars worth of non-military items year round. The items sold include cars, vans, trucks, boats, household and office furniture, computers, printers, copiers, recreational and athletic equipment, cameras, projectors, tools, plumbing, heating and electrical equipment, paper products, farm machinery, and many other items of interest to individuals and businesses. The items are generally sold in "as is" condition, which can range from excellent to poor. Prospective bidders are given the opportunity to inspect sale property before making an offer.

Surplus personal property is sold by sealed bid, auction, spot bid, and fixed price sales. While some sales are advertised in trade journals, national newspapers and periodicals, the GSA generally uses mailing lists to alert potential bidders to up coming sales. The mailing lists are intended for "frequent purchasers" of government property. Occasional buyers can get information about future sales by calling the GSA telephone hotlines (listed below) for recorded messages.

The GSA advertises sales of national interest in the U.S. Department of Commerce publication, "Commerce Business Daily." This publication is available at many libraries and local Chambers of Commerce. If you're interested in getting a subscription to the "Commerce Business Daily,"contact the Superintendent of Documents, U.S. Government Printing Office, Washington, DC 20402 or call the U.S. Government Printing Officeorder line at (202) 783-3238.

To get general information on GSA sales of used federal personal property, or to be placed on a mailing list, write to Personal Property Sales, U.S. GSA, at the appropriate address listed below. Keep in mind that mailing lists are for those indviduals who make frequent purchases. Recorded information about upcoming GSA sales is available by calling the "hotline" telephone numbers listed at the end of each address.

Region 1: CT, ME, MA, NH, RI, VT; 10 Causeway Street, 9th Floor, Boston, MA 02222-1076; (617) 565-7326.

Region 2: NJ, NY, Puerto Rico, Virgin Islands; Room 20-112, Box 10, 26 Federal Plaza, New York, NY 10278; (212) 264-4823; (800) 488-7253.

Region 3: DE, MD, VA, PA, WV; P.O. Box 40657, Philadelphia, PA 19107-3396; (215) 597-7253.

Region 4: AL, FL, GA, KY, MS, NC, SC, TN; Peachtree Summit Building, 401 West Peachtree Street, Atlanta, GA 30365-2550; (404) 331-5177.

Region 5: IL, IN, MI, MN, OH, WI; 230 South Dearborn Street, Chicago, IL 60604; (312) 353-0246.

Region 6: IA, KS, MO, NB; 4400 College Boulevard, Suite 175, Overland Park, KS 66211; (913) 236-2565.

Region 7: AR, LA, NM, OK, TX; 819 Taylor Street, Fort Worth, TX 76102-6105; (817) 334-2351.

Region 8: CO, MT, ND, SD, UT, WY; Denver Federal Center, Building 41, Denver, CO 80225-0506; (303) 236-7705.

Region 9: AZ, CA, HI, NV; 525 Market Street, San Francisco, CA 94105; (415) 744-5120; (800) 676-7253.

Region 10: AK, ID, OR, WA; 400 15th Street, SW, Auburn, WA 98001-6599; (206) 931-7566.

National Capital Region: Washington, DC metropolitan area; 470 L'Enfant Plaza East, SW, Suite 8214, Washington, DC 20407; (703) 557-7796.

* U.S. Real Property Sales

By authority of the Federal Property and Administrative Services Act of 1949, the GSA sells most surplus government real estate. The surplus real estate is marketed in all 50 states, the District of Columbia, Puerto Rico, the Virgin Islands, and the U.S. Pacific territories.

While GSA real estate sales properties vary widely in value and type, you'll often find some outstanding bargains. Past sales have featured small parcels of unimproved land, individual residences confiscated by law enforcement officials, high-rise building sites, warehouses, and military housing complexes. Generally, major properties are sold at auction, and less expensive properties are disposed of by sealed bid.

You can contact one of the GSA's regional or field offices (listed below) or call (800) 472-1313 for information about the government's real property sales program. You also can write to the Consumer Information Center, Department 514A, Pueblo, CO 81009, and request a free copy of "U.S. Real Property Sales List." The "Sales List" is published by the GSA and features government property listings in all 50 states. Past issues of the "Real Property Sales List" have featured listings for a residential ocean-front lot in Hawaii; a 13-acre trailer park in Oregon; single-family residences in Alaska; family residences, townhouses, apartment complexes, unimproved lots and farm land in California; and a four bedroom residence in Pennsylvania.

If you have access to a computer equipped with a modem, you also can get information on federal real estate sales from the Federal Real Estate Bulletin Board. To access the bulletin board, set your communications software to 8 data bits, no parity, and i stop bit. Dial 1 (800) 776-7872.

The GSA's regional real estate sales offices and field offices are located across the United States. Here are the addresses and telephone numbers for those offices:

Regional Offices

— Office of Real Estate Sales, U.S. GSA, 10 Causeway Street, Boston, MA 02222; (617) 556-5700.

— Office of Real Estate Sales, U.S. GSA, Peachtree Summit Building, 401 West Peachtree Street, Atlanta, GA 30365-2550; (404) 331-5133.

— Office of Real Estate Sales, U.S. GSA, 819 Taylor Street, Ft. Worth, TX 76102; (817) 334-2331.

— Office of Real Estate Sales, U.S. GSA, 525 Market Street, San Francisco, CA 94105; (415) 744-5952.

Field Offices

— Office of Real Estate Sales, U.S. GSA, 230 South Dearborn Street, Room 3864, Chicago, IL 60604; (312) 353-6045.

— Office of Real Estate Sales, U.S. GSA, 400 15th Street, SW, Room 1138, Auburn, WA 98001-6599; (206) 931-7547.

* Military Property Sales

The Department of Defense (DoD), through its Defense Logistics Agency, sells personal property. The property is sold by the Agency's Defense Reutilization and Marketing Service through its regional offices worldwide. The list of sale items includes hand tools, passenger vehicles, trucks, motorcycles, communications equipment, lighting fixtures and lamps, tents, household and office furniture, textiles, clothing, sports equipment, musical instruments, photographic equipment, office machinery and supplies, maps, flags, and many other items. Sorry, no material of primarily military application, such as weapons, is sold.

For additional information and a list of Defense Reutilization and Marketing Service regional offices, call (800) 222-3767 and ask for a copy of the booklet, "How To Buy

Surplus Property from the U.S.Department of Defense". The booklet, which is free, also explains how to buy DoD surplus personal property, and provides 20 categories of sale items. You also can get information by writing or calling Defense Reutilization and Marketing Service, National Sales Office, P.O. Box 5275 DDRC, 2163 Airways Boulevard, Memphis, TN 38114-5201; (901) 775-6427.

* Forfeited And Confiscated Property Sales

If you've heard about people buying diamond rings, luxury cars and other expensive items at government auctions at unbelievably low prices, it's a good bet they bought forfeited property. Most of this property is seized and confiscated from convicted drug dealers and other lawbreakers. It's then sold to the public by the U.S. Marshal's Service and the U.S. Customs Service.

While you won't be able to buy a new Mercedes for $100, you can get some great bargains on a host of items for your personal use. Past sales have included cars, boats, jewelry, clothing, household items, art and antiques, furniture, and hundreds of other items. With a little patience and effort, you could land some sensational bargains buying forfeited property.

You can get information on sales conducted by the U.S. Marshal's Service, by contacting the U.S. Marshal's Service, National Seized Assets and Forfeiture Service, 600 Army Navy Drive, Arlington, VA 22202-4201; (202) 307-9087.

To get information on sales by the U.S. Customs Service, contact E.G. Dynatrend, Inc.; U.S. Customs Service Support

Division; 2300 Clarendon Avenue, Suite 705; Arlington, VA 22201; (703) 351-7887.

Free Stuff From The Internal Revenue Service

Many people aren't aware that the IRS is one government agency that offers a variety of free services and publications. In many cases, the free assistance and/or information provided by the IRS can help you prepare your own tax return, saving you $50 to $100 you might otherwise pay a professional tax return preparer.

All the assistance programs and materials listed below are available free of charge through the IRS. Most are available year-round.

* Toll-Free Telephone Assistance

The IRS offers toll-free telephone assistance in all 50 states, as well as the District of Columbia, Puerto Rico, and the U.S. Virgin Islands. By taking advantage of this free assistance, you can get answers to any tax questions you might have.

— General Tax Information and Notice Inquiries, (800) 829-1040. Call this number for free assistance whenever you have questions about your tax account, tax rules, or for general information about IRS procedures and services.

— Tele Tax Recorded Tax Information (800), 829-4477. This service provides recorded tax information and automated refund information. The Recorded Tax Information includes nearly 140 topics covering many federal tax questions. You can listen to up to three topics on each call you make. The Automated Refund Information enables you to check the status of your refund.

— Free forms and Publications orders, (800) 829-3676. See the list of free IRS publications at the end of this chapter.

— Telephone Service for the Hearing Impaired, (800) 829-4059. Deaf and hearing-impaired individuals who have access to telecommunications device for the deaf (TDD) equipment can call this toll-free number for telephone tax assistance.

Free Tax Return Preparation Services

The IRS offers several programs which provide free assistance with tax return preparation and/or tax counseling. The programs use volunteers who are trained by the IRS. Some of the most popular free assistance programs include the following:

— Tax Counseling for the Elderly (TCE). This program provides free tax assistance to people age 60 or older. Contact your local IRS office for information on this program and to find locations of TCE help in your area.

— Volunteer Income Tax Assistance (VITA). This volunteer program provides free tax help to people who cannot afford professional tax assistance, people with disabilities, the elderly, and others with special needs. VITA sites can generally be found at libraries, schools, community centers, shopping malls, and other convenient community locations.

— Student Tax Clinics: Sponsored by law and graduate accounting schools, these clinics are staffed by volunteers who provide free tax assistance. The assistance is available to people who can not afford counsel when faced with a tax examination or audit.

— Free Tax Preparation Materials. The IRS supplies many libraries, post offices, banks, military bases, community colleges, technical schools, and other locations with free tax preparation materials. Libraries which receive these materials have available tax forms (which can be copied), audiovisual materials, and general tax information. Other sites have available Forms 1040, 1040A, 1040EZ as well as the instructions and related schedules.

— Community Outreach Tax Education. This program offers two kinds of free assistance: line-by-line self-help income tax return preparation for individuals who want to prepare their own returns, and tax seminars on assorted tax topics. The program is available to retired people, farmers, small business owners, employees, and other groups of people who share common tax concerns.

— Walk-In Tax Preparation Service. While they cannot prepare your return for you, assistors at most IRS offices can provide line-by-line self-help tax return assistance for you in a group setting. They can give you guidance with your individual federal tax return. Most IRS offices also have available, free of charge, tax forms and useful publications.

Free Tax Publications

The IRS produces a number of free publications designed to help you fill out your own tax return and to answer your tax questions. Listed below are several useful publications which can be ordered at no charge by calling the IRS toll-free at (800) 829-3676.

— Publication 1, "Your Rights As A Taxpayer": Explains your rights in the tax process, step-by-step.

— Publication 4, "Student's Guide To Federal Income Tax":Explains students' responsibilities to pay taxes, how to file returns, and how to get help.

— Publication 17, "Your Federal Income Tax (For Individuals)":Provides step-by-step instructions on how to pre-pare your individual tax return. This publication also explains the tax laws in understandable language.

— Publication 463, "Travel, Entertainment and Gift Expenses": This publication identifies business-related travel, entertainment, gift and local transportation expenses that you may be able to deduct.

— Publication 501, 'Exemptions, Standard Deduction, and Filing Information."

— Publication 502, "Medical and Dental Expenses": Identifies which medical and dental expenses are deductible and how to deduct them.

— Publication 504, "Divorced or Separated Individuals."

— Publication 505, "Tax Withholding and Estimated Tax."

— Publication 508, "Educational Expenses": Explains work-related educational expenses that may be deductible.

— Publication 521, "Moving Expenses": Identifies certain expenses of moving which are deductible.

— Publication 523, "Selling Your Home": Explains how to handle any gain or loss from selling your main home.

— Publication 524, "Credit for the Elderly or the Disabled": Explains who is eligible for this tax credit.

— Publication 525, "Taxable and Nontaxable Income."

— Publication 526, "Charitable Contributions."

— Publication 529, "Miscellaneous Deductions": Identifies expenses you may be able to take as miscellaneous deductions on form 1040 (Schedule A).

— Publication 530, "Tax Information for First-Time Homeowners."

— Publication 533, "Self-Employment Tax": Explains payment of self-employment tax.

— Publication 535, "Business Expenses."

— Publication 550, "Investment Income and Expenses."

— "Publication 554, "Tax Information for Older Americans."

— Publication 560, "Retirement Plans for the Self-Employed."

— Publication 583, "Taxpayers Starting a Business."

— Publication 587, "Business Use of Your Home": Explains the rules for claiming a deduction for business use of your home and identifies what expenses may be deducted.

— Publication 596, "Earned Income Credit": Identifies who may receive this credit, how to figure and claim the credit, and how to receive advance payments of the credit.

— Publication 908, "Tax Information on Bankruptcy."

— Publication 910, "Guide To Free Tax Services."

— Publication 911, "Tax Information for Direct Sellers": Explains how to figure income from direct sales and identifies deductible expenses.

— Publication 917, "Business Use of A Car."

— Publication 929, "Tax Rules For Children and Dependents": Explains the filing requirements and the standard deduction amounts for dependents.

— Publication 936, "Home Mortgage Interest Deduction."

Social Security Administration Giveaways

Free Informational Booklets

The Social Security Administration, in cooperation with the Health Care Financing Administration, produces a number of publications and fact sheets designed to help explain various Social Security programs. The publications and fact sheets are available free of charge at any Social Security Office or by calling 1-800-772-1213. Here are a few of the free publications you may find helpful:

— "A Guide For Representative Payees" (Publication No. 05-10076). A guide to receiving benefits on behalf of another individual.

— "Disability" (Publication No. 05-10029). Offers information about Social Security Disability benefits.

— "If You're Self-Employed" (Publication No. 05-10022). Provides information about self-employment tax rates.

— "Medicare" (Publication No. 05-10043). A guide to the Medicare program.

— "Personal Earnings and Benefits Statement." Provides a

detailed, personal estimate of your Social Security retirement, disability and survivor benefits.

— "Retirement" (Publication No. 05-10035). Explains Social Security retirement benefits.

— "SSI" (Publication No. 05-11000). A guide to the Supplemental Security Income program.

— "Survivors" (Publication No. 05-10084). Information concerning Social Security survivor benefits.

— "The Appeals Process" (Publication No. 05-10041). Explains the appeals procedure you may use if you disagree with a Social Security Administration decision regarding your eligibility for Social Security or SSI benefits.

Free And Low-Cost Federal Consumer Publications

Free and low-cost timely and helpful information on virtually any consumer topic is available through scores of federal consumer publications. The publications are listed in "The Consumer Information Catalog," which is published quarterly by the Consumer Information Center of the U.S. General Services Administration. You can get a free copy of the most recent "Consumer Information Catalog" by writing to: Consumer Information Catalog, Pueblo, CO 81009.

The publications listed in the catalog address a wide variety of consumer-related topics including car-buying and maintenance, employment, federal programs and benefits, health , housing, money management, and much more. Many of the publications are free. Others cost from 50 cents to several dollars. There's a $1.00 service fee when you order any of the free publications.

Listed below is a sample of the many free and low-cost booklets available as of the summer 1995 "Consumer Information Catalog." To order any of the free booklets, send the item numbers of the booklets you want (listed at the end of each booklet description), along with your name and address and the $1.00 service fee to S. James, Consumer Information Center, 5C, P.O. Box 100, Pueblo, CO 81002. If ordering both free and sales booklets, send the above information along with your payment and service fee to R. Woods at the same address.

Cars

— "Buying A Safer Car": This 12-page booklet provides comprehensive charts which compare safety features and crash test results of 1995 model year vehicles. It also identifies vehicle theft rates. (1994) 501B. Free.

— "Collecting Used Oil For Recycling": This is a six-page booklet from the Environmental Protection Agency which discusses how and why oil recycling helps the environment and saves energy. (1994) 502B. Free.

— "New Car Buying Guide": This three-page booklet from the Federal Trade Commission discusses pricing terms, financing options, and various contracts. It also provides a worksheet to help you get a better bargain. (1995) 305B. 50 cents.

— "Consumer Tire Guide": This 12-page booklet from the Department of Transportation provides useful information on how to check for proper air pressure and signs of uneven wear. It also explains how and why to rotate your tires; special cold-weather care, and more. (1990) 302B. 50 cents.

Children

— "Read It Before You Eat It!": From the Food and Drug Administration— this 8-page booklet helps children learn how to read the new nutrition labels. The booklet includes fun activities to test kids' nutrition knowledge. (1995) 590B. Free.

— "Helping Your Child Get Ready for School": This booklet (56 pp.)provides a variety of activities from birth to age five to help children develop socially, mentally and physically. It also offers guidelines for what to expect from children at each age level. (1992) 309B. 50 cents.

— "Helping Your Child Learn Responsible Behavior": This 46-page booklet is designed for children up to nine years old to help develop fairness, respect, courage, honesty, compassion, and more. (1993) 313B. 50 cents.

— "Timeless Classics": This is a 3-page booklet which lists nearly 400 books published before 1960 for children of all ages. (1994) 384B. 50 cents.

Employment

— "The GED Diploma": This 16-page booklet provides information on how to earn your General Education Development diploma. The booklet includes what the tests cover, how to prepare, and where to get more information. (1991) 512B. Free.

— "Health Benefits Under COBRA (Consolidated Omnibus Budget Reconciliation Act)": This 24-page booklet from the Department of Labor provides information on how to keep or buy coverage for yourself and family after a job loss, reduced work hours, divorce, or death. (1994) 513B. Free.

— "How To File a Claim for Your Benefits": This is a two-page booklet from the Department of Labor which explains what to do if your claim or appeal for health, disability, vacation, or severance benefits is denied. It covers what the law does, waiting periods, and more. (1991) 514B. Free.

— "Resumes. Application Forms, Cover Letters, and Interviews": This 8-page publication from the Department of Labor features tips on how to tailor your resume for specific jobs and how to score higher on employment tests. It also includes sample interview questions and more. (1987) 105B. $1.00.

Federal Programs

— "U.S. Real Property Sales List": Produced by the General Services Administration,, this 16-page booklet lists government properties for sale that are sold by auction or sealed bid. It also tells how to get more information on specific properties. (Revised quarterly) 515B. Free.

— "How To Buy Surplus Personal Property from the Department of Defense": This 51-page booklet lists types of items for sale and includes a bidders application. (1992) 110B. $1.00.

— "How You Can Buy Used Federal Personal Property": This is an 8-page booklet that explains how the U.S. General Services Administration advertises and sells used government equipment and industrial items. It also lists where to call for more information. (1994) 319B. 50 cents.

— "Your Social Security Number": This is a 10-page booklet produced by the Social Security Administration. It explains why we have social security numbers, when and how to get one, and how to protect its privacy. (1993) 516B. Free.

Federal Benefits

— "Advanced Earned Income Credit": This 4-page IRS publication explains the Advanced Earned Income tax credit, who qualifies and how to claim the credit. (1995) 517B. Free.

— "Medicare Q & A": More than 80 commonly asked questions about Medicare are answered in this 5-page booklet. Learn about eligibility, enrollment, who pays deductibles, services, benefits and more. (1994) 523B. Free.

— "Request for Earnings and Benefit Statement": This 3-page

booklet from the Social Security Administration provides a form to complete and return to Social Security to get your earnings history and an estimate of future benefits. (1993) 524B. Free.

— "Understanding Social Security": Learn about retirement, disability, survivor's benefits, Medicare coverage, Supplemental Security Income, and more in this 41-page booklet from the Social Security Administration. (1993) 525B. Free.

Health

— "Decoding the Cosmetic Label": This 4-page booklet from the Food And Drug Administration provides a list of common cosmetic ingredients and their usual functions to help you select safe products. (1994) 620B. Free.

— "Healthy Tan: A Fast-Fading Myth": Learn the symptoms of skin cancer and the benefits of protecting your skin from the sun in this 3-page booklet from the Food and Drug Administration. (1989) 614B. Free.

— "Aspirin: A New Look at an Old Drug": This 3-page booklet explains the history of aspirin, how it works, and its use in disease prevention and treatment. (1994) 601B. Free.

— "Buying Medicine? Help Protect Yourself Against Tampering": This is a 2-page booklet produced by the Food and Drug Administration. (1992) 539B. Free.

— "Cancer Tests You Should Know About: A Guide for People 65 & Over": The National Cancer Institute produced the 16-

page booklet which describes six tests that can help detect cancer early. (1992) 540B. Free.

— "Choosing a Contraceptive": This 8-page booklet compares 12 methods of birth control according to effectiveness, health risks, convenience, availability, and how well they protect you from sexually transmitted diseases. (1993) 541B. Free.

— "Hocus-Pocus As Applied To Arthritis": This is a 7-page booklet produced by the Food and Drug Administration. It discusses fraudulent cures and medically sound treatments for arthritis, rheumatism and gout. (1989) 605B. Free.

— "Some Things You Should Know About Prescription Drugs": This 4-page booklet offers tips for safe use of potentially dangerous prescription drugs. (1984). 607B. Free.

— "Using Over-the-Counter Medications Wisely": Learn how to use OTC medications for colds, coughs and dieting safely with the information provided in this 3-page booklet. (1991) 549B. Free.

Housing

— "The HUD Home Buying Guide": This 14 page booklet produced by the Department of Housing and Urban Development offers step-by-step instructions for finding and financing a HUD home. (1995) 635B. Free.

— "A Consumer's Guide to Mortgage Refinancings": The information in this 8-page booklet can help you determine the costs involved and whether or not the time is right to refinance your home. (1988) 336B. 50 cents.

— "The Home Inspection and You": Get answers to 11 questions about how and why you should get a professional home inspection before you buy or sell. (1993) 337B. 50 cents.

Money Management And Financial Planning

— "Shopping With Your ATM Card": This 28-page booklet describes the new and expanded ways you can use an ATM card. It also provides safety precautions and a listing of ATM networks and affiliated shopping services by state. (1995) 565B. Free.

— "Deposits and Investments": Produced by the Treasury department, this 9-page booklet explains the differences between bank deposits and investments. (1993) 567B. Free.

— "Direct Loan Consolidation": This 18-page booklet explains the benefits of consolidating your federal student loans into a single Individual Education Account. It also describes types of repayment plans available. (1995). 611B. Free.

— "Facts About Financial Planners": This Federal Trade Commission publication (14 pp.) explains what financial planners can and can't do. It also identifies what credentials to ask for, and what costs to expect. (1995) 388B. 50 cents.

— "Investors' Bill of Rights": This 7-page booklet offers tips to help you make an informed decision when making investments. (1993) 596B. Free.

— "Your Guaranteed Pension": This 14-page booklet provides answers to frequently asked questions about the federal agency that insures private pension plans including benefits and plan termination. (1995) 571B. Free.

Miscellaneous Consumer Booklets

— "At-Home Shopping Rights": This 5-page booklet explains how to deal with late deliveries, unordered merchandise, billing errors and more when buying by mail or phone order. (1994) 373B. 50 cents.

— "Protecting Your Privacy": Learn how to check your credit file and medical record, handle telephone sales, and have your name removed from mailing lists with the information provided in this 5-page booklet. (1990) 579B. Free.

— "Finding Legal Help": This 20-page booklet provides tips for reducing the costs of legal help. It also provides practical information for older people on public and private resources. (1994) 390B. 50 cents.

— "A Consumer's Guide To Postal Services": Produced by the U.S. Postal Service, this 37-page booklet explains the various product and service options the Postal Service offers to help you choose the right service to save you time and money. (1994) 582B. Free.

— "Getting Information From the FDA": This 4-page booklet covers food, drugs, pesticides, medical devices, radiation safety, pet foods, and more. (1994) 585B. Free.

— "U.S. Government TDD Directory": This 72-page publication from the General Services Administration lists telephone numbers of agencies and congressional offices with Telecommunications Devices for the Deaf. (1994) 588B. Free.

NOTES

_____

_____

_____

_____

_____

_____

_____

C H A P T E R   1 0   **10**

CHEAPIES, FREE GOODIES
AND GIVEAWAYS

Miscellaneous Cheapies & Free Stuff

W hat follows is a pot-pourri of cheapies and free stuff—everything from free and low-cost legal help to over 60 sources of wholesale bargains on an assortment of personal use products. Using the savvy consumer techniques described throughout this book, you may be able to take advantage of the information provided in this chapter and find some extra special cheapies.

How To Get Free and Low-Cost Legal Help

Depending on your circumstances, you may be able to take advantage of free or low-cost legal services which are available nationwide. Federally funded programs which may provide such services are available in every state. Some states also provide free or reduced fee attorney programs as well as legal hotlines which provide free "call-in" legal advice.

Hopefully, you'll never need the services of an attorney, but if you do, the programs and services described below may provide you with a source of affordable legal help.

Legal Aid Offices

More Than 1000 Legal Aid offices around the country offer free legal help to low-income people of all ages. These offices are funded by a variety of sources, including federal, state and local governments and private donations, and are staffed by lawyers, paralegals and law students. Many of the nation's law schools operate clinics in which law students, as part of their training, assist practicing attorneys with Legal Aid cases.

The assistance offered by Legal Aid offices generally includes problems such as landlord-tenant disputes, credit, utilities, divorce, adoption (and other family issues), foreclosure and home equity fraud, social security, welfare, unemployment, workmen's compensation, and other non-criminal cases. Each Legal Aid office has its own board of directors which determines the priorities of the office and the types of cases handled as well as eligibility requirements.

If the Legal Aid office in your area doesn't handle your type of case, it may be able to refer you to other local, state or national organizations which can offer assistance. Look in your telephone directory under "legal aid" or "legal services" to find the address and telephone number of the Legal Aid office in your area. You also may be able to get this information by contacting your local bar association.

You also can get a directory of Legal Aid offices throughout the United States by contacting the National Legal Aid and Defender Association, 1625 K Street, N.W., 8th Floor, Washington, DC 20006; Phone: (202) 452-0620.

Legal Services Corporation

The Legal Services Corporation (LSC), a non-profit organization created by Congress in 1974, is another potential source of free legal help. The LSC offers non-criminal legal assistance to people who can't afford to hire their own lawyers. The LSC has offices in all 50 states, Puerto Rico, the Virgin Islands, Guam and Micronesia. To locate an office in your area, call the LSC Public Affairs Office at (202) 863-4089. The LSC also offers for sale, a full directory of its programs. To buy a copy of the LSC directory, contact Public Affairs, Legal Services Corporation, 400 Virginia Avenue, S.W., Washington, DC 20024-2751.

Older Americans Act Legal Services

Under the Older Americans Act (OAA) state offices on aging are required to fund local Area Agency on Aging (AAA) programs to provide free legal help to many older Americans.

These programs provide free legal help on civil matters (not criminal) to people 60 years of age and older. In some states, the AAAs contract with programs which are funded by the Legal Services Corporation. Other AAAs operate their own programs or contract with private attorneys to provide free legal services to eligible older persons.

Generally, there are no income guidelines older persons must meet to be eligible for the free legal services provided by the OAA. The help is available to people age 60 or older regardless of income. However, many of the over 600 local AAAs give special consideration to those older persons who can least afford legal help.

You can find programs and offices which provide OAA-mandated free legal services by contacting your local Area Agency on Aging. Look in the government section of your local phone directory.

The American Bar Association also has available a national directory, "Law and Aging Resource Guide," which provides a state-by-state listing of OAA legal service providers. Individual state profiles are free and the complete directory, listing addresses and phone numbers for OAA programs in all 50 states, is $20. To order the directory, write to the American Bar Association Commission on Legal Problems of the Elderly, 1800 M. Street, NW, Suite 200, Washington, DC 20036.

Pro Bono And Reduced-Fee Attorney Panels

You may be able to get free legal help through special "pro bono"panels offered by many legal aid offices and some bar associations. Such "pro bono" (free) legal help is provided as a public service by many private attorneys. If an attorney agrees to handle your case "pro bono," his/her services are free but you may still be responsible for court costs and other costs related to the case.

Some private attorneys also offer reduced-fee legal assistance to clients who may not be able to afford an attorney otherwise. The fees are substantially lower than the private attorney "usually" charges to handle a case of the same type.

The purpose of the special panels is to "connect" people who need legal help with attorneys who have made it known they are willing to provide some free or reduced-fee services. It's then up to the attorney to decide whether or not to handle a case.

To find out whether or not there is a program— either "pro bono" or reduced-fee attorney panels— in your area, contact local legal aid offices or bar associations. Both should be listed in the yellow or white pages of your telephone book.

Legal Advice Hotlines

Free legal advice may be available over the phone through legal hotlines sponsored by bar associations and other agencies and organizations. For example, the American Association of Retired Persons (AARP) and the federal government's Administration on Aging (AoA) both sponsor legal hotlines. People age 60 or older— regardless of income or legal problems—can call these hotline numbers and receive free legal advice from qualified attorneys. The attorneys also may send informational materials or make referrals to special "pro bono" or reduced-fee attorney panels in cases where services beyond advice may be required.

While legal hotlines are not available in all areas of the country, most of those that are operating provide legal advice free. Most also offer only limited hours of operation. To find out whether or not a legal hotline is available in your area, contact your Area Agency on Aging or local bar association.

Here are several statewide legal hotlines currently in operation:

ARIZONA: Legal Hotline for the Elderly, 64 Broadway, Tucson, AZ 85701; (800) 231-5441 (in AZ); (602) 623-5137 (Tucson and out-of-state). Hours: 8 a.m. - 4 p.m. MST.

NORTHERN CALIFORNIA: Senior legal Hotline, Legal Services of Northern California, 1004 18th Street, Sacramento, CA 95814; (800) 222-1753. Hours: 9 a.m. - 5 p.m. PST.

DISTRICT OF COLUMBIA: Legal Counsel for the Elderly, 601 E Street, NW, Washington, DC 20049; (202) 434-2170 (in DC). Hours: 9 a.m. - 4 p.m. EST.

FLORIDA: Legal Hotline for Older Floridians, P.O. Box 370705, Miami, FL 33137; (800) 252-5997 (in FL); (305) 576-5997 (Dade county and out-of-state). Hours: 9 a.m. - 5 p.m. EST.

MAINE: Legal Hotline for the Elderly, P.O. Box 2723, 72 Winthrop Street, Augusta, ME 04338-2723; (800) 750-5353 (in ME); (207) 623- 1797 (Augusta and out-of-state). Hours: 9

a.m. - 4 p.m. EST.

MICHIGAN: Legal Hotline for Older Michiganians, 115 West Allegan Street, Suite 720, Lansing, MI 48933; (800) 347-5297 (in MI); (517) 372-5959 (Lansing and out-of-state). Hours: 9 a.m. - 5 p.m. EST.

NEW MEXICO: State Bar of New Mexico, Special Project, Inc., Lawyer Referral for the Elderly Program, P.O. Box 25883, Albuquerque, NM 87125; (800) 876-6657 (in NM); (505) 842-6252 (Albuquerque and out-of-state). Hours: 8 a.m. - 5 p.m. MST.

OHIO: Pro Seniors Hotline, Legal Hotline for Ohioans, Enquirer Building, Suite 900, 617 Vine Street, Cincinnati, OH 45202; (800) 488-6070 (in OH); (513) 621-8721 (Hamilton county and out-of-state). Hours: 8:30 a.m. - 4:30 p.m. EST.

PENNSYLVANIA: AARP/Legal Counsel for the Elderly, Legal Hotline for Older Pennsylvanians, Law & Finance Building, 429 4th Avenue, Suite 1706, P.O. Box 23180, Pittsburgh, PA 15219; (800) 262-5297 (in PA); (412) 261-5297 (Allegheny county and out-of-state). Hours: 9 a.m. - 5 p.m. EST.

TEXAS: Legal Hotline for Older Texans, 815 Brazos, Suite 1002, Austin, TX 78701; (800) 622-2520 (in TX); (512) 477-3950 (Travis county and out-of-state). Hours: 9 a.m. - 5 p.m. CST.

Small Claims Courts

Small Claims courts also can provide a source of inexpensive legal help. These courts were established to resolve disputes involving claims for small debts and accounts. The maximum amounts that can be claimed or awarded in small claims courts differ from state to state, but court procedures are generally "simple, inexpensive, quick and informal." In fact, the court is so informal you won't need a lawyer. In some states, lawyers aren't even allowed in small claims court.

Keep in mind however, that even though the court is informal, its ruling must be followed, just like the ruling of any other court. Whether you win or lose, you must follow the court's decision.

If you think your problem could be settled in such a fashion, check your local telephone book under the municipal, county or state government headings for small claims court offices. When you contact the court, ask the court clerk how to use the small claims court. In some areas, state and local consumer agencies have consumer education material to help prepare you for small claims court (see the Appendix for a state-by-state-listing of consumer protection agencies).

One way to find out how small claims court works is to sit in on a session before you take your case to court. Some small claims courts have dispute resolution programs which help contesting parties resolve their disputes. The dispute resolution processes, which involve mediation and conciliation, often simplify the process by helping the parties involved create their own agreement.

You can get more information about dispute resolution from the American Bar Association, Standing Committee on Dispute

Resolution, 1800 M Street, N.W., Washington, DC 20036.

Cheaper Wills

Most lawyers charge a minimum of around $150 to pre-
pare even the most basic wills. You can save $100 or more by
preparing your own will using a kit or computer program. These
do-it-yourself will kits and programs are available at most sta-
tionery or office supply stores for $20 to $40. They're especially suitable for single people who have limited assets and no children.

Of course, your will should reflect both your financial and
personal life, so you should read the information printed on the
packaging before you buy a do-it-yourself will kit. Make sure the
kit is suitable for your particular needs.

Unclaimed Money Windfall

Believe it or not, you may be overlooking thousands of dollars that are rightfully yours. There are over 5 billion dollars
worth of forgotten bank accounts, uncashed dividends, insurance payments, passbook savings, checking accounts, utility
deposits, travelers checks, money orders and other income waiting to be claimed in state Abandoned Property offices. The property goes unclaimed for a number of reasons— people move,
change their names, lose track of investments, or die. Whatever
the reason, after three to five years the unclaimed assets are

turned over to the state. The state then makes an effort to locate the rightful owner or heir and return the money. Sometimes the state doesn't try very hard.

If you think some of this unclaimed property may be rightfully yours, you can take matters into your own hands by contacting the appropriate "Unclaimed Property" office in your state and any other state where you or your family may have held assets (see the Appendix for a state-by-state listing of Unclaimed Property offices) to find out whether or not your name is listed as an owner or an heir. But don't try to pull a fast one. Make sure you have a valid claim before you contact your state office.

Free Home Energy Audit

You may be eligible for a free or low-cost home energy audit. Many utilities and some state and local governments provide free energy audits and home energy ratings. In some areas there may be a nominal charge for this service, but it's well worth the cost. By having an energy audit you can determine the energy efficiency of your home's construction and condition, enabling you to make any needed energy improvements. The result will be lower utility bills.

You can find out whether or not this energy-auditing service is available in your area by contacting your local utility.

More Home Energy Cost-Cutters

There are several easy ways you can conserve energy and take a chunk off your utility bills. Here are several proven cost-cutters:

— Reduce your water-heating costs by 10 to 15 percent by reducing your water-heater temperature from 145 degrees F to 120 degrees F.

— Plug up leaks by weather-stripping, caulking and insulating. You also can save up to 7 percent on heating costs by replacing storm windows or covering windows with plastic film.

— Reduce your water-consumption by up to 50 percent by installing a low-flow shower head.

— Fix all leaky faucets immediately. Just one drop per second can use up to eight gallons of water per week.

— Save up to 20 cents a load by washing your clothes in cold water.

— Save up to 40 cents an hour by turning off your air conditioner when you leave home.

— Switch to fluorescent light bulbs and save up to $40 per month on your electric bill. Fluorescent bulbs last from 10 to 14 times longer than incandescent bulbs and use up to 75 percent less electricity, making them a better bargain.

— Hang your clothes to dry on an old-fashioned clothes line and save $10 to $20 per month on your electric bill. Using your dryer is a costly way to accomplish something mother nature will do free.

— Cut your electricity bill by purchasing energy-efficient appliances. That's especially important when buying a new air conditioner and/or furnace. Information on the energy efficiency of major appliances is found on Energy Guide Labels which are required by federal law. Your local electric utility also may have a program to help reduce the cost of any energy efficient appliance purchase. Contact your electric utility for information.

— Enroll in cost-saving programs offered by your electric utility. Load management programs and off-hour rate programs offered by your electric utility may save you up to $100 a year on your electric bill. Contact your electric utility for information about these cost-saving programs.

Cheaper Long Distance Telephone Service

Here are three easy ways to cut your long distance telephone bills by 15 percent or more:

— Avoid calling long distance on weekdays. Long distance calls made at night or on weekends can cost much less than calls made during weekdays.

— Consider subscribing to a calling plan. This is especially good advice if you make several long distance calls each month. Contact several long distance carriers and find out which one has the least expensive plan for the number of calls you make.

— Dial your long distance calls directly whenever possible. You spend an extra $1 to $3 by using the operator to complete your long distance call.

— Review your bill carefully every month. If you discover unfamiliar long distance charges on your bill, notify the phone company immediately.

Free Pets

If you're looking for a family pet, say a dog or cat, stay away from pet stores. Consider instead a visit to your local animal shelter. Animal shelters provide "temporary" homes for dogs and cats that are usually mixed breed. Most of these animals would make wonderful family pets and are available free or for a small nominal adoption fee.

The Humane Society of the United States, (202) 452-1100, can provide you with information and help you locate an animal shelter in your area.

Computer Cheapies That Can Save You 50% And More

Shopping for a computer can be a harrowing experience, especially if you're on a tight budget. To get the type of system and all of the goodies you want and need, you'll likely have to spend $1,500 to $2,000. That's if you buy from a typical retail outlet. However, if you're willing to settle for a slightly outdated or reconditioned computer, mail-order computer factory outlets can offer you savings of up to 60% off average list prices.

Most PC users don't need to invest in expensive, "cutting-edge" computer equipment. A brand name PC that's a year old or are conditioned model will do just fine, especially considering the deep discounts offered by most factory outlets. Monitors, printers, and an assortment of peripherals also are available at discounts.

Listed below are four of the biggest computer factory outlets that offer deep discounts on their own computers and peripherals. Since factory outlet inventories change frequently, you should call for information about current models and prices.

— Compaq Works Factory Outlet, Houston, TX; (800) 318-6919. This outlet offers savings of 20% to 60% off original list prices on certain Compaq 486 computers, notebook computers, laser printers and other equipment.

— Dell Factory Outlet, Austin, TX; (512) 728-5656. Dell's outlet offers savings of over 60% off list prices on reconditioned Dell computers and peripherals.

— IBM PC Factory Outlet, Morrisville, NC; (800) 426-3395. IBM's outlet offers most IBM PCs, monitors, and peripherals at savings of 20% to 50% off original list prices.

— Zeos Computer Factory Outlets, Arden Hills, MN; (612) 486-1900; (612) 541-1900 (in Golden Valley, MN). Savings of up to

50% are available on reconditioned Zeos computers.

—·Gateway 2000 Factory Outlet, N. Sioux City, SD; (605) 232-2454; (605) 357-1001 (in Sioux Falls, SD). While no phone orders are taken at Gateway's outlets, you can save up to 20% on Gateway computers, notebooks and peripherals if you can travel to the outlet locations.

Save 70% And More On All Magazine Subscriptions

If your coffee table is buried beneath stacks of magazines, you're probably paying a pretty penny in subscription rates. You can reduce those costs or eliminate them altogether and still enjoy your favorite magazines by taking advantage of the following money-saving suggestions:

1) Let your local library pay for your magazine subscriptions. True, library copies aren't yours to keep, but you can check out 5 to ten magazines at a time. You can keep them for a week or longer, and you can read every article in the comfort of your own home without having to pay for a subscription. You'll save a bundle of money by avoiding outlandish subscription rates.

2) Take advantage of free issues. As an enticement to get you to subscribe, many magazines offer free trial subscriptions. Such a trial subscription may consist of one or more free issues of a particular magazine. The offer may direct you to write "cancel" on the first bill if you aren't satisfied— otherwise, you'll be billed a

regular six month to one-year subscription rate. This is a good way to examine magazines you've never seen before or to get a copy or two of your favorite magazine(s) without paying a cent.

Just make sure you write "cancel" on the first bill you receive. And don't be surprised if more than one payment-due notice arrives before you receive the first trial issue. Write "cancel" on these payment-due notices.

3) Consider subscribing through a magazine clearing house. Usually, when you buy something direct from the manufacturer you get the lowest price. That's because you don't have to deal with a middleman and a middleman's markup. In the case of magazines however, buying subscriptions directly from publishers may cost you a good deal more than subscribing through a middleman.

Before ordering from a publisher or before you renew a subscription, compare subscription rates for the same publications at magazine clearing houses. In some cases, clearing houses, such as those listed below, can save you as much as 70% off regular subscription rates.

— American Family Publishers, P.O. Box 30640, Tampa, FL 33662-0640; Phone: (800) 237-2400. This magazine clearing-house offers savings of up to 70% on subscriptions to many of today's most popular magazines. Contact the company for information.

— Magazine Warehouse; Phone: (800) 728-3728. The Magazine Warehouse offers substantial savings on subscription rates to many of the most widely-read magazines. Call the toll-free number for information.

— Publisher's Clearing House, 101 Winners Circle, Port Washington, NY 11050; Phone: (800) 645-9242. Publisher's Clearing House offers savings of up to 50% off regular subscription rates on many popular and special interest magazines. Call or write the company for details.

4) Wait until your subscription has almost expired before you renew. Many times, magazines will offer a special subscriber's rate if you renew right away. The nearer your subscription comes to running out, the more "special" the renewal rate may become. You may be offered a special renewal rate that is significantly lower than the regular renewal rate.

5) Resubscribe at a lower rate. If your favorite magazine offers new subscribers a low introductory rate, you may consider letting your subscription expire and then resubscribe as a new reader. You may save several dollars off the subscription rate you had been paying.

Free Cable TV Hookup

If you're patient, you may be able to get cable without paying the installation fee. Most cable companies offer occasional specials that sometimes include free installation. These specials often require you to buy one or more pay channels, such as the Disney Channel, Showtime or HBO, for a month in order to get free hookup. You can take advantage of such a special, get free installation, and cancel the pay channel(s) after the month is up, if you wish.

Cheaper-By-Mail Wholesale Sources

Shopping by mail is one of the easiest, most convenient and cheapest ways to buy virtually everything you need. From the comfort of your own home you can browse through product catalogs, find what you want, make one phone call and place your order. You don't have to fight bumper-to-bumper traffic, use a tank of gas to find a parking space, or go elbow to elbow with scores of other bargain hunters. And, if you find the right mail-order source, you can save 80 percent or more off typical retail prices.

Whether you're looking for a new set of tires for your car or a fine set of china, there's a mail-order company that has what you want. The following mail-order sources offer an assortment of products, most of which are priced well below average retail prices. Most of the companies have product catalogs, brochures, price lists and other informational material you can order free of charge. You may have to send a nominal fee to get some of the product catalogs, but in many cases those charges are refundable when you place your first order.

Send away for as many catalogs as you like. That way you can shop around and compare products, prices and services. And before you place an order, remember to take the precautions described in chapter 3.

Automotive

— J.C. Whitney, 1917-19 Archer Avenue, P.O. Box 8410, Chicago, IL 60680; (312) 431-6102. Offers savings of up to 40 percent on a complete line of automotive parts and accessories. Whitney stocks parts for all makes and models of cars, vans, trucks, motorcycles and RVs. Call or write the company and request a product catalog.

— Belle Tire Distributors, Inc., Wholesale Division, 3500 Enterprise Drive, Allen Park, MI 48101; (313) 271-9400. Offers discounts of up to 35 percent off average retail prices on new tires. Brand names include Bridgestone, Firestone, B.F. Goodrich, Goodyear, Kelly Springfield, Michelin, Pirelli, Uniroyal, Yokohama and others. Call or write the company and request a price quote.

— Car Racks Direct, 82 Danbury Road, Wilton, CT 06837; (800) 722-5734. Offers discount prices on an assortment of car racks to secure luggage, bicycles, skis, etc. Accessories, such as locks, straps, security cables, cross bars, and brackets also are available. Call or write the company and request a free catalog.

Carpeting

— Advantage Carpets, Box 1777, Dalton, GA 30720; (800) 743-4762. Offers first-quality carpeting, padding and vinyl floor covering at wholesale prices. Call the company for more information.

— Carpet Wholesale Outlet, Dalton, GA 30720; (800) 628-

4412. Offers deep discounts on quality carpeting and hand-made and machine-crafted rugs. Call or write for information.

— Designer Carpet, Dalton, GA 30720; (800) 253-7239. Offers quality designer carpeting at wholesale prices. Call the company and request a customized sample package.

— Johnson's Carpets, Inc., 3239 S. Dixie Highway, Dalton, GA 30720; (800) 235-1079 ext 532. Offers discounts of up to 80 percent on direct-from-the-mill carpeting. Carpet padding, vinyl flooring and custom area rugs also are available. Call or write the company and request a free brochure. Free price quotes and samples also are available. Provide a specific manufacturer, style name or number, and the square yardage you need for a price quote.

— Paradise Mills, Inc., P.O. Box 2488, Dalton, GA 30722; (800) 338-7811. Offers discounts of up to 60 percent on carpeting and vinyl and wood flooring. Brand names include Aladdin, Cumberland, Diamond, Horizon, Philadelphia, Queen, World, and many others. The company also offers its own line of carpeting and customized rugs. Call or write the company and request a free brochure. A free buyer's guide and samples also are available.

— Village Carpet, 3203 Highway 70 S.E., Newton, NC 28658; (704) 465-6818. Offers discounts up to 50 percent off average retail prices on first-quality carpeting. Brand names include Bigelow, Aladdin, Cumberland, Mohawk, Sutton, and many others. Call or write the company and ask for a free brochure.

China, Crystal and Silver

— Barrons, P.O. Box 994, Novi, MI 48736-0994; (800) 762-7145. Offers savings of up to 40 percent on fine tableware, giftware and collectibles. Brand names include Oneida, Noritake, Gorham, Lenox, Johnson Brothers, Royal Doulton, Towne, and many others. Call or write and request a free product catalog.

— Buschemeyer Silver Exchange, 515 S. Fourth Avenue, Louisville, KY 40202; (800) 626-4555. Offers savings of 50 percent on flatware by famous manufacturers, such as Oneida, Lunt, Gorham, Wallace and others. They also can match patterns of discontinued or customized flatware. Call for price quotes on specific brand names and patterns and for information about the company's custom matching service.

— China Marketing, P.O. Box 33, Cheltenham, PA 19012; (800) 599-4900. Offers deep discounts on over 100,000 pieces of discontinued china and crystal. Contact the company for more information.

— The China Warehouse, P.O. Box 21807, Cleveland, OH 44121; (800) 321-3212. Offers discounts of up to 70 percent off typical retail prices of china, crystal, flatware, stemware, dishes, and brand-name gift collectibles. Brand names include Waterford, Lenox, Noritake, Baccarat, and many others. Call or write to request a free catalog.

— The Yellow Door, 1308 Ave. M, Brooklyn, NY 11230; (718) 998-7382. Offers savings of up to 30 percent off typical retail prices on brand-name china, crystal and silver. Brand names include Royal Worcester, Port Merion, Gorham, Orrefors,

Retrenou, Lalique, and many others. Call or write with brand name and style number and request a price quote.

Computer Hardware And Supplies

— Computer Discount Warehouse, CDW Computer Centers, Inc., 2840 Maria Avenue, Northbrook, IL 60062-2026; (800) 800-4CDW. Offers savings of up to 50 percent on computers, peripherals, software and related items. Brand names include Acer, Epson, Hewlett-Packard, IBM, Intel, Logitech, Maxtor, NEC, WordPerfect and many more. Call or write the company and request a free product catalog.

— Dayton Computer Supply, 6501 State Rte. 123 N., Franklin, OH 45005; (800) 735-3272. Offers savings of up to 50 percent on a variety of computer supplies including printer ribbons, toner cartridges, diskettes, surge protectors, mice, printer stands, cables and more. Call or write and request a free product catalog.

— PC & Mac Connection Catalog, 6 Mill Street, Marlow, NH 03456; (800) 800-1111. Offers discount prices on personal computer products, accessories, games and upgrades for IBM, IBM-compatible, Macintosh, and multimedia CD-Rom. Also offers a 24-hour customer-service telephone hotline to answer your questions before and after you buy. Call or write the company and request a free catalog.

— Rocky Mountain Computer Outfitters, 100 Financial Drive, Kalispell, MT 59901; (800) 367-4222. Offers an assortment of brand name computer hardware, software, peripherals and accessories. Brand names include NEC, Radius, Daystar and many others. Call or write the company and request a free product catalog.

Cosmetics and Toiletries

— Beautiful Visions, 810 S. Broadway, Hicksville, NY 11801; (516) 576-9000. Offers name brand cosmetics and toiletries at discount prices. Contact the company to request a free catalog.

— Beauty Boutique, P.O. Box 94520, Cleveland, OH 44101-4520; 216) 826-3008. Write the company to request a free catalog featuring name brand toiletries and cosmetics at discount prices.

— Common Scents, 3920 A 24th Street, San Francisco, CA 94114; (415) 826-1019. Offers a fine line of bath and skin care products at discount prices. Contact the company and request a product catalog.

— New York Cosmetics and Fragrances, 318 Brannan Street, San Francisco, CA 94107; (415) 896-0373. Offers discounts of up to 70 percent off average retail prices on quality cosmetics, fragrances and beauty treatments. Brand names include Opium, Paris, Private Collection, Decadence, Elizabeth Arden, Knowing and many others. Send $2 for a product catalog.

Eyewear

— Contact Lens Discount Center, (800) 780-5367. Offers prescription contact lenses at savings of up to 75 percent. Brand names include, Bausch & Lomb, Cooper Vision, Barnes Hind, and many others. A product brochure is available free upon request.

— House of Eyes II, Greensboro, NC 27420; (800) 331-4701. Offers savings of up to 70 percent on brand name eyewear and frames. Both fashion and sport styles are available. Call or write and request a free catalog and/or a price quote.

— Lens First, 400 Galleria #400, Southfield, MI 48034; (800) 388-2400. Offers the same contact lenses prescribed by your doctor. All lenses are shipped in factory-sealed vials at a savings of up to 75 percent off typical retail prices. Call or write the company and request a free color catalog and/or an instant price quote.

— National Contact Lens Center, 3527 Bonita Vista Drive, Santa Rosa, CA 95404-1506; (800) 326-6352. Offers savings of 70 percent and more on soft contact lenses, hard lenses, and gas-permeable lenses for experienced wearers. Brand names include American Hydron, Aquaflex, Boston, Bausch & Lomb, Ciba, Johnson & Johnson, Cooper Vison, and others. Call or write the company and request a free brochure.

— Sunglasses USA, 469 Sunrise Highway, Lynbrook, NY 11563; (800) 872-7297. Offers a wide selection of sunglasses by Ray Ban, Bausch & Lomb, and other famous makers at discount prices. Send $2 (refundable with first order) for a catalog and price list.

— The Ultimate Contact, 721 North Beers Street, Holmdel, NJ

07733; (800) 432-5367. Offers savings of up to 70 percent off typical retail prices on all brand-name lenses. The selection includes disposable, soft, hard, gas permeable and toric lenses. Call or write for information.

Fabrics

— B. Wilk Fabrics, 618 S. Fourth Street, Philadelphia, PA 19147; (215) 627-1146. Offers up to 50 percent off retail prices on overruns and closeouts of name-brand fabrics for drapes and slipcovers. Some special order fabrics also are discounted. Call with the exact lot number and request a price quote, or send a swatch of your fabric to the above address.

The Fabric Center, Inc., 485 Electric Avenue, Fitchburg, MA 01420; (508) 343-4402. Offers fine quality fabrics for home decorating at discounts of up to 50 percent off typical retail prices. Brand names include American Textile, Robert Allen, Peachtree, Waverly and others. Send $2 for a product catalog.

— The Fabric Outlet Store, 30 Airport Road, West Lebanon, NH 03784; (800) 635-9715. Offers savings of up to 60% off typical retail prices on fabrics sold by the yard. Discounts are available on brand name fabrics by Duralee, Kravet, Robert Allen, Waverly and many others. Call with a brand name, pattern description and color and request a price quote.

— Lorraine Fabrics, 593 Mineral Spring Avenue, Pawtucket, RI 02860; (401) 722-9500. Offers a wide range of fabrics, including cottons, silks and upholstery fabrics at discount prices. Send the company a swatch of your fabric and request a price quote.

Furniture

— European Furniture Importers, 2145 West Grand Avenue, Chicago, IL 60612; (800) 283-1955. Offers mail-order discounts on chairs, tables and other European furniture pieces by Le Corbusier, Mackintosh, and Miles Van Der Rohe. The company also will special order pieces at no extra cost. Send $3 for a product catalog and/or call or write for special order information. Include a description and a brand name.

— Homeway Furniture Company, P.O. Box 1548, Mt. Airy, NC 27030; (800) 334-9094. Offers factory-direct savings on first-quality furniture from over 400 manufacturers. Call or write the company and request a free brochure.

— James Roy Furniture Company, 15 E 32nd Street, New York, NY 10016; (212) 679-2565. Offers discounts of up to 50 percent on a large selection of furniture and bedding by famous manufacturers. Call or write the company and request a free brochure.

— The Lamp Warehouse, 1073 39th Street, Brooklyn, NY 11219; (800) 525-4837. Offers an assortment of lighting products including halogens and table lamps at discounts up to 50 percent off retail prices. Ceiling fans also are available. Call the company with brand names and description and request a price quote.

— Loftin-Black, 111 Sedgehill Drive, Thomasville, NC 27360; (212) 679-2565. Save 30 to 50% off the manufacturer's suggested retail prices on most major brands of furniture, bedding and accessories. Call or write and request a free brochure.

— North Carolina Showrooms, Hickory, NC; (800) 227-6060. Offers savings of up to 50 percent on hundreds of furniture items by famous manufacturers. Call with the brand name and style number you want.

— St. Charles Furniture Company, P.O. Box 2144, Greensboro, NC 27161; (800) 545-3287. Offers discounts of up to 40 percent on brand name home and office furniture. Also available are accessories, such as lamps, bedding, table pads, and clocks. Price quotes are available by calling the company with the brand and model you're considering.

— Quality Furniture of Lenoir, 2034 Hickory Boulevard SW, Lenoir, NC 28645; Phone: (704) 728-2946. Quality Furniture offers deep discounts on furniture and bedding from a number of famous manufacturers. Call or write the company to request a free price quote.

Kitchenware

— Bridge Kitchenware, 214 E. 52nd Street, New York, NY 10022; (800) BRIDGE-K. Offers discounts on a selection of copper and stainless-steel cookware. A product catalog is available free upon request.

— Fivenson Food Equipment, Inc., 324 S. Union Street, Traverse City, MI 49684; (800) 632-7342. Offers discounts of up to 50 percent off typical retail prices on brand-name kitchenware, including frying pans, restaurant-style glass dishes, European coffee mugs, and other items. The company also offers discounts on refrigerators, stoves and other kitchen appliances. Send $3 for a product catalog.

— Commercial Culinary, P.O. Box 7258, Arlington, VA 22207; (800) 999-4949. Save up to 40 percent on brand name cookware, cutlery and kitchen appliances. Call or write the company and request a free product catalog.

— Professional Cutlery Direct, 170 Boston Port Road, Suite 135, Madison, CT 06443; (800) 859-6994. Offers savings of 40 percent and more on a complete line of cookware and cutlery. A product catalog is available free upon request.

— Lamalle Kitchenware, 36 W. 25th Street, New York, NY 10010; (800) 660-0750. Offers discounts on a fine line of kitchen tools and cookware. Choose from copper cookware, ovenware, pastry utensils, and many other items. Send $3 for a product catalog.

Linens

— Bedroom Secrets, P.O. Box 529, Freemont, ME 68025; (800) 955-2559. Offers savings of up to 40 percent on towels, sheet and comforter sets, window treatments, and wallpaper and borders. Designer linens by Laura Ashley, Croscill and other famous designers also are available at discount prices. Send $2 for a product catalog.

— Eldridge Textile Company, 277 Grand St., New York, NY

10002; (212) 925-1523. Offers a large selection of bed, bath and table linens at discounts of up to 40 percent. Choose from brand names such as Bill Blass, Laura Ashley, Crown Crafts, Springmaid, Fieldcrest, Wamsutta and many others. Send $3 (refundable with first order) for a product catalog.

— The Linen Source, 5401 Hangar Ct., P.O. Box 31151, Tampa, FL 33631-3152; (800) 431-2620. Offers discounts of up to 40 percent on brand name bed linens and home accessories, such as quilts, rugs, lamps, and window treatments. Brand names include Burlington House, Dakotah, Springmaid, Laura Ashley, Wamsutta, and many others. A free product catalog is available upon request.

Photography And Video Equipment

— Adorama, 42 W. 18th Street, New York, Ny 10011; (800) 223-2500. Offers discount prices on name brand cameras, lenses, film, camcorders, darkroom supplies, and other related items. Call or write and request a catalog and/or a price quote.

— Camera World, 500 S.W. 5th Ave, Portland, OR 97204; (800) 222-1557. Offers an assortment of cameras, lenses, camcorders, accessories and other related equipment at discount prices. Call the company and request a price quote.

— Focus Camera, 4419-12 13th Avenue, Brooklyn, NY 11219; (800) 221-0828. Offers discounts on cameras, lenses, film, darkroom supplies, camcorders and related accessories. Contact the company for more information.

Sporting Goods And Equipment

— The Austad Company, P.O. Box 1428, Sioux Falls, SD 57196-1428; (605) 336-3135. Best known for discounts on quality golfing equipment and supplies, Austad offers a variety of other sporting goods at savings of up to 40 percent off average retail prices. Also offers some overstocked and closeout items. A product catalog is available free upon request.

— Cabela's, Inc., 812 13th Avenue, Sidney, NE 69160; (308) 254-5505. Offers a great selection of brand name hunting and fishing gear at savings of up to 40 percent off typical retail prices.Send $2 for a product catalog.

— Las Vegas Discount & Tennis, 5325 South Valley Boulevard, Las Vegas, NV 89118; (702) 798-6847. Offers deep discounts on a wide variety of name brand sports equipment. Save on golf clubs and golfing equipment, tennis racquets and other racquet equipment, and many other items. Call or write the company and request a free catalog and/or a price quote. Include a SASE.

Wallcovering Bargains

— American Blind & Wallpaper Factory, 28237 Orchard Lake Road, Farmington Hills, MI 48334; (800) 567-2034. This company offers savings of up to 80% off typical retail prices on blinds by Levolor and Del Mar. Also has blinds by Bali, Graber, Duette, Hunter Douglas, Joanna and other manufacturers. American also offers savings of 75% and more on all national brands of wallpaper and a free wallpaper catalog.

— American Discount Wall and Window Coverings, 1411 Fifth Avenue, Pittsburgh, PA 15219; (800) 777-2737. Offers deep discounts of 70 percent and more on brand-name wall coverings and window treatments. Save 70 percent and more on brand names, such as Levelor, Graber, Sunwall, and Imperial. Call or write with a brand name and pattern number and request a price quote.

— Bennington's, 1271 Manheim Pike, Lancaster, PA 17601; (800) 252-5060 Ext. 15. Bennington's offers savings of up to 80% on brand name wallpaper. Also specializes in customer service.

— Headquarters Window & Walls, 8 Clinton Place, Morristown, NJ 07960; (800) 338-4882. Headquarters offers first-quality major brand name wallcoverings at savings of up to 78%. Call with book name and pattern number. Also save over 80% on all major brand name blinds.

— Harmony Supply, Inc., P.O. Box 313, Medford, MA 02155; (617) 395-8218. Offers wall coverings and window treatments by Laura Ashley, Duette and Crystal Pleat at 60 percent below typical retail prices. Call or write the company with brand name, style code and window dimensions and request a price quote.

—National Blind & Wallpaper Factory, 400 Galleria, Southfield, MI 48034; (800) 477-8000. National has merged with Safe Wallcovering and Mary's Wallpaper to become one of the largest discounters of blinds and wallpaper. Save up to 80% on brand name blinds and wallpaper.

— Nationwide Wholesaler, P.O. Box 40, Hackensack, NJ 07602; (800) 488-9255. Nationwide offers savings of 50% to 75% on a large selection of wallcoverings, fabrics and blinds. Call the toll-free number for a price quote.

— Number One Wallpaper, 2914 Long Beach Road, Oceanside, NY 11572; (800) 423-0084; (516-678-4445 in New York state). Number One offers wholesale discounts of up to 80% on wallpaper. Over 100,000 rolls are in stock. Call the toll-free number for a free price quote. Have the name of the book and the pattern number handy when you call.

— Peerless Wallpaper & Blind Depot, 39500 14 Mile Road, Walled Lake, MI 48390; (800) 999-0898. Offers 1st quality wallpaper and blinds at discounts of up to 80% off retail prices.

— Silver's Wholesale Club, 3001-15 Kensington Ave., Philadelphia, PA 19134; (800) 426-6600. This wholesale club offers savings of over 80% on all brands of wallcoverings and blinds.

— Worldwide Wallcoverings & Blinds, 333 Skokie Blvd., Northbrook, IL 60062; (800) 322-5400. Worldwide offers deep discounts of up to 80% off retail prices on brand name blinds and wallcoverings. You can get a free ordering kit for blinds and special case discounts for wallpaper.

CHAPTER 11

11

CHEAPIES, FREE GOODIES AND GIVEAWAYS

Free Stuff: 190 Products And Publications You Can Get Absolutely Free

If, as the saying goes, "the best things in life are free," this final chapter of "Cheapies and Free Stuff" should provide a good deal of pleasure. That's because we've listed more than 190 items, including sample products, recipes, posters, toys, and educational and informational publications that are available absolutely free. Consumer booklets that might ordinarily cost you $1.50 to $5.00 can be yours for nothing more than the 32 cent postage stamp used to mail your letter of request. Sample products can be yours for the asking or for merely the cost of postage and handling. And in some cases, free stuff is just a toll-free phone call away.

Before you send away for any of the items in this chapter, there are a few things you should keep in mind about the offers themselves. First of all, some of the offers require that you include a self-addressed, stamped envelope (SASE) with your request. When a SASE is required it's important that you send the exact size specified by the organization or company making the offer.

The free item will be sent to you in your SASE, so make sure you follow all directions and instructions accompanying a "free" offer carefully.

Other offers require that you send enough money to cover postage and handling. The items themselves are free, but the sponsors must receive enough money to cover the cost of shipping you their products and publications. Again, follow all directions exactly.

Finally, no offer—free or otherwise—lasts forever. Most offers are available in limited quantities and are available to those people who request them right away. In fact, by the time you read this, some of the offers listed in this chapter may no longer be available. Don't be discouraged if this happens with an item you wanted. There will be many other items available if you persist and mail out your letters of request.

You also should be patient. It may take several weeks before a free item you send for arrives in the mail.

Consumer Information

— "Too Good To Be True": Learn how to detect mail order and telemarketing fraud before you get taken, by requesting a free copy of this booklet from the Consumer Information Center, Pueblo, CO 81009.

— Lemon Law Update: Lemon Laws are a consumer's best defense against getting stuck with a new car that turns out to be a lemon. These laws allow new car owners to receive refunds or replacements if their new vehicles have substantial problems which aren't fixed within a reasonable number of attempts. "The Lemon Law Summary" can provide you with the latest information about these laws and how they can help you. To get a free copy of the "Lemon Law Summary", write to the Center for Auto Safety, 2001 S Street, N.W., Suite 410, Washington, DC 20009.

— Car-Leasing Guide: Get the low-down on car-leasing in a free publication available from the Federal Trade Commission, Public Reference Section, 6th and Pennsylvania Avenue, N.W., Room 130, Washington, DC 20580; Phone; (202) 326-2222.

You also can contact the Federal Trade Commission at the above address for free publications on car rental, vehicle repossessions, buying a used car, and much more.

— "Shopping for a Safer Car" and "Teenage Drivers": These two publications on car safety are available free upon request from the Insurance Institute for Highway Safety, 1005 N. Glebe Road, Suite 800, Arlington, VA 22201.

— Electronic Equipment Service Brochures: If you've had problems getting electronic equipment repaired, the following brochures could prove helpful: " Getting Good Service For Electronic Equipment"; "Extended Warranty Service Contracts: Good or Bad?"; "Consumer Complaint Checklist for Electronic

Equipment." You can get the brochures free by sending a SASE to the National Electronics Service Dealers Association (NESDA), 2708 West Berry Street, Fort Worth, TX 76109.

— "Consumer Guide to Finding Reputable Service Companies": To get a free copy of this brochure, write to the Professional Service Association, 71 Columbia Street, Cohoes, NY 12047.

— Radon Update: Get more information about radon in "The Home Buyer's and Seller's Guide to Radon," published by the U.S. Environmental Protection Agency (EPA). To get a free copy of this informative booklet, write to the EPA Public Information Center, PM-211B, 401 M Street S.W., Washington, DC 20460; Phone: (800) SOS-RADON.

— Home Security Brochure: Home security is a major concern of every homeowner. "Home Security Basics" is a free brochure which provides valuable information on easy and inexpensive ways you can make your home more secure. To get a copy of the brochure, write to the Insurance Information Institute, 110 William Street, New York, NY 10038.

— Home Buying Tips: The U.S. Department of Housing and Urban Development (HUD) publishes a helpful booklet for prospective first-time home-buyers. The booklet, "A Home of Your Own: Helpful Advice from HUD on Choosing, Buying and Enjoying a Home," is available free upon request from the Consumer Information Center, HUD, Department 568Z, Pueblo, CO 81009.

— Life Insurance Buying Guide: Find out how to get the best, affordable life insurance coverage in the booklet, "How To Save

Money on Life Insurance." To get a copy of this booklet, write to the National Consumers Organization, 121 North Payne Street, Alexandria, VA 22314.

— Toy Safety Tips: Find out how to select appropriate toys for children of different ages and abilities by sending for the free brochure, "Which Toy for Which Child." Write to: U.S. CPSC, Washington, DC 20207.

— Lead Alert: The Food and Drug Administration offers a free pamphlet concerning lead in crystal, ceramic ware, cans, and wine bottles. The pamphlet, "What You Should Know About Lead In China Dishes," is available upon request from the Office of Consumer Affairs, HFE-20, Food and Drug Administration, 5600 Fishers Lane, Room 1685, Rockville, MD 20857.

— Travel Tips: The U.S. Department of Transportation publishes a series of fact sheets, titled "Plane Talk." The information in these fact sheets includes tips on avoiding baggage problems, and frequent flyer programs. To get a free copy of "Plane Talk," write to the Office of Consumer Affairs, I-125, U.S. Department of Transportation, 400 7th Street, S.W., Washington, DC 20590.

— Air Travel Consumer Report: Produced monthly by the Department of Transportation's Office of Consumer Affairs, this report is designed to assist consumers with information on the quality of services provided by airlines. The report focuses on flight delays, mishandled baggage, oversales and consumer complaints. For a free copy of this report, write to the Office of Consumer Affairs, U.S. Department of Transportation, 400 7th Street, S.W., Room 10405, Washington, DC 20590.

— Free Credit Report: You can get a free report on your credit status from TRW Consumer Assistance. To get your free report, send your full name, address(s) of the past five years, Social Security number, year of birth, and, if married, spouse's name, to TRW Consumer Assistance, Box 2350, Chatsworth, CA 91313. Also include a bill or another document that includes your name and address to prevent unauthorized release of your credit information.

— "Buy Recycled": All sorts of everyday products are being made from materials that have been recycled. You can find out about recycling and the number of products made from recycled materials you can buy in this free brochure from the Environmental Defense Fund, 257 Park Ave. South, New York, NY 10010; Phone (800) CALL-EDF.

— Motor Oil Recycling Booklet: When improperly disposed of, oil can contaminate the soil and surface and ground waters. Recycling oil can help preserve our natural resources, protect the environment and save consumers' money. The Resource Conservation Hotline and Recovery Act (RCRA) offers several free publications which deal with recycling used oil. The free publications include, "How To Set Up Local Programs To Recycle Used Oil"; "Recycling Used Oil: 10 steps to change your oil"; "Recycling Used Oil: What Can You Do." To get free copies of these and other booklets, contact RCRA Hotline, U.S. EPA, 401 M Street, S.W., Washington, DC 20460; Phone: (800) 424-9346.

— "The Guide To Consumer Product Information": This free 272-page consumer product directory includes tips on drugs, pain-treatment, personal care and household cleaning products.

There's also a resource directory of over 90 major national health organizations. For a free copy, write to Bristol-Myers Company Guide To Consumer Product Information, Box 14177, Baltimore, MD 21268.

— "Consumer Information Catalog": This catalog lists nearly 20 free or low-cost federal booklets with helpful information for consumers. Topics include careers and education, cars, child care, the environment, federal benefits, financial planning, food and nutrition, health, housing, small business, and more. The catalog is free and it is published quarterly by the Consumer Information Center of the U.S. General Services Administration. You may order a copy of the catalog by sending your name and address to Catalog, Consumer Information Center, Pueblo, CO 81009 or by calling (719) 948-4000.

Food Preparation, Handling And Storage

— Food preservation: You can get free information about canning and freezing, including how to make pickles, jellies and jams by writing Kerr Consumer Affairs, 2444 West 16th Street, Chicago, IL 60608.

— Meat and poultry: For a booklet on the proper handling of meat and poultry, write to The Meat and Poultry Hotline USDA-FSIS, Room 1165-S, Washington, DC 20250; or call the Hotline at (800) 535-4555 between 10 a.m. and 4.p.m on weekdays. Ask for "A Quick Consumer's Guide to Safe Food Handling."

— Food labeling: "Labeling Logic" is a brochure featuring timely information on what you need to know about food labeling. To get a free copy, send a SASE to "Labeling Logic", American Dietetic Association, P.O. Box 39101, Chicago, IL 60639.

— "Food Safety": To get this free brochure of general food safety information, write to "Food Safety", Consumer Affairs Office (HFE-88), Food and Drug Administration, 5600 Fishers Lane, Rockville, MD 20857.

— Seafood Safety: The Public Voice for Food and Health Policy offers a free two-page tip sheet on seafood safety. For a copy of the tip sheet, write to Public Voice, 1001 Connecticut Avenue, N.W., Suite 522, Washington, DC 20036. Include a SASE.

Free Stuff For Infants and Children

— "Help Your Child": This is a series of 10 books, available free from the U.S. Department of Education. The books are designed to help parents teach children to read, learn geography and use the library. To get copies of these books, write to the U.S. Department of Education, Office of Educational Research and Improvement, 555 New Jersey Ave., N.W., Washington, DC 20208-5641.

— Puzzle Kit: Your kids can create their very own miniature solar system with the free "Solar System Puzzle Kit." For your free puzzle kit, write to National Aeronautics & Space Administration Educational Publications, Code FEO-2, Washington, DC 20546.

— Presidential picture: You can get a picture of President Clinton and/or a picture of Socks, the White House cat, by writing to the Office of Presidential Correspondence, White House,

Washington, DC 20500.

— Coloring Book: The American Dental Association offers a free 26-page coloring book, "The ABC's of Good Oral Health." To get a copy, write to the Association at 211 E. Chicago Avenue, Chicago, IL 60611.

— Removable Dinosaur Tattoos: Get two, 2" removable dinosaur tattoos free by sending a written request to the Alvin Peters Company, P.O. Box 2400, Empire State Plaza, Albany, NY 12220. Include a business-size SASE with your request. Only one request per address.

— Six-Inch Ruler: Get this combination plastic ruler and book-mark free by writing to: Union Label Department, ILGWU, 1710 Broadway, New York, NY 10019. Include a business-size SASE with your request.

— "Astronaut Fact Book": This free book features biographical information about all of the U.S. astronauts— past and present. To get your free copy, write to the National Aeronautics and Space Administration Educational Publications, Code FEO-2, Washington, DC 20546.

— Free poster: A four-color 25" x 32" poster is available free upon request from the U.S. Arboretum Publications Department, 3501 New York Ave. N.E., Washington, DC 20002.

— Money Management Guide: Information on budgeting, sav-ings, inflation and other money matters are featured in "Kids and Money: A Learning Guide for Children." Activity sheets and directions also are included. For a free copy, write to Fidelity

Investments, "Kids and Money Guide," Box 770001, Cincinnati, OH 45277.

— Bike Safety Coloring Book: Get a free coloring book, which focuses on bicycle safety, by writing to Sandoz-Triaminic, Route 10 East, E. Hanover, NJ 07936. Request the "Bike Safety Coloring Book."

— Math Activities Booklet: Believe it or not, you can have fun learning basic math. This free booklet shows you how. To get a copy, send a SASE to: National Council of Math Teachers, 1906 Association Drive, Reston, VA 22091. Request the "Family Math Activities" booklet.

Health Concerns

The National Cancer Institute (NCI) OF Bethesda, Maryland offers free of charge the following booklets: "Facing Forward: A Guide For Cancer Survivors"; "Radiation Therapy and You: A Guide to Self-Help During Treatment"; "Taking Time: Support for People With Cancer and the People Who Care About Them"; "What Are Clinical Trials All About?"; "What You Need To Know About Melanoma"; "What You Need To Know About Moles and Dysplastic Nevi"; and "When Cancer Recurs: Meeting the Challenge Again".

To get any or all of the free booklets, contact the NCI at (800) 4-CANCER (422- 6237).

— "A Guide To Your Child's Hearing": This free guide for parents is published by the Better Hearing Institute. The guide is designed to help parents become more aware of possible hearing problems in their children and also provides sources of help available. Write the Better Hearing Institute, P.O. Box 1840, Washington, DC 20013.

— Hearing Aid Advice: 3M Hearing Health offers a free booklet, "Choices," that gives advice on hearing aids and how to select a hearing specialist. For a copy, write to 3M Hearing Health, 260-6A-19, St. Paul, MN 55144 or call (800) 882-3636.

— "Newborn Feeding Guide": To get a free copy of this guide, write to Evenflo Products, 771 N. Freedom Street, Ravenna, OH 44266.

— "Guide To Eating for a Healthy Heart": To get a free copy of this booklet, send a SASE to Merck Sharp & Dohme, Health Information Dept., P.O. Box 1486, West Point, PA 19454.

— Healthier living guide: Menus, charts and tips on how to lead a healthier lifestyle are featured in "A Guide for Healthier Living." The guide is produced by the makers of Stouffer's Lean Cuisine, and is available free upon request from the Stouffer Food Corporation, Consumer Information Department, 5750, Harper Road, Solon, OH 44139-1880.

— "Calories and Weight": You need to consume the proper amount of calories each day in order to maintain the ideal weight for your height and build. This guide provides nutritional information that can help you achieve your proper body weight. For a free copy, write to the Office of Communication, Publications Division, U.S. Department of Agriculture,

Washington, DC 20250. Ask for "Calories and Weight: The USDA Pocket Guide."

— Registered Dietician Directory: More and more people are getting nutritional counseling from registered dieticians. These people know that good nutrition translates into good health and lower medical costs. To get a free list of registered dieticians in your area, contact the American Diabetes Association at (800) 366-1655.

— First Aid: Traveler's Insurance Company offers a free first aid summary chart and an emergency telephone card. To get a chart and a card, write to Travelers Insurance Company, Women's Information Bureau, One Tower Square, Hartford, CT 06115.

— "Your Health Information Belongs To You": This free brochure provides information on how you can gain access to your own medical records. To get a copy, send a SASE to the American Medical Record Association, 919 North Michigan Avenue, Suite 1400, Chicago, IL 60611.

— Stress booklet: Learn the three stages of physical and mental stress from information provided in the free booklet, "Plain Talk About Stress." The booklet also provides expert advice on how to cope with daily stress. To get a copy, write to Public Inquiries, National Institute of Mental Health, Room 7C-02, 5600 Fishers Lane, Rockville, MD 20857.

— Over 40 Exercise Booklet: If you're over 40, this exercise booklet provides several safe and effective exercises that can help keep you fit. To get a free copy of the booklet, write to Staying Fit Over 40, Advil Forum on Health Education, 1500

Broadway, 25th Floor, New York, NY 10036.

— "How To Take Your Medicines": The Office of Consumer Affairs has compiled a series of informative articles in this free booklet. The articles explain how to organize your medicine cabinet and offer tips on how to prevent taking medications that are out of date or taking drugs in the wrong combination. For a free copy, write to the Office of Consumer Affairs, Food and Drug Administration, 5600 Fishers Lane, HFE-88, Rockville, MD 20857.

— Medical history checklist: Learn how to keep a record of your medical history, including immunizations and health problems you experience with the information provided in this free checklist. To get a free copy, write to Safety Education Division, Area 2C, Metlife, One Madison Avenue, New York, NY 10010. Include a business-size SASE with your request.

— "An FDA Consumer Special Report: Focus on Food Labeling": This free booklet from the Food and Drug Administration includes information on ingredient labeling. To get a copy, write to the FDA, HFE-88, 5600 Fishers Lane, Rockville, MD 20857.

— "The Facts About Weight Loss Products and Programs": This informative and helpful brochure is available free upon request from the Food and Drug Administration, Consumer Affairs and Information, 5600 Fishers Lane, HFC-110, Rockville, MD 20857.

— Vitamin/Mineral Brochure: You can get this free guide dealing with vitamin and mineral requirements, by writing to the United States Pharmacopeia (USP), 12601 Twinbrook Parkway, Rockville, MD 20852.

— Meal Planner: Are you consuming the recommended daily servings of fruits and vegetables? If not, the "5-A-Day Weekly Planner" can help you change your eating habits and maintain a well-balanced diet. To get a planner, write to the California Grape Commission, P.O. Box 5498, Five-A-Day Planner, Fresno, CA 93755.

— "A Quick Consumer Guide to Safe Food Handling": This valuable booklet is available free upon request from the Consumer Information Center, 574-X, Pueblo, CO 81009.

— Cold Brochure: "The Cold Hard Facts: Blasting 10 Myths About The Common Cold" is a free brochure which debunks 10 frequent misconceptions about colds. Send for the brochure and also get a 25-cents-off coupon for Halls cough medication. Write to: The Cold Hard Facts, 500 N. Michigan Avenue, Ste. 200, Chicago, IL 60611.

— Fitness Booklet: This free booklet provides advice on how to develop a fitness and nutrition plan designed for your individual lifestyle. To get a free copy, write to Melbra Fit-Informed Free Brochure Offer, P.O. Box 3931, Schaumberg, IL 60168-3931.

— Food Guide Pyramid: A new brochure developed by the International Food Information Council Foundation, Food Marketing Institute and the U.S. Department of Agriculture Center for Nutrition Policy provides information that could help you follow a healthful diet. To get a free copy of "The Food Guide Pyramid: Your Personal Guide to Healthful Eating," send a business-size SASE to: The Food Guide Pyramid Brochure, P.O. Box 1144, Rockville, MD 20850.

— "A Consumer's Guide To Fats (item 599B)": This free guide provides helpful information on cholesterol testing, how to lower your risk for heart disease and reduce the level of "bad" (LDL) cholesterol. To get your free copy, write to: Consumer Information Center, Department 599B, Pueblo, CO 81009.

— "Eating Defensively: Food Safety Advice For Persons With AIDS": This brochure is available free upon request from the AIDS Information Clearinghouse, P.O. Box 6003, Rockville, MD 20850.

— Heart attack risk pamphlet: The makers of Bayer Aspirin offer a free pamphlet, "Getting to the Heart of the Family: Know Your Risk For Heart Disease." For a free copy, write to the Bayer Company, 90 Park Avenue, New York, NY 10016; or call (800) 332-2253.

Investment Guides and Financial Booklets

— The Investment Institute in Washington, DC publishes several consumer brochures dealing with the basics of investing for beginners. The material is available free upon request and includes the following brochures:

"What Is A Mutual Fund?"— Provides basic information for investing in mutual funds. This illustrated leaflet also shows how to read mutual fund share quotes and explains the potential risks and rewards of investing in mutual funds.

"Reading The Mutual Fund Prospectus"— This illustrated

30-page guide explains what to look for when examining a prospectus.

"Money Market Mutual Funds"— This guide explains, in understandable language, money market mutual funds.

"Planning For College?"— Explains how to use mutual funds to meet the rising costs of higher education.

"Investing: Start Now!"— A "plain-English" guide for beginners.

" A Close Look At Closed-End Funds"— This 12-page brochure is a primer for investing in closed-end funds.

To receive free copies of these and other brochures, write to Consumer Brochures, Investment Company Institute, P.O. Box 27850, Washington, DC 20038-7850.

— The Consumer Information Center has free (and low-cost) federal publications on investing, and many other topics. Publications include "Investors' Bill of Rights"; "Building Your Future With Annuities: A Consumer's Guide"; and "Staying Independent: Planning For Financial Independence in Later Life". To get a free copy of the most current catalog of booklets available, write the Consumer Information Catalog, Pueblo, CO 81009.

— Investment guides: The National Association of Securities Dealers (NASDAQ), a self-regulating organization of the securities industry, offers two free investment guides. To get free copies of "Guide To Information and Services" and "NASDAQ Fact

Book," , contact the National Association of Securities Dealers, Inc., 1735 K Street N.W., Washington, DC 20006.

— "Consumers Financial Guide": Find out how to choose investments and keep them safe, how to trade securities and more in this free investment guide. Write to Publications Section, Printing Branch, Stop C-11, Securities and Exchange Commission, 450 5th Street, N.W., Washington, DC 20549.

— "Keeping Your Financial Balance": This free booklet provides valuable financial information and advice. For a free copy, write to "Keeping Your Financial Balance," Citibank, P.O. Box 17029, Baltimore, MD 21203.

— "Credit and Charge Card Fraud"; "Fair Credit Billing"; "Credit Billing Blues": These three brochures, dealing with ATM card fraud and credit card billing problems are available free upon request. Write to: Public Reference, Federal Trade Commission, Washington, DC 20580.

— "Investment Swindles: How They Work and How to Avoid Them": This free booklet provides helpful information on detecting and avoiding investment scams. For a free copy, write to the National Futures Association, 200 West Madison Street, Suite 1600, Chicago, IL 60606-3447; Phone: (800) 572-9400.

— "What Every Investor Should Know": This free booklet, available from the Securities and Exchange Commission (SEC), provides useful information for beginning investors. For a free copy, contact the SEC Public Reference Branch, Stop 1-2, 450 5th Street N.W., Washington, DC 20549: Phone: (202) 272-7460.

— Mortgage Guide: The Federal Trade Commission offers "The Money Management Guide", a free booklet for home buyers. For a free copy, write to the FTC, Consumer Protection Department, Washington, DC 20580.

Lawn & Garden

— "Efficient Use of Water in the Garden and Landscape": This free booklet provides information about proper techniques for watering your lawn and garden. To get a copy of the booklet, write to the Texas Water Development Board, P.O. Box 13231, Capitol Station, Austin, TX 78711.

— "The Citizen's Guide To Pesticides": The Environmental Protection Agency offers this free booklet, which provides information on how to choose and use pesticides wisely. To get a copy, write to the EPA, Office of Pesticide Programs, H7502C, 401 M Street S.W., Washington, DC 20460.

— Seed Catalogs: Many nurseries and seed companies offer seed catalogs free of charge or for a nominal fee to cover postage and handling. The catalogs list a wide assortment of flower and vegetable seeds as well as yard and gardening equipment, much of which is available at discount prices. You can write or call the following companies to request their seed catalogs:

* W. Atlee Burpee & Company, 300 Park Avenue, Warminster, PA 18991-0001; (800) 888-1477.

* Henry Field's Seed & Nursery Company, 415 N. Burnett,

Shenandoah,IA 51602; (605) 665-9391.

* J.W. Jung Seed & Nursery Company, 335 South High Street, Randolph, WI 53956; (800) 247-5864.

* Northwoods Retail Nursery, 27635 S Oglesby Road, Canby, OR 97013; (503) 266-5432.

* Miller Nurseries, 5060 West Lake Road, Canandaigua, NY 14420; (800) 836-9630.

* Park Seed, Cokesbury Road, Greenwood, SC 29647-0001; (800) 845-3369.

* Shepard's Garden Seeds, 30 Irene Street, Torrington, CT 06790; (203) 482-3638.

* Stokes Seeds, Inc., Box 548, Buffalo, NY 14240-0548.

* Thompson & Morgan, P.O. Box 1308, Jackson, NJ 08527-0308; (908) 363-2225.

Pets

— Pet Selection Brochure: The first step in selecting a pet is knowing what type of pet is right for you. The American Veterinary Medical Association (AVMA) publishes a free brochure titled "The Veterinarian's Way of Selecting A Proper Pet", which provides expert information to help you make the right choice. To get a copy of the brochure, write to the AVMA, Public Information Department, 1931 North Meacham Road, Schaumburg, IL

60173.

— Travel Tips: If air travel is in your pet's future, you may want to consult the Air Transport Association of America's brochure, "Air Travel For Your Dog or Cat". To get a free copy of the brochure, write to the Association at 1709 New York Avenue N.W., Washington, DC 20006-5206.

— Summer Pet Care: The American Kennel Club offers a free pamphlet, "Fun In The Sun." The pamphlet provides tips on summer care, fitness and travel for dogs. To get a free copy of the pamphlet, write to AKA Fulfillment, "Fun In The Sun," 5580 Centerview Drive, Raleigh, NC 27606.

— Traveling with your pet: The American Society for the Prevention of Cruelty to Animals (A.S.P.C.A.), has a free booklet, "Air Travel Tips (for pets)." To get a copy of this booklet, send a long SASE to the A.S.P.C.A., Education Department, 424 E. 92nd Street, New York, NY 10128.

— "Coping With Pet Odors": If your pet is a real stinker, this booklet can provide some helpful information. It explains how to remove pet odors from carpeting and upholstery. To get a free copy of this booklet, write to "Coping With Pet Odors," Church & Dwight Company, P.O., P.O. Box 7648, Princeton, NJ 08543. Include a business-size SASE with your request.

Product Samples

— Sweet 'N Low pocket carrier: Get a free pocket carrier for sweetener packets by sending 50 cents (for postage and handling) to Sweet 'N Low, 60 Flushing Ave., Brooklyn, NY 11205. For free samples of Sweet 'N Low, write to the manufacturer, 2 Cumberland St., Brooklyn, NY 11205.

— Seasoning packets: For $1.50 postage and handling you can get a catalog of seasonings, coupons, and sample packets of seasoning. To get these items, write to Magic Seasonings Blends, P.O. Box 23342, New Orleans, LA 70183-0342.

— Tea For Two: Sample Lipton's Cinnamon Apple herbal and Orange and Spice-flavored "Soothing Moments" teas. To get these two free tea samples, write to Lipton Soothing Moments Sample Offer, P.O. Box 1206, Grand Rapids, MN 55745-1206.

— Nuts to you: Get a sample bag of nuts along with "nutty" information about almonds and pistachios by writing to Buchanan Hollow Nut Co., Box 227, Le Grand, CA 95333. Include $1 shipping and handling.

— Blistex: For a free sample packet of Blistex Lip Ointment, write to Blistex Sample Offer, 1800 Swift Drive, Oak Brook, IL 60521. Include a SASE.

— Spruce tree seeds: You can get free Colorado Spruce tree seeds by writing to the Waukesha Seed Company, P.O. Box 1820, Waukesha, WI 53187. Include 50 cents for postage and handling.

— Folded Animal Patterns: Contact the Winslow Publishing Company to get several free patterns for folded animals. Write to: P.O. Box 38012-AP, 500 Eglinton Ave., West Toronto, ON , M5N 3A8, Canada. Be sure to use the correct first-class postage on your request.

— Flower painting and patterns: Discover the artist in yourself with a rose painting and patterns. The painting and patterns are available free upon request from Norwegian Rosemaling, 1506 Lynn, Marquette, MI 49855.

— Shampoo: A free sample of Neutrogena Shampoo is available by writing to: Neutrogena Shampoo Offer, Department 1765, P.O. Box 45062, Los Angeles, CA 90045. Include $1.00 for postage and handling.

— Cleaning products: Household clean-up jobs can be a breeze with "Colonel Brassy" and "General Clean-Up". Free samples of these cleaning products are available from Vertex Industries, P.O. Box 297, Farmingville, NY 11738. Include $1.00 for shipping and handling.

— Hagerty's Silver Polish: Get a free sample of this product by writing to: W.J. Hagerty LTD., Box 1496, 3801 W. Linden Avenue, South Bend, IN 46624.

— Potpourri Packet: This free packet including sample potpourri oils, herbs, and flowers is available from Tradewinds, P.O. Box 52, Moorcraft, WY 82721. Include $1 for postage and handling.

— Bacon Flavor Dog Treats: Purina offers a free 3 ounce sample of "Beggin' Strips" dog treats. To get the free sample, send a written request to: Beggin' Strips Sample Offer, P.O. Box 15510, Mascoutah, IL 62224.

— International Currency: You can get samples of paper money from a number of nations by writing to Jolie Company, P.O. Box 399, Roslyn Heights, NY 11577. Include $1 for shipping and handling.

— Denture Adhesive Powder: The makers of Klutch Denture Adhesive Powder offer free samples to denture wearers. Write to Klutch Free Sample Offer, I. Putnam, Inc., P.O. Box 444, Big Flats, NY 14814.

— Bird Food: Free samples of Super Preen bird foods and supplements, and a bird care booklet are available upon request from RHB Labs, 1640 E. Ediger Ave, Santa Ana, CA 92705.

— Oil of Olay Bath Bar: Get a free sample bath bar by sending 50 cents for postage and handling to Oil of Olay Sample Offer, P.O. Box 5767, Clinton, IA 52736.

— Wheat Germ: A free packet of wheat germ and a brochure, "Growing Younger: Eating and Exercising Smart after 50," is available upon request from Kretschmer Wheat Germ, P.O. Box 530, Barrington, IL 60011.

Recipes

— Baking soda secrets: Get a free copy of "Arm & Hammer Great Recipes With Baking Soda" by sending a SASE to Church and Dwight, P.O. Box 853, Young America, MN 55399.

— Microwave cheese treats: The Wisconsin Milk Marketing Board offers free "Microwaveable Cheese Recipes." To get the recipes, write to the Board at 8414 Excelsior Drive, Madison, WI 60473.

— Apricot sensations: Recipes using fresh, canned and dried apricots are featured in "Simply Sensational California Apricots." To ge a free copy, send a business-size SASE to California Apricot Advisory Board, 1280 Boulevard Way, Walnut Creek, CA 94595.

— Egg tricks: Get several free egg recipes by sending a SASE to The American Egg Board, 1460 Renaissance, Park Ridge, IL 60068.

— Mexican meals: "Food Secrets of Mexico" features recipes from south of the border. The recipes are available upon request from La Victoria Recipes, P.O. Box 3884, City of Industry, CA 91744.

— French favorites: If French cooking makes your mouth water, send for a free copy of "Favorite French Recipes." Write to: Air France, 1350 Avenue of the Americas, New York, NY 10019.

— Teen treats: Get a free copy of "Fast and Easy Recipes for Teens" from California Cling Peaches. Send a SASE to Fast & Easy, CFPS Inc., P.O. Box 7111, San Francisco, CA 94120-7111.

— Here's the beef: Seven beef recipes for the grill plus tips for successful barbequing are featured in "Grilled Beef Easy and Delicious." For a free copy of this booklet, send a business-size SASE to Meat Board Test Kitchens, Department GB, 444 N Michigan Ave, Chicago, IL 60611.

— Dream grill: The makers of Kingsford Charcoal offer a free leaflet of recipes and grilling tips. To get a copy of this leaflet, send a business-size SASE to Kingsford Easy BBQ Tips and Recipes, P.O. Box 14335, Baltimore, MD 21268.

— Turkey tempters: Free turkey recipes are available for the asking (and a SASE) from the National Turkey Federation, Consumer Dept., 11319 Sunset Hills Road, Reston, VA 22090.

— Born to be wild rice: For free recipes using wild rice, send a SASE to Wild Rice National Directory Offer, 1306 W. Country Road, F, #109, St. Paul, MN 55112.

— New England edibles: Seafood recipes from New England are available free upon request from the Maine Department of Marine Resources, State House, Augusta, ME 04333.

— Chef's recipes: The featured ingredient in the chef's recipes found in "America's Chefs Cook at Home," is butter. To get a free copy of this leaflet, send a business-size SASE to America's Dairy Farmers, c/o Lewis & Neale Inc., 928 Broadway, Box AC, New York, NY 10010.

— Mushroom magic: "Recipes for Mushroom Lovers" is available free upon request from the American Mushroom Institute, P.O. Box 373, Kennet Square, PA 19348.

— Tasty Tomatoes: Get several free recipes using tomatoes by writing to the Florida Tomato Committee, Dept. NP, P.O. Box 140533, Orlando, FL 32814-0533.

— "Basic Recipes for Those With Allergies": This leaflet features recipes plus substitute information for people with food allergies. For a free copy, write to USA Rice, P.O. Box 740121, Houston, TX 77274. Include a business-size SASE.

— "Red Ripe Tomato Salads: Rich In Vitamin C": Mediterranean Pasta Salad and BLT Slaw are just two of the tempting recipes featured in this leaflet available free from Tomato Salads, P.O. Box 140635, Orlando, FL 32814. Include a SASE.

— "Delicious Beef Recipes": This leaflet provides seven recipes using beef from the National Live Stock and Meat Board cookbook "Skinny Beef." Also featured are tips for trimming fat. To get a free copy, send a business-size SASE to Meat Board Test Kitchens, 444 N. Michigan Avenue, Chicago, IL 60611.

— Brown Rice Bonanza: Find out how to prepare Nutty Vegetable Pilaf and Hot To Go Thai Salad and many other tasty recipes featured in "Brown Rice: The Whole Grain". You can get this free recipe brochure by sending a business-size SASE to USA Rice, P.O. Box 7401, Houston, TX 77274.

— Sugar Substitute: Sweet One granulated sugar substitute is featured in the free leaflet, "Fabulous Finales." Four recipes and a conversion chart are included. For a free copy, write to Sweet One, Stadt Corporation, P.O. Box 2160, Great Neck, NY 11021; or call the Sweet One Hotline, (800) 544-8610 Monday through Friday 9 a.m. to 5 p.m..

— "Cheese: The Menu Star": This free brochure from the National Cheese Institute features nutritional information and four recipes using cheese. For a free copy, send a business-size SASE to Cheese: The Menu Star, The National Cheese Institute, 1250 H Street, N.W. Suite 900, Washington, DC 20005.

Sports

— Sports Cards: Get baseball or football cards to add to your collection, by writing to Danors, 5721 Funston Street, Bay 14, Hollywood, FL 33023. Be sure to specify which cards you prefer— baseball or football. Also include a SASE and 50 cents to cover postage and handling.

— Archery Tips: Get a copy of the booklet "Archery Made Easy" by writing to Ben Pearson Inc., Pine Bluff, AR 71601.

— Basketball booklet: The Basketball Hall of Fame offers a free booklet, "Basketball Was Born Here," a Hall of Fame building brochure, and a Hall of Fame membership brochure. To get this basketball package, write to Basketball Was Born Here, Basketball Hall of Fame, 1150 W. Columbus Avenue, Springfield, MA 01101. Include $1 for postage and handling.

— Table Tennis Guide and Rules: Learn the finer points of table tennis with the information provided in the U.S. Table Tennis Association's free table tennis guide. To get a copy, send a SASE to U.S. Table Tennis Association, Box 815, Orange, CT 06477.

— Rules for Horseshoes: The official rules for horseshoe pitching are available free from the National Horseshoe Pitcher's Association, Rt. 2, Box 178, Lamonte, MO 65337.

— Row, Row, Row Your Boat: Get free information on canoe safety and the sport of canoeing in the free pamphlet, "Welcome Paddler," available from Jim Mack, U. S. Canoe Association, 606 Ross Street, Middletown, OH 45044-5062. Include a long SASE with your request.

— Exercise Posters: The President's Council On Fitness and Sports offers free exercise posters and pictures. To get these items, write to the President's Council on Physical Fitness and Sports, 450 Fifth Street, S.W., Suite 7103, Washington, DC 20001.

— Baseball Fan Mail Packages: Team decals, schedules, photos of your favorite players, and other baseball items are available in fan mail packages from all 27 major league baseball teams. Send your request for fan mail packages to the "Fan Mail Department" at any of the following addresses. Include a SASE with your request.

National League

* ATLANTA BRAVES: 521 CApitol Avenue, SW, Atlanta, GA 30312.

* CHICAGO CUBS: 1060 West Addison Street, Chicago, IL 60613.

* CINCINNATI REDS: 100 Riverfront Stadium,

Cincinnati, OH 45202.

* COLORADO ROCKIES: 1700 Broadway, Denver, CO 80290.

* FLORIDA MARLINS: 2267 NW 199th Street, Miami, FL 33056.

* HOUSTON ASTROS: P.O. Box 288, Houston, TX 77001.

* LOS ANGELES DODGERS: Dodger Stadium, 1000 Elysian Park Ave., Los Angeles, CA 90012.

* MONTREAL EXPOS: P.O. Box 500, Station M, Montreal, Que. H1V 3P2.

* NEW YORK METS: Shea Stadium, Flushing, NY 11368.

* PHILADELPHIA PHILLIES: P.O. Box 7575, Philadelphia, PA 19101.

* PITTSBURGH PIRATES: Three Rivers Stadium, Pittsburgh, PA 15212.

* ST. LOUIS CARDINALS: Busch Memorial Stadium, St. Louis, MO 63102.

* SAN DIEGO PADRES: P.O. Box 2000, San Diego, CA 92122.

* SAN FRANCISCO GIANTS: Candlestick Park, San Francisco, CA 94124.

American League

* BALTIMORE ORIOLES: 333 W. Camden Street, Baltimore, MD 21202.

* BOSTON RED SOX: 24 Yawkey Way, Boston, MA 02215.

* CALIFORNIA ANGELS: P.O. Box 2000, Anaheim Stadium, Anaheim CA 92803.

* CHICAGO WHITE SOX: 333 W. 35th Street, Chicago, IL 60616.

* CLEVELAND INDIANS: 2401 ONtario Street, Cleveland, OH 44115.

* DETROIT TIGERS: Tiger Stadium, 2121 Trumbull Ave., Detroit, MI 48216.

* KANSAS CITY ROYALS: P.O. BOX 419969, Kansas City, MO 64141.

* MILWAUKEE BREWERS: Milwaukee County Stadium, Milwaukee, WI
53214.

* MINNESOTA TWINS: 501 Chicago Ave., South,

Minneapolis, MN 55415.

* NEW YORK YANKEES: Yankee Stadium, Bronx, NY 10451.

* OAKLAND ATHLETICS: Oakland Coliseum, Oakland, CA 94621.

* SEATTLE MARINERS: P.O. Box 4100, Seattle, WA 98104.

* TEXAS RANGERS: P.O. Box 90111, Arlington, TX 76004.

* TORONTO BLUE JAYS: 1 Blue Jays Way, Toronto, Ont. M5V 1J1.

Odds 'N Ends

— Free poster: You can get a free copy of the wall poster titled, "Freedom from Hunger" by contacting the Food and Agriculture Organization of the U.N., 1325 "C" Street S.W., Washington, DC 20437.

— Traveling tips: Learn how to prepare for a trip, handle money and stay safe while traveling with the information provided in the "Travel Safety Guide." To get a free copy of the Guide, write to American Express Travelers Cheques Travel Safety Guide, 307 W. 36th Street, 8th Floor, New York, NY 10018.

— "Your House Is On Fire": Aetna Insurance offers this free

booklet, which explains how to prevent fires. The guide also features escape plans and a fire safety quiz. To get a free copy, write to Aetna Insurance, Public Relations Department C., 1922 F Street, Washington, DC 20006-4387. Include a SASE with your request.

— Garage Sale Tips: Make money by holding your own garage sale. The free booklet, "How To Hold A Garage Sale," tells you everything you need to know. For a copy of this booklet, write to United Van Lines, One United Drive, Consumer Services, Fenton, MO 63026.

— Termite control tips: "Tips on Subterranean Termite Control" is a free booklet designed for homeowners who are worried about termite infestation. For a free copy of the booklet, send a business-size SASE to: Termite, ODA Pesticide Regulation, 8995 E. Main Street, Reynoldsburg, OH 43068-3399.

— Home Security Test: The maker of Segal locks offers a free home security test for homeowners who want to find out whether or not their homes are secure. You can get a copy of this home security test by writing to the New England Lock Company, Box 544, S. Norwalk, CT 06856.

— Environmental guide: For a free copy of the booklet, "Protecting the Environment," write to MOBIL, Box EL, 3225 Gallows Road, Fairfax, VA 22037.

— Mini Sewing Kit: This free sewing kit features thread, needles, measuring tape, button, safety pin, and more. The kit is available for $1.00 postage and handling from Assiduity Industries, P.O. Box 1147, Willis, CA 95490.

— Chess rules: Improve your chess prowess with the information provided in the free booklet, "World Chess Championship Play." Write to the U.S. Chess Federation, Department 68, Rt. 9W, New Windsor, NY 12550.

— Child Safety Booklet: "Help Save A Child's Life" is a free booklet that provides parents with information on what to do with discarded refrigerators and freezers and other measures to "childproof" a home. For a free copy, send a SASE to Home Appliance Manufacturers, 20 North Wacker Drive, Chicago, IL 60602.

— "Long-Term Care Insurance Buying Guide": This booklet is available upon request from the National Association of Insurance Commissioners (NAIC), 120 West 12th Street, Suite 1100, Kansas City, MO 64105.

— Plant A Tree: Get a free tree to plant in your yard from the National Arbor Day Foundation. You can plant the free tree as part of the national "Trees For America" program. Request a free tree by writing to the National Arbor Day Foundation, Arbor Avenue, Nebraska City, NE 68410.

— Renting guide: Get a free booklet, "A Guide to Renting an Apartment," featuring tips on what to look for and what to avoid when choosing an apartment to rent. The guide also features a rating system to help you choose the right apartment. For a free copy, write to State Farm Insurance, Public Relations Department, One State Farm Plaza, Bloomington, IL 61701.

— Outdoor recreation guide: "A Guide To Your National

Forests" features addresses and phone numbers for more than 150 National forests. The guide also lists regional Forest Service offices. You can get a free copy of this guide by writing to: Forest Service, U.S. Department of Agriculture, 12th and Independence, S.W. P.O. Box 96090, Washington, DC 20090.

— Financial Aid For College: "The Student Guide: Five Federal Financial Aid Programs": This free booklet, is available from the Federal Student Financial Aid Information Center, P.O. Box 84, Washington, DC 20044; Phone: (800) 333-4636.

— Recycling Bag: The makers of Reynolds Wrap offer a free recycling kit. The kit includes a recycling bag for collecting used aluminum, a refrigerator magnet, an informational brochure, and a coupon for Reynolds Wrap. To get a free kit, call (800) 344-9727.

— Braille Alphabet: You can get a card that features the entire braille alphabet and number system by sending your request on a postcard to the American Foundation for the Blind, 15 West 16th Street, New York, NY 10011. Ask for the "Braille Alphabet Card."

— Household Management Guide: Whirlpool offers various tips to help you manage your home better in the free Time Smart Guide. To get a copy of the guide, call toll-free (800) 253-1301.

A P P E N D I X

CHEAPIES, FREE GOODIES AND GIVEAWAYS

National Consumer Organizations

The defined mission (based on information provided in the "Consumer's Resources Handbook" from the Office of Consumer Affairs) of the following organizations includes developing and distributing consumer education and information materials. While many of these materials are available free, there is sometimes a nominal charge. You should contact the organization to find out.

— American Association of Retired Persons (AARP), Consumer Affairs Section, 601 E Street, N.W., Washington, DC 20049

AARP's Consumer Affairs section develops and distributes consumer information about the specific needs of older consumers. Materials on housing, insurance, eligibility for public benefits, financial security and other matters are developed and distributed.

— Bankcard Holders of America (BHA), Suite 120, 560 Herndon Parkway, Herndon, VA 22070; Phone (703) 481-1110.

BHA is a non-profit organization which assists consumers in saving money on credit, getting out of debt and resolving credit problems. It offers lists of low-rate and secured credit cards for a small charge (see chapter 5), more than 20 guidebooks and educational brochures on credit topics, and other materials.

— Consumer Action (CA), 116 New Montgomery, Suite 233, San Francisco, CA 94105.

Among the services of Consumer Action are surveys of banks and long distance telephone companies. CA offers free information on its surveys as well as a variety of consumer education materials.

—- Consumer Federation of America (CFA), 1424 16th Street, N.W., Suite 604, Washington, DC 20036; Phone: (202) 387-6121.

The CFA is comprised of more than 240 organizations which represent over 50 million consumers. As part of its mission, the CFA develops and distributes studies of various consumer issues, as well as consumer guides in book and pamphlet form.

— National Consumers League (NCL), 815 15th Street, N.W., Suite 928-N, Washington, DC 20005; Phone: (202) 639-8140.

Founded in 1899, the NCL is a non-profit membership organization working for consumer health and safety protection and fairness in the marketplace and workplace. It also develops consumer education materials and a newsletter.

— National Insurance Consumer Organization (NICO), P.O. Box 15492, Alexandria, VA 22309; Phone: (703) 549-8050.

NICO is a non-profit organization which, among other services offered, develops and distributes consumer information on insurance. The materials distributed include information designed to educate consumers on buying insurance.

— Public Voice for Food and Health Policy, 1001 Connecticut Avenue, N.W., Suite 522, Washington, DC 20036; Phone: (202) 659-5930; Fax: (202) 659- 3683.

Public Voice develops and distributes consumer information materials on nutrition labeling, seafood safety and pesticide reduction.

State-by-State Consumer Protection Agencies

State consumer protection offices provide consumers with important services. They might mediate complaints, conduct investigations, and provide educational materials, among many other services offered.

If you have a consumer complaint, call the office before sending it in writing. Find out if the office handles the type of complaint you have or if complaint forms are provided. Many state offices also distribute "consumer alerts" on a variety of consumer issues. You can contact your state agency to obtain available educational information on your consumer problem.

ALABAMA: Consumer Affairs Division, Office of Attorney General, 11 South Union Street, Montgomery AL 36130; Phone: (205) 242-7334; (800) 392-5658 (in AL)

ALASKA: The Consumer Protection Section, formerly in the Attorney General's Office has been closed. Consumers with complaints are being referred to the Better Business Bureau, small claims court and private attorneys.

ARIZONA: Consumer Protection, Office of the Attorney General, 1275 West Washington Street, Room 259, Phoenix, AZ 85007; Phone (602) 542-3702; (800) 352-8431 (in AZ).

ARKANSAS: Consumer Protection Division, Office of Attorney General, 200 Tower Building, 323 Center Street, Little Rock, AR 72201; (501) 682-2341; (800) 482- 8982 (in AR).

CALIFORNIA: California Department of Consumer Affairs, 400 R Street, Suite 1040, Sacramento, CA 95814; Phone: (916) 445-1254 (for consumer information); (800) 344-9940 (in CA).

Office of Attorney General, Public Inquiry Unit, P.O. Box 944255, Sacramento, CA 94244-2550; Phone: (916) 322-

3360; (800) 952-5225 (in CA).

COLORADO: Consumer Protection Unit, Office of Attorney General, 1525 Sherman Street, 5th Floor, Denver, CO 80203; Phone: (303) 866-5189.

CONNECTICUT: Department of Consumer Protection, 165 Capitol Avenue, Hartford, CT 06106; Phone: (203) 566-2534; (800) 842-2649 (in CT).

DELAWARE: Division of Consumer Affairs, Department of Community Affairs, 820 North French Street, 4th Floor, Wilmington, DE 19801; Phone: (302) 577-3250.

DISTRICT OF COLUMBIA: Department of Consumer and Regulatory Affairs, 614 H Street, N.W., Washington, DC 20001; Phone: (202) 727-7120.

FLORIDA: Department of Agriculture and Consumer Services, Division of Consumer Services, 407 South Calhoun Street, Mayo Building, 2nd Floor, Tallahassee, FL 32399-0800; Phone: (904) 488-2221; (800) 435-7352 (in FL).

GEORGIA: Governors Office of Consumer Affairs, 2 Martin Luther King, Jr. Drive, S.E., Plaza Level-East Tower, Atlanta, GA 30334; Phone: (404) 651-8600; (800) 869-1123 (in GA).

HAWAII: Office of Consumer Protection, Department of Commerce and Consumer Affairs, 828 Fort St. Mall, Suite 600B, P.O. Box 3767, Honolulu, HI 96812-3767; Phone: (808) 586-2636.

IDAHO: Deputy Attorney General, Office of the Attorney General, Consumer Protection Unit, Statehouse, Room 119, Boise, ID 83720-1000; Phone: (208) 334-2424; (800) 432-3545 (in ID).

ILLINOIS: Consumer Protection Division, Office of Attorney General, 100 West Randolph, 12th Floor, Chicago, IL 60601; (312) 814-3000.

Department of Citizen Advocacy, 100 West Randolph, 13th Floor, Chicago, IL 60601; (312) 814-3289.

INDIANA: Chief Counsel and Director, Consumer Protection Division, Office of Attorney General, 219 State House, Indianapolis, IN 46204; (317) 232-6330; (800) 382-5516 (in Indiana).

IOWA: Assistant Attorney General, Consumer Protection Division, Office of Attorney General, 1300 East Walnut Street, 2nd Floor, Des Moines, IA 50319; (515) 281-5926.

KANSAS: Deputy Attorney General, Consumer Protection Division, Office of Attorney General, 301 West 10th, Kansas Judicial Center, Topeka, KS 66612-1597; (913) 296-3751; (800) 432-2310 (in Kansas).

KENTUCKY: Consumer Protection Division, Office of Attorney General, 209 Saint Clair Street, Frankfort, KY 40601-1875; (502) 564-2200; (800) 432-9257 (in Kentucky).

Consumer Protection Division, Office of Attorney General, 107 South 4th Street, Louisville, KY 40202; (502) 595-3262; (800)

432-9257 (in Kentucky).

LOUISIANA: Consumer Protection Section, Office of Attorney General, State Capitol Building, P.O. Box 94095, Baton Rouge, LA 70804-9095; (504) 342-9638.

MAINE: Superintendent, Bureau of Consumer Credit Protection, State House Station No. 35, Augusta, ME 04333-0035; (207) 582-8718; (800) 332-8529 (in Maine).

Consumer and Antitrust Division, Office of Attorney General, State House Station No. 6, Augusta, ME 04333; (207) 626-8849.

MARYLAND: Consumer Protection Division, Office of Attorney General, 200 St. Paul Place, Baltimore, MD 21202-2021; (410) 528-8662; (410) 565-0451 (in DC metro area).

Consumer Affairs Specialist, Eastern Shore Branch Office, Consumer Protection Division, Office of Attorney General, 201 Baptist Street, Suite 30, Salisbury, MD 21801-4976; (401) 543-6620.

Consumer Protection Division, Office of Attorney General, 138 East Antietam Street, Suite 210, Hagerstown, MD 21740-5684; (301) 791-4780.

MASSACHUSETTS: Consumer Protection Division, Department of Attorney General, 1 Ashburton Place, Boston, MA 02103; (617) 727-8400.

Assistant Attorney General, Western Massachusetts Consumer

Protection Division, Department of Attorney General, 436 Dwight Street, Springfield, MA 01103; (403) 784-1240.

MICHIGAN: Assistant in Charge, Consumer Protection Division, Office of Attorney General, P.O. Box 30213, Lansing, MI 48909; (517) 373-1140.

MINNESOTA: Consumer Services Division, Office of Attorney General, 1400 NCL Tower, 445 Minnesota Street, St. Paul, MN 55101; (612) 296-3353.

MISSISSIPPI: Special Assistant Attorney General, Director, Office of Consumer Protection, P.O. Box 22947, Jackson, MS; (601) 354-6018.

Bureau of Regulatory Services, Department of Agriculture and Services, Department of Agriculture and Commerce, 500 Greymont Avenue, P.O. Box 1609, Jackson, MS 39215-1609; (601) 354-7063.

MISSOURI: Office of Attorney General, Division of Consumer Protection, P.O. Box 899, Jefferson City, MO 65102; (314) 751-3321; (800) 392-8222 (in Missouri).

MONTANA: Consumer Affairs Unit, Department of Commerce, 1424 Ninth Avenue, Box 200501, Helena, MT 59620-0501; (406) 444-4312.

NEBRASKA: Assistant Attorney General, Consumer Protection Division, Department of Justice, 2115 State Capitol, P.O. Box 98920, Lincoln, NE 68509; (402) 471-2682.

NEVADA: Commissioner of Consumer Affairs, Department of Commerce, State Mail Room Complex, Las Vegas, NV 89158; (702) 486-7355; (800) 992-0900 (in Nevada).

Consumer Affairs Division, Department of Commerce, 4600 Kietzke Lane, B-113, Reno, NV 89502; (702) 688-1800; (800) 992-0900 (in Nevada).

NEW HAMPSHIRE: Consumer Protection and Antitrust Bureau, Office of Attorney General, State House Annex, Concord, NH 07101; (603) 271-3641.

NEW JERSEY: Division of Consumer Affairs, P.O. Box 45027, 124 Halsey Street, 7th Floor, Newark, NJ 07101; (201) 504-6534.

Deputy Attorney General, New Jersey Division of Law, P.O. Box 45029, 124 Halsey Street, 5th Floor, Newark, NJ 07101; (201) 648-7579.

NEW MEXICO: Consumer Protection Division, Office of Attorney General, P.O. Drawer 1508, Santa Fe, NM 87504; (505) 827-6060; (800) 678-1508 (in New Mexico).

NEW YORK: Assistant Attorney General, Bureau of Consumer Frauds and Protection, Office of Attorney General, State Capitol, Albany, NY 12224; (518) 474-5481.

NORTH CAROLINA: Special Deputy Attorney General, Consumer Protection Service, Office of Attorney General, Consumer Protection Section, Office of Attorney General, Raney Building, P.O. Box 629, Raleigh, NC 27602; (919) 733-7741.

NORTH DAKOTA: Office of Attorney General, 600 East Boulevard, Bismarck, ND 58505; (701) 224-3404; (800) 472-2600 (in North Dakota).

Consumer Fraud Section, Office of Attorney General, 600 East Boulevard, Bismarck, ND 58505; (701) 224-3404; (800) 472-2600 (in ND).

OHIO: Consumer Frauds and Crimes Section, Office of Attorney General, 30 East Broad Street, State Office Tower, 25th Floor, Columbus, OH 43266-0410; (614) 466-4986 (complaints); (800) 282-0515 (in Ohio).

Office of Consumers' Counsel, 77 South High Street, 15th Floor, Columbus, OH 43266-0550; (614) 466-9605; (800) 282-9448 (in Ohio).

OKLAHOMA: Assistant Attorney General, Office of Attorney General, Consumer Protection Division, 4545 N. Lincoln Blvd., Suite 260, Oklahoma City, OK 73105; (405) 521-4274.

OREGON: Financial Fraud Section, Department of Justice, 1162 Court Street N.E., Salem, OR 97310; (503) 378-4732.

PENNSYLVANIA: Bureau of Consumer Protection, Office of Attorney General, Strawberry Square, 14th Floor, Harrisburg, PA 17120; (717) 787-9707; (800) 441-2555 (in Pennsylvania).

RHODE ISLAND: Consumer Protection Division, Department of Attorney General, 72 Pine Street, Providence, RI 02903; (401) 274-4400; (800) 852-7776 (in Rhode Island).

SOUTH CAROLINA: Assistant Attorney General, Consumer Fraud and Antitrust Section, Office of Attorney General, P.O. Box 11549, Columbia, SC 29211; (803) 734-3970.

Department of Consumer Affairs, P.O. Box 5757, Columbia, SC 29250-5757; (803) 734-9452; (800) 922-1594 (in South Carolina).

SOUTH DAKOTA: Division of Consumer Affairs, Office of Attorney General, 500 East Capitol, State Capitol Building, Pierre, SD 57501-5070; (605) 773-4400.

TENNESSEE: Division of Consumer Protection, Office of Attorney General, 450 James Robertson Parkway, Nashville, TN 37243-0600; (615) 741-3491.

Division of Consumer Affairs, 500 James Robertson Parkway, Nashville, TN 37243-0600; (615) 741-4737; (800) 342-8383 (in Tennessee).

TEXAS: Assistant Attorney General and Chief, Consumer Protection Division, Office of Attorney General, P.O. Box 12548, Austin, TX 78711; (512) 463-2070.

Assistant Attorney General, Consumer Protection Division, Office of Attorney General, 714 Jackson Street, Suite 800, Dallas, TX 75202-4506; (214) 742-8944.

UTAH: Division of Consumer Protection, Department of Commerce, 160 East 3rd South, P.O. Box 45804, Salt Lake City, UT 84145-0804; (801) 530-6001.

VERMONT: Assistant Attorney General and Chief, Public Protection Division, Office of Attorney General, 109 State Street, Montpelier, VT 05609-1001; (802) 828-3171.

VIRGINIA: State Division of Consumer Affairs, Department of Agriculture and Consumer Services, Room 101, Washington Building, P.O. Box 1163, Richmond, VA 23209; (804) 786-2042.

WASHINGTON: Consumer Protection Division, Office of the Attorney General, P.O. Box 40118, Olympia, WA 98504-0118; (206) 753-6210.

Director of Consumer Services, Consumer and Business Fair Practices Division, Office of the Attorney General, 900 Fourth Avenue, Suite 2000, Seattle, WA 98164; (206) 464-6684; (800) 551-4636 (in Washington).

WEST VIRGINIA: Consumer Protection Division, Office of Attorney General, 812 Quarrier Street, 6th Floor, Charleston, WV 25301; (304) 558-8986; (800) 368-8808 (in WV).

WISCONSIN: Division of Trade and Consumer Protection, Department of Agriculture, Trade and Consumer Protection, 801 West Badger Road, P.O. Box 8911, Madison, WI 53708; (608) 266-9836; (800) 422-7178 (in Wisconsin).

WYOMING: Assistant Attorney General, Office of Attorney General, 123 State Capitol Building, Cheyenne, WY 82002; (307) 777-7874.

State Insurance Departments (see chapters 4 and 5)

Each state has its own laws and regulations governing homeowner, health, automobile and other types of insurance. Listed below are the addresses and phone numbers of the individual state departments which enforce those laws. State regulators also can provide you with information to help you save money by making informed insurance buying decisions.

ALABAMA: Insurance Commissioner, 135 South Union Street #200, Montgomery, AL 36130; (205) 269-3550.

ALASKA: Director of Insurance, P.O. Box 110805, Juneau, AK 99811-0805; (907) 465-2515.

ARIZONA: Director of Insurance, 3030 North Third Street, Suite 1100, Phoenix, AZ 85012; (602) 255-5400.

ARKANSAS: Insurance Commissioner, 1123 S. University Avenue, Suite 400, University Tower Building, Little Rock, AR 72204-1699; (501) 686-2900.

CALIFORNIA: Commissioner of Insurance, 770 L Street, Suite 1120, Sacramento, CA 95814; (800) 927-5357.

COLORADO: Commissioner of Insurance, 1560 Broadway St, Suite 850, Denver, CO 80202; (303) 894-7499.

CONNECTICUT: Insurance Commissioner, P.O. Box 816, Hartford, CT 06142-0816; (203) 297-3800.

DELAWARE: Insurance Commissioner, 841 Silver Lake Boulevard, Dover, DE 19901; (302) 739-4251; (800) 282-8611 (toll free in Delaware).

DISTRICT OF COLUMBIA: Superintendent of Insurance, 441 4th Street, N.W., One Judiciary Square, 8th Floor, Washington, DC 20001; (202) 727-8000.

FLORIDA: Insurance Commissioner, Plaza Level Eleven-The Capitol, Tallahassee, FL 32399-0300; (904) 922-3100; (800) 342-2762 (toll free in Florida).

GEORGIA: Insurance Commissioner, 2 Martin L. King, Jr. Drive, Atlanta, GA 30334; (404) 656-2056.

HAWAII: Insurance Commissioner, P.O. Box 3614, Honolulu, HI 96811-3614; (808) 586-2790.

IDAHO: Director of Insurance, 700 W. State Street, Boise, ID 83720; (208) 334-4250.

ILLINOIS: Director of Insurance, 320 West Washington Street, Springfield, IL 62767; (217) 782-4515.

INDIANA: Commissioner of Insurance, 311 West Washington Street, Indianapolis, IN 46204-2787; (317) 232-3520; (800) 622-4461 (toll free in Indiana).

IOWA: Insurance Commissioner, Lucas State Office Building, 6th Floor, Des Moines, IA 50319; (515) 281-5705.

KANSAS: Commissioner of Insurance, 420 S.W. 9th Street, Topeka, KS 66612; (913) 296-3071; (800) 432-2484 (toll free in Kansas).

KENTUCKY: Insurance Commissioner, 229 West Main Street, P.O. Box 517, Frankfort, KY 40602; (502) 564-3630.

LOUISIANA: Commissioner of Insurance, P.O. Box 94214, Baton Rouge, LA 70804-9214; (504) 342-5900.

MAINE: Superintendent of Insurance, State House Station 34, Augusta, ME 04333-0034; (207) 582-8707.

MARYLAND: Insurance Commissioner, Maryland Insurance Administration, 502 St. Paul Place, 7th Floor, Baltimore, MD 21202; (410) 333-6300.

MASSACHUSETTS: Commissioner of Insurance, 280 Friend Street, Boston, MA 02114; (617) 727-7189, ext. 300.

MICHIGAN: Commissioner of Insurance, Insurance Bureau, P.O. Box 30220; (517) 373-9273.

MINNESOTA: Commissioner of Commerce, 133 East 7th Street, St.Paul, MN 55101; (612) 296-2594.

MISSISSIPPI: Commissioner of Insurance, 1804 Walter Sillers Building, 550 High Street, Jackson, MS 39201-1190; (601) 359-3569; (800) 562-2957.

MISSOURI: Director of Insurance, 301 West High Street, Room 630, P.O. Box 690, Jefferson City, MO 65102; (314) 751-4126;

(800) 726-7390 (toll free in Missouri).

MONTANA:Commissioner of Insurance, P.O. Box 4009, Helena, MT 59604-4009; (406) 444-2040; (800) 332-6148 (toll free in Montana).

NEBRASKA: Director of Insurance, 941 "O" Street, Suite 400, Lincoln, NE 68508; (402) 471-2201.

NEVADA: Commissioner of Insurance, 1665 Hot Springs Road #152, Capitol Complex, Carson City, NV 89710; (702) 687-4270; (800) 992-0900 (toll free in Nevada).

NEW HAMPSHIRE: Insurance Commissioner, 169 Manchester Street, Concord, NH 03301; (603) 271-2261; (800) 852-3416 (toll free in New Hampshire).

NEW JERSEY: Commissioner, Department of Insurance, 20 West State Street, CN325, Trenton, NJ 08625; (609) 292-5363.

NEW MEXICO: Superintendent of Insurance, PERA Building, Room 428, P.O. Drawer 1269, Santa FE, NM 87504-1269; (505) 827-4500.

NEW YORK: Superintendent of Insurance, 160 West Broadway, New York, NY 10013-3393; (212) 602-0429; (800) 342-3736 (toll free in New York).

NORTH CAROLINA: Commissioner of Insurance, Dobbs Building, P.O. Box 26387, Raleigh, NC 27611; (919) 733-7343; (800) 662-7777 (toll free in North Carolina).

NORTH DAKOTA: Commissioner of Insurance, Capitol Building, 5th Floor, 600 East Boulevard Avenue, Bismarck, ND 58505-0320; (701) 224-2440; (800) 247-0560 (toll free in North Dakota).

OHIO: Director of Insurance, 2100 Stella Court, Columbus, OH 43266-0566; (614) 644-2672; (800) 686-1526 (toll free in Ohio).

OKLAHOMA: Insurance Commissioner, P.O. Box 53408, Oklahoma City, OK 73152-3408; (405) 521-2828; (800) 522-0071 (toll free in Oklahoma).

OREGON: Insurance Commissioner, 21 Labor and Industries Building, Salem, OR 97310-0765; (503) 378-4120.

PENNSYLVANIA: Insurance Commissioner, Strawberry Square, 13th Floor, Harrisburg, PA 17120; (717) 783-0442.

RHODE ISLAND: Insurance Commissioner, 233 Richmond Street, Providence, RI 02903; (401) 277-2246.

SOUTH CAROLINA: Chief Insurance Commissioner, P.O. Box 100105, Columbia, SC 29202-3105; (803) 737-6117; (800) 768-3467 (toll free in South Carolina).

SOUTH DAKOTA: Director of Insurance, Insurance Building, 910 East Sioux Avenue, Pierre, SD 57501-3940; (605) 773-3563.

TENNESSEE: Commissioner of Insurance, 500 James Robertson Parkway, Nashville, TN 37243-0565; (615) 741-2241; (800) 342-4029 (toll free in Tennessee).

TEXAS: Associate Commissioner, Consumer Services, Texas Department of Insurance, P.O. Box 149091, Austin, TX 78714-9091;(512) 463-6500; (800) 252-3439 (toll free in Texas).

UTAH: Commissioner of Insurance, 3110 State Office Building, Salt Lake City, UT 84114; (801) 538-3804.

VERMONT: Commissioner, Department of Banking, Insurance and Securities, 89 Main Street, Drawer 20, Montpelier, VT 05620-3101; (802) 828-3301.

VIRGINIA: Commissioner of Insurance, Tyler Building, P.O. Box 1157, Richmond, VA 23209; (804) 371-9741; (800) 552-7945 (toll free in Virginia).

WASHINGTON: Insurance Commissioner, Insurance Building, P.O. Box 40255, Olympia, WA 98504-0255; (206) 753-7301; (800) 562-6900 (toll free in Washington).

WEST VIRGINIA: Insurance Commissioner, 2019 Washington Street, East, P.O. Box 50540, Charleston, WV 25305-0540; (304) 348-3394; (800) 642-9004 (toll free in West Virginia).

WISCONSIN: Commissioner of Insurance, P.O. Box 7873, Madison, WI 53707-7873; (608) 266-3585; (800) 236-8517 (toll free in Wisconsin).

WYOMING: Commissioner of Insurance, Herschler Building, 122 West 25th Street, Cheyenne, WY 82002-0440; (307) 777-7401; (800) 438-5768 (toll free in Wyoming).

State-by-State Contacts For College Financial Aid Information (see chapter 8)

The agencies listed below can provide you with individual state financial aid information as well as information about specific colleges and universities. They also can provide you with referrals for more information.

ALABAMA: Executive Director, Commission of Higher Education, 3465 Norman Bridge Road, Montgomery, AL 36105; (205) 281-1921.

ALASKA: Executive Director, Alaska Commission of Postsecondary Education, 3030 Vintage Boulevard, Juneau, AK 99801-7109; (907) 465-2962.

ARIZONA: Executive Director, Arizona Board of Regents, 2020 North Central, Suite 230, Phoenix, AZ 85004; (602) 229-2500.

ARKANSAS: Director, Department of Higher Education, 114 East Capitol, Little Rock, AR 72201; (501) 324-9300.

CALIFORNIA: Executive Director, California Postsecondary Education Commission, 1303 J. Street, 5th Floor, Sacramento, CA 95814-2938; (916) 445-1000.

California Student Aid Commission, P.O. Box 510845; Sacramento, CA 94245-0845; (916) 445-0880.

COLORADO: Executive Director, Commission on Higher

Education, 1300 Broadway, 2nd Floor, Denver. CO 80203; (303) 866-4034.

CONNECTICUT: Commissioner of Higher Education, Department of Higher Education, 61 Woodland Street, Hartford, CT 06105; (203) 566-5766.

DELAWARE: Executive Director, Delaware Higher Education Commission, 820 North French Street, 4th Floor, Wilmington, DL 19801; (302) 577-3240.

DISTRICT OF COLUMBIA: Chief, Office of Postsecondary Education Research and Assistance, 2100 M.L. King Ave., S.E. 401, Washington, DC 20020; (202) 727-3685.

FLORIDA: Executive Director, Postsecondary Education Planning Commission, Florida Education Center, Collins Building, Tallahassee, FL 32399; (904) 488-7894.

Office of Student Financial Assistance, Florida Department of Education, Florida Education Center, Suite 1344, Tallahassee, FL 32399-0400; (904) 488-1034.

GEORGIA: Chancellor, Board of Regents, University System of Georgia, 244 Washington Street, S.W., Atlanta, GA 30334; (404) 656-2202.

Georgia Student Finance Commission, 2082 East Exchange Place, Tucker, GA 30084; (404) 414-3200.

HAWAII: President, University of Hawaii System, 2444 Dole Street, Bachman Hall, Room 202, Honolulu, HI 96822; (808)

956-8213.

IDAHO: Executive Director for Higher Education, State Board of Education, P.O. Box 83720, Boise, ID 83720-0037; (208) 334-2270.

ILLINOIS: Executive Director, Board of Higher Education, 4 West Capitol Plaza, Room 500, Springfield, IL 62701; (217) 782-2551.

Illinois Student Assistance Commission, Executive Offices, 500 West Monroe St., Third Floor, Springfield, IL 62704; (217) 782-6767.

INDIANA: State Student Assistance Commission of Indiana, 150 West Market Street, Suite 500, Indianapolis, IN 46204; (317) 232-2350.

IOWA: Executive Director, State Board of Regents, Old Historical Building, East 12th & Grand Avenue, Des Moines, IA 50319; (515) 281-3934.

Iowa College Student Aid Commission, 914 Grand Avenue, Suite 201, Des Moines, IA 50309; (515) 281-3501.

KANSAS: Executive Director, Kansas Board of Regents, 700 SW Harrison, Suite 1410, Topeka, KS 66603-3760; (913) 296-3421.

KENTUCKY: Executive Director, Council on Higher Education, 1050 U.S. 127 South, Suite 101, Frankfort, KY 40601; (502) 564-3553.

Kentucky Higher Education Association Authority, 1050 U.S. 127 South, Suite 102, Frankfort, KY 40601; (502) 564-7990.

LOUISIANA: Commissioner, Board of Regents, 150 Third Street, Suite 129, Baton Rouge, LA 70801-1303; (504) 342-4253.

Office of Student Financial Assistance Commission, P.O. Box 91202, Baton Rouge, LA 70821-9202; (504) 922-1011.

MAINE: Financial Authority of Maine, Maine Education Assistance Division, One Weston Court, State House, Station 119, Augusta, ME 04333; (207) 287-2183

MARYLAND: Secretary of Higher Education, Maryland Higher Education Commission, 16 Francis Street, Annapolis, MD 21401; (410) 974-2971.

MASSACHUSETTS: Massachusetts State Scholarship Office, 330 Stuart Street, Boston, MA 02116; (617) 727-9420.

MICHIGAN: Michigan Higher Education Assistance Authority, P.O. Box 30008, Lansing, MI 48909; (517) 373-3394.

MINNESOTA: Executive Director, Higher Education Coordinating Board, 400 Capital Square Building, 550 Cedar Street, St. Paul, MN 55101; (612) 296-9665.

MISSISSIPPI: Commissioner, Board of Trustees of State Institutions of Higher Learning, 3825 Ridgewood Road, Jackson, MS 39211-6453; (601) 982-6611.

MISSOURI: Commissioner of Higher Education, Coordinating Board for Higher Education, 3515 Amazonas, Jefferson City, MO 65109; (314) 751-2361.

MONTANA: Commissioner of Higher Education, Montana University System, 33 South Last Chance Gulch, Helena, MT 59620; (406) 444-6570.

NEBRASKA: Executive Director, Coordinating Commission for Postsecondary Education, P.O. Box 95005, Lincoln, NB 68509-5005; (402) 471-2847.

NEVADA: Chancellor, University of Nevada System, 2601 Enterprise Road, Reno, NV 89512; (702) 784-4901.

NEW HAMPSHIRE, Executive Director, New Hampshire Postsecondary Education Commission, Two Industrial Park Drive, Concord, NH 03301-8512; (603) 271-2555.

NEW JERSEY: New Jersey Department of Higher Education, Office of Student Assistance and Information Systems, 4 Quakerbridge Plaza, CN 540, Trenton, NJ 08625; (800) 792-8670; (609) 584-9618.

NEW MEXICO: Executive Director, Commission on Higher Education, 1068 Cerrillos Road, Santa Fe, NM 87501-4295; (505) 827-7383; (505) 827-7383.

NEW YORK: Deputy Commissioner for Higher and Professional Education, Room 5B28 Cultural Education Department, Albany, NY 12230; (518) 474-5851.

NORTH CAROLINA: North Carolina State Education Assistance Authority (NCSEAA), P.O. Box 2688, Chapel Hill, NC 27515-2688; (919) 549-8614.

College Foundation, Inc., P.O. Box 12100, Raleigh, NC 27605; (919) 821-4771.

NORTH DAKOTA: Chancellor, North Dakota University System, 600 East Boulevard Avenue, Bismarck, ND 58505; (701) 224-2960.

OHIO: Chancellor, Ohio Board of Regents, 30 East Broad Street, 36th Floor, Columbus, OH 43266-0417; (614) 466-0887.

OKLAHOMA: Chancellor, State Regents for Higher Education, 500 Education Building, State Capitol Complex, Oklahoma City, OK 73105; (405) 524-9100.

OREGON: Oregon State Scholarship Commission, 1500 Valley River Drive, Suite 100, Eugene, OR 97401: (503) 687-7400.

PENNSYLVANIA: Pennsylvania Higher Education Assistance Agency, 1200 North 7th Street, Harrisburg, PA 17102; (717) 257-2850.

RHODE ISLAND: Rhode Island Higher Education Assistance Authority, 560 Jefferson Boulevard, Warwick, RI 02886; (401) 736-1100.

SOUTH CAROLINA: South Carolina Higher Education Tuition Grants Commission, P.O. Box 12159, Columbia, SC 29211; (803) 734-1200.

SOUTH DAKOTA: Executive Director, Board of Regents, 207 East Capitol Ave., Pierre, SD 57501-3159; (605) 773-3455.

TENNESSEE: Tennessee Student Assistance Corporation, Parkway Towers, Suite 1950, 404 James Robertson Parkway, Nashville, TN 37243-0820; (615) 741-1346.

TEXAS: Commissioner, Texas Higher Education Coordinating Board, P.O. Box 12788, Austin, TX 78711; (512) 483-6101.

UTAH: Commissioner of Higher Education, Utah System of Higher Education, 3 Triad Center, Suite 550, Salt Lake City, UT 84180-1205; (801) 321-7101.

VERMONT: Vermont Student Assistance Corporation, P.O. Box 2000, Champlain Mill, Winooski, VT 05404-2601; (802) 655-9602.

VIRGINIA: Director, State Council of Higher Education, 101 North 14th Street, Richmond, VA 23219; (804) 225-2600.

WASHINGTON: Executive Director, Higher Education Coordinating Board, 917 Lakeridge Way, P.O. Box 43430; Olympia, WA 98504-3430; (206) 753-3241.

WEST VIRGINIA: Chancellor, State College System of West Virginia, 1018 Kanawha Boulevard, East, Charleston, WV 25302; (304) 558-0699.

WISCONSIN: Higher Education Aids Board, P.O. Box 7885, Madison, WI 53707; (608) 267-2206.

WYOMING: The Community College Commission, 122 West 25th Street, Herschler Building, 1W, Cheyenne, WY 82002; (307) 777-7763.

President, University of Wyoming, Box 3434, University Station, Laramie, WY 82071; (307) 766-4121.

State-By-State Listing of Unclaimed Property Offices (see Chapter 10)

ALABAMA: Department of Revenue, Unclaimed Property Division, P.O. Box 327580, Montgomery, AL 36132-7580; (205) 242-9614.

ALASKA: Alaska Department of Revenue, Income and Excise Audit Division, Unclaimed Property Section, 1111 West 8th Street, Room 106, Juneau, AK 99801; (907) 465-4653.

ARIZONA: Arizona Department of Revenue, Unclaimed Property Division, 1600 West Monroe, Room 610, Phoenix, AZ 85007; (602) 542-3908.

ARKANSAS: Auditor of the State, Unclaimed Property Division, 230 State Capitol, Little Rock, AR 72201; (501) 324-9670.

CALIFORNIA: Unclaimed Property Office, P.O. Box 942850, Sacramento, CA 94250-5873; (916) 323-2827.

COLORADO: Colorado State Treasurer, Division of

UnclaimedProperty, 1560 Broadway, Suite 630, Denver, CO 80202; (303) 894-2449.

CONNECTICUT: Treasury Department, Unclaimed Property Division, 55 Elm Street, Hartford, CT 06106; (203) 566-5516.

DELAWARE: Delaware State Escheator, Abandoned Property Division, P.O. Box 8931, Wilmington, DE 19899; (302) 577-3349.

DISTRICT OF COLUMBIA: Department of Finance and Revenue, Unclaimed Property Division, 300 Indiana Avenue, N.W., Room 5008, Washington, DC 20001; (202) 727-0063.

FLORIDA: Office of Comptroller, Division of Finance, Abandoned Property Section, Tallahassee, FL 32311-0350; (904) 487-0510.

GEORGIA: Georgia Department of Revenue, Unclaimed Property Section, 270 Washington Street, Room 405, Atlanta, GA 30334; (404) 656-4244.

HAWAII: Director of Finance, State of Hawaii Unclaimed Property Section, P.O. Box 150, Honolulu, HI 96810; (808) 586-1590.

IDAHO: State Tax Commission, Unclaimed Property Division, 700West State Street, P.O. Box 36, Boise, ID 83722-2240; (208) 334-7623.

ILLINOIS: Department of Financial Institutions, Unclaimed Property Division, 500 Iles Park Place, Suite 510, Springfield, IL

62718; (217) 782-8463.

INDIANA: Office of Attorney General, Unclaimed Property Division, 219 State House, Indianapolis, IN 46204-2794; (317) 232-6348.

IOWA: Great Iowa Treasure Hunt, State Treasurer's Office, Hoover State Office Building, Des Moines, IA 50319; (515) 281-5540.

KANSAS: State Treasurer's Office, Unclaimed Property Division, 900 Southwest Jackson, Suite 201, Topeka, KS 66612-1235; (913) 296-3171; (800) 432-0386 (KS only).

KENTUCKY: Abandoned Property Unit, Station 62, Frankfort, KY 40601; (502) 564-6823.

LOUISIANA: Louisiana Department of Revenue and Taxation, Unclaimed Property Division, P.O. Box 91010, Baton Rouge, LA 70821-9010 ; (504) 925-7425.

MAINE: Treasury Department, Abandoned Property Division, Station 39, Augusta, ME 04333; (207) 289-2771.

MARYLAND: Comptroller of the Treasury, Unclaimed Property Section, 301 West Preston Street, Baltimore, MD 21201; (410) 225-1700.

MASSACHUSETTS: Commonwealth of Massachusetts Treasury Department, Unclaimed Property Division, One Ashburton Place, Room 1207, Boston, MA 02108; (617) 367-3900.

MICHIGAN: Michigan Department of the Treasury, Escheats Division,Lansing, MI 48922; (517) 334-6550.

MINNESOTA: Minnesota Department of Commerce, Office of Unclaimed Property, 133 East 7th Street, St. Paul, MN 55101-2362; (612) 296-2568; (800) 652-9747 (in MN).

MISSISSIPPI: Mississippi Treasurer's Office, Unclaimed Property Division, P.O.Box 138, Jackson, MS 39205; (601) 359-3600.

MISSOURI: Department of Economic Development, Unclaimed Property, Box 1272, Jefferson City, MO 65102; (314) 751-0840.

MONTANA: State of Montana, Department of Revenue, Abandoned Property Section, Mitchell Building, Helena, MT 59620; (406) 444-2425.

NEBRASKA: Nebraska State Treasurer's Office, Property Capitol Building, P.O. Box 94788, Lincoln, NE 68509; (402) 471-2455.

NEVADA: State of Nevada, Unclaimed Property Division, State Mail Room, Las Vegas, NV 89158; (702) 486-4140; (800) 521-0019 (in NV).

NEW HAMPSHIRE: New Hampshire State Treasurer's Office, Abandoned Property Division, 25 Capitol Street, State House Annex Room 121, Concord, NH 03301; (603) 271-2619.

NEW JERSEY: Department of Treasurer, Unclaimed Property, CN-214, Trenton, NJ 08646; (609) 292-9200.

NEW MEXICO: New Mexico Taxation and Revenue Department, P.O. Box 25123, Santa Fe, NM 87504-5123; (505) 827-0767.

NEW YORK: Administrator, Office of Unclaimed Funds, Alfred E. Smith Building, 9th Floor, Albany, NY; (518) 474-4038; (800) 211-9311 (in New York).

NORTH CAROLINA: Administrator, Escheat and Abandoned Property Section, Department of State Treasurer, 325 N. Salisbury St., Raleigh, NC 27603-1388; (919) 733-6876.

NORTH DAKOTA: North Dakota Unclaimed Property Division, 918 East Divide Ave., Suite 410, P.O. Box 5523, Bismarck, ND 58502; (701) 224-2805.

OHIO: Division of Unclaimed Funds, Department of Commerce, 77 South High Street, 20th Floor, Columbus, OH 43266-0545; (614) 466-4433.

OKLAHOMA: Oklahoma Tax Commission, Unclaimed Property Section, 2501 Lincoln Blvd., Oklahoma City, OK 73194-0010; (405) 521-4275.

OREGON: Oregon Division of State Lands, 775 Summer Street NS, Salem, OR 93710; (503) 378-3805.

PENNSYLVANIA: Supervisor, Abandoned and Unclaimed Property Section, Philadelphia Department of Revenue, 2850 Turnpike Industrial Park, Middletown, PA 17057; (717) 986-4641; (800) 222-2046 (in PA).

RHODE ISLAND: State of Rhode Island, Unclaimed Property

Division, 40 Fountain Street, Providence, RI 02903; (401) 277-6505.

SOUTH CAROLINA: Abandoned Property Office, South Carolina Tax Commission, P.O. Box 125, Columbia, SC 29214; (803) 737-4771.

SOUTH DAKOTA: Abandoned Property, State Treasurer's Office, 500 East Capitol, Pierre, SD 57501; (605) 773-3378.

TENNESSEE: State of Tennessee, Unclaimed Property Division, Andrew Jackson State Office Building, 11th Floor, Nashville, TN 37243-0242; (615) 741-6499.

TEXAS: Unclaimed Money Fund, P.O. Box 12019, State Treasurer's Office, Austin, TX 78711; (512) 444-7833; (800) 321-CASH (in TX).

UTAH: Utah Unclaimed Property Division, 341 South Main Street, 4th Floor,Salt Lake City, UT 84114; (801) 533-4101.

VERMONT: State Treasurer's Office, Unclaimed Property Division, 133 State Street, Montpelier, VT 05633-6200; (802) 533-4101.

VIRGINIA: Department of the Treasury, Division of Unclaimed Property, P.O. Box 2478, Richmond, VA 23207; (804) 225-2393; (800) 468-1088 (in VA).

WASHINGTON: State of Washington Department of Revenue, Unclaimed Property Division, P.O. Box 448, Olympia, WA 98507; (206) 586-2736.

WEST VIRGINIA: Treasurer of the State, Unclaimed Property Division, Building 1, Suite E145, State Capitol, Charleston, WV 25305; (304) 343-4000.

WISCONSIN: Office of the State Treasurer, Unclaimed Property Division, P.O. Box 2114, Madison, WI 53701-2114; (608) 267-7977.

WYOMING: Unclaimed Property Division, Wyoming State Treasury Office, State Capitol, Cheyenne, WY 82002; (307) 777-5590.